# Intimate Partner
# Sexual Violence

*of related interest*

**Counselling Skills for Working with Trauma**
**Healing From Child Sexual Abuse, Sexual Violence and Domestic Abuse**
*Christiane Sanderson*
ISBN 978 1 84905 326 6
eISBN 978 0 85700 743 8

**Good Practice in Promoting Recovery and Healing for Abused Adults**
*Edited by Jacki Pritchard*
ISBN 978 1 84905 372 3
eISBN 978 0 85700 723 0
Part of the Good Practice in Health, Social Care and Criminal Justice series

**Picking up the Pieces After Domestic Violence**
**A Practical Resource for Supporting Parenting Skills**
*Kate Iwi and Chris Newman*
ISBN 978 1 84905 021 0
eISBN 978 0 85700 533 5

**Violence Against Women**
**Current Theory and Practice in Domestic Abuse, Sexual Violence and Exploitation**
*Edited by Nancy Lombard and Lesley McMillan*
ISBN 978 1 84905 132 3
eISBN 978 0 85700 330 0
Part of the Research Highlights in Social Work series

**Rebuilding Lives after Domestic Violence**
**Understanding Long-Term Outcomes**
*Hilary Abrahams*
ISBN 978 1 84310 961 7
eISBN 978 0 85700 320 1

**Supporting Women after Domestic Violence**
**Loss, Trauma and Recovery**
*Hilary Abrahams*
ISBN 978 1 84310 431 5
eISBN 978 1 84642 615 5

**Narrative Therapy for Women Experiencing Domestic Violence**
**Supporting Women's Transitions from Abuse to Safety**
*Mary Allen*
*Foreword by Ravi K. Thiara*
ISBN 978 1 84905 190 3
eISBN 978 0 85700 420 8

# Intimate Partner Sexual Violence

## A MULTIDISCIPLINARY GUIDE TO IMPROVING SERVICES AND SUPPORT FOR SURVIVORS OF RAPE AND ABUSE

Edited by Louise McOrmond-Plummer, Patricia Easteal AM, and Jennifer Y. Levy-Peck

FOREWORD BY RAQUEL KENNEDY BERGEN

Jessica Kingsley *Publishers*
London and Philadelphia

Figure 9.1 is reproduced on p.111 with kind permission from
202 East Superior Street, Duluth, MN 55802
218-722-2781, www.theduluthmodel.org

First published in 2014
by Jessica Kingsley Publishers
73 Collier Street
London N1 9BE, UK
and
400 Market Street, Suite 400
Philadelphia, PA 19106, USA

*www.jkp.com*

**Library of Congress Cataloging in Publication Data**
Intimate partner sexual violence : a multidisciplinary
guide to improving services and support for
survivors of rape and abuse / edited by Louise McOrmond-
Plummer, Patricia Easteal and Jennifer Y.
Levy-Peck ; foreword by Raquel Kennedy Bergen.
pages cm
Includes bibliographical references and index.
ISBN 978-1-84905-912-1
1. Intimate partner violence. 2. Sexual abuse victims--
Counseling of. I. McOrmond-Plummer, Louise,
1966- editor of compilation.
HV6626.I5835 2013
362.883--dc23
2013019205

**British Library Cataloguing in Publication Data**
A CIP catalogue record for this book is available from the British Library

ISBN 978 1 84905 912 1
eISBN 978 0 85700 655 4

Printed and bound in Great Britain by Bell & Bain Ltd, Glasgow

We, the editors, dedicate this book to: Diana E.H. Russell, trailblazer in addressing the issue of intimate partner sexual violence (IPSV), and the survivors of IPSV who have fallen through the service provision cracks, or been actively harmed and further endangered when they reached out for professional help. We hope this will no longer be the case.

# Contents

## PART 3 INTIMATE PARTNER SEXUAL VIOLENCE AND BEST PRACTICE SERVICE RESPONSE

## PART 4 REACHING AND ASSISTING DIFFERENT POPULATIONS

## PART 5 CONCLUSION

# Foreword

Raquel Kennedy Bergen

It is almost 30 years ago to the day when I first wrote the words, "There is a dearth of information about the serious problem of rape in marital relationships." At that time, I was completing my undergraduate thesis, which was a study of how service providers in the fields of medicine, law, and crisis counseling perceived the problem of rape in marriage. I was shocked and appalled that women who had been raped by their intimate partners were routinely denied services by local rape crisis centers because they were not perceived as victims of "real rape," and that some local battered women's programs would not include marital rape survivors in their groups because they just "didn't fit." Prosecutors could not take cases of rape by intimate partners because it was not a prosecutable offense where I lived at the time.

Today I continue to work on this topic and to be shocked and appalled! Certainly some progress has been made. For example, forced sexual violence by a marriage partner has been criminalized in at least some circumstances, in every state in the US, and more than 100 countries around the world. Despite public outcry, countries such as Thailand have seen marital rape legislation enacted and cases prosecuted (China Post 2007). Intimate partner sexual violence (IPSV) has been analyzed from a global perspective by the World Health Organization (2005) in their fantastic multi-country study of violence against women.

While progress is certainly being made, even today I would still argue vehemently that there is a long way to go. The recent parliamentary panel decision in India against criminalizing rape in marriage because it would threaten the traditional family maintains the status quo and continues to signify that rape by an intimate partner is not "real rape" (Bhattacharjee 2013). In failing to criminalize this horrific form of violence against women, abusers who perceive a sense of entitlement to sex in their intimate partnerships are empowered while the victims are silenced. As a society, we continue to perpetuate the archaic message that with marriage (or previous sexual contact) a woman gives up her right to freely consent to sex (Bergen 1996).

In the historic words of Matthew Hale (1736), "The husband cannot be guilty of a rape committed by himself upon his lawful wife, for by their mutual matrimonial consent and contract, the wife hath given up herself in this kind unto the husband which she cannot retract." This understanding that rape in marriage is an impossibility continues to be prevalent today. If you ask anyone who works in this field, they can tell you how often they hear, "You study (or help or treat or prosecute…) what? How can a man rape his wife?"

This is a form of violence against women that to this day remains difficult yet vitally important to address. By asking questions about women's experiences of sexual violence at the hands of their partners, we are lifting the veil of secrecy on the most private of domestic spheres—the family bedroom. When we ask about the prevalence of women's experiences of IPSV, the causes and consequences, and how we can best meet the needs of this population, we legitimize women's experiences and make a statement that this horrific type of violence against women must be stopped. This book plays an important role in making such a statement.

While progress has been made in providing services to survivors of IPSV, there is still much work to be done. A study that I did several years ago of rape crisis centers, battered women's programs, and combination programs in the US indicated that services to survivors of IPSV had improved, including providing shelter to them and specifically addressing the issue of intimate partner rape in the mission statement of the organization. However, substantial progress was still needed with regard to educating staff and volunteers about IPSV (only 60% of programs provided this training) and in routinely asking women about their experiences of sexual violence with their partners. Only half of programs indicated that they did this on a regular basis (Bergen 2005).

The need for service providers and practitioners to engage with survivors of IPSV is a central theme of this book. Importantly, the American College of Obstetricians and Gynecologists recently issued a *Futures Without Violence* report, which calls on practitioners to routinely address intimate partner violence, sexual coercion, and reproductive coercion among their patients (Chamberlain and Levenson 2012). Such recommendations are critically important given that medical practitioners have a unique opportunity to help identify and assist survivors of IPSV, many of whom may never have shared their experiences of victimization with anyone.

As I argued 30 years ago, there is still a dearth of information about the subject of intimate partner rape. There are few monographs which are devoted specifically to the topic of IPSV and even fewer which address rape in heterosexual marital relationships, or in the LGBTQ (lesbian, gay, bisexual, transgender, queer/questioning) community. However, what McOrmond-Plummer, Easteal, and Levy-Peck have done is to assemble into one volume interdisciplinary and international perspectives about IPSV from the leading experts in the field. This excellent volume provides important information about how women around the world experience IPSV and the horrific responses that they too frequently receive from service providers. As the authors write in Chapter 1, "Women seeking help from advocates, counseling professionals, law enforcement, religious leaders, and medical professionals may receive treatment ranging from ignorance to seeming cruelty." The chapters on service provision provide excellent insight on the best ways to assist women (and men) who have been victimized by their partners, validating their experiences and helping them down the path of healing.

Far too often we fail to realize how many survivors of IPSV are with us. The first step in truly working to end this form of violence against women is to open the door to hearing about individuals' experiences. It is critical that we validate women's experiences of IPSV and work with them in ways which acknowledge the severity of this abuse. This book also provides cutting-edge research on the risks, causes, and—far too often—deadly consequences of IPSV. It is an important resource for anyone who works with survivors of IPSV or who has a family member, friend, or loved one who is a survivor.

The book that you are about to read is a critically important step in acknowledging the life-damaging impact of IPSV and helps to give voice to this group of survivors who have been too long silenced. I am deeply thankful to the authors for their contribution to this field and hope that in another 30 years I can cheerfully write the words, "There is no longer a dearth of information about this serious problem."

*Raquel Kennedy Bergen*
*St. Joseph's University, Philadelphia, Pennsylvania, USA*

# References

Bergen, R.K. (1996) *Wife Rape: Understanding the Response of Survivors and Service Providers.* Thousand Oaks, CA: Sage.

Bergen, R.K. (2005) *Still a Long Way to Go: Comparing Services for Marital Rape Survivors from 1994 and 2004.* Unpublished.

Bhattacharjee, A. (2013) *The Non-Criminalisation of Marital Rape.* Ultra Violet: Indian Feminists Unplugged. Available at www.ultraviolet.in/2013/03/06/the-non-criminalization-of-marital-rape-by-anwesha-bhattacharjee, accessed March 14, 2013.

Chamberlain, L. and Levenson, R. (2012) *Addressing Intimate Partner Violence, Reproductive and Sexual Coercion: A Guide for Obstetric, Gynecologic and Reproductive Health Care Settings.* Washington, DC: American College of Obstetricians and Gynecologists. Available at www.acog.org/About_ACOG/ACOG_Departments/Violence_Against_Women/~/media/Departments/Violence%20Against%20Women/Reproguidelines.pdf, accessed March 15, 2013.

China Post (2007) *Thailand Outlaws Marital Rape.* Available at www.chinapost.com.tw/asia/2007/06/22/113083/Thailand-outlaws.htm, accessed March 14, 2013.

Hale, M. (1736) *Historia Placitorum Coronae: The History of the Pleas of the Crown.* Edited by S. Emlyn, 2 vols, London. (Reprint 1971. Classical English Law Texts. London: Professional Books Ltd.)

World Health Organization (2005) *WHO Multi-Country Study on Women's Health and Domestic Violence Against Women: Summary Report of Initial Results on Prevalence, Health Outcomes, and Women's Responses.* Geneva, Switzerland: World Health Organization. Available at www.who.int/gender/violence/who_multicountry_study/en/, accessed March 15, 2013.

# Acknowledgments

The editors would like to acknowledge Raquel Kennedy Bergen for her guidance in putting together a prospectus, Charles Peck for excellent editorial suggestions, Cassandra Beaumont of Forensic and Medical Sexual Assault Clinicians Australia (FAMSAC) for finding just the right doctor/authors for us, and Lori B. Girshick and Claire Renzetti for their helpful direction.

We thank Stephen Jones from Jessica Kingsley Publishers for recognizing the importance of this book, and for his valuable and insightful suggestions. Thanks also to Caroline Walton for her assistance.

We are grateful to our terrific team of contributing authors, each with invaluable expertise and insights, without whom this work would have been impossible.

Lastly, we the editors acknowledge each other—the Sisterhood of the Coven (SOC) as we have come to identify ourselves—for an incredibly supportive collaboration with wonderful communication, cohesion, flexibility, mutual encouragement, respect, and affection. We had a dream and it has now been actualized.

# PART 1

# Introduction
# and
# Overview

# CHAPTER 1

# Introduction

## THE NECESSITY OF APPROPRIATE SERVICE RESPONSE TO INTIMATE PARTNER SEXUAL VIOLENCE

Louise McOrmond-Plummer, Patricia Easteal AM, and Jennifer Y. Levy-Peck

This book is about intimate partner sexual violence (IPSV). With an international focus, it contains multidisciplinary advice for professionals—such as advocates, mental health professionals, health practitioners, religious leaders, lawyers, police, and the judiciary—who interact with individuals (primarily women) who have experienced IPSV. We locate IPSV within the context of domestic and sexual violence—as both/and, rather than either/or—and give IPSV service provision priority.

## What is intimate partner sexual violence?

IPSV is sexual assault by a current or former intimate partner, and includes sexual coercion in teen dating relationships, as well as what was formerly known as marital rape, and sexual assault in same-sex intimate relationships. Perpetrators have a range of ways to force or coerce partners or ex-partners into nonconsensual sex acts. These may include the following:

- *Physical force:* Holding down or otherwise restraining the victim, using superior physical strength to overcome refusal. May include beating or weapons.

- *Threats of harm to the victim or a third party:* May include pets, and often includes children or other family members with whom the victim has a bond. It is important to note here that a threat may not need to be expressly uttered; for example, if the sexual assault coexists with battery, there may be an implicit undertone of menace that forestalls refusal. Or, the perpetrator

has raped the victim before and, as a result, she knows that refusal is pointless (Easteal and McOrmond-Plummer 2006).

- *Verbal badgering and blackmail:* Not allowing the victim to say no to sexual activity without unpleasant consequences such as withdrawal of affection, withholding of housekeeping money, or refusal of help with children. The perpetrator may threaten to seek sex outside the relationship. A teenager may be blackmailed with having rumors spread that she is promiscuous, or a same-sex partner may threaten to "out" the victim to work colleagues (Easteal and McOrmond-Plummer 2006; Winters 2009).

IPSV may include any of the following acts that are perpetrated without consent:

- Anal or vaginal penetration with finger, penis, or object.
- Oral rape: forced or coerced fellatio or cunnilingus.
- Touching the victim in a sexual way or forcing the victim to touch the perpetrator.
- Making the victim available to other people for the purpose of gang-rape or prostitution.
- Forced sexual contact with animals.
- Forcing or coercing a partner into viewing pornography.
- Filming or otherwise recording sex acts without a partner's consent.
- Verbal sexual humiliation or degradation.
- Reproductive coercion (such as forcing a partner to become pregnant, to carry a pregnancy to term, or to abort).
- Deliberate exposure to sexually transmitted infections.

Importantly, not all forms of IPSV may meet legal definitions of criminality—for example, calling a partner degrading names such as "slut" or "whore" is also a form of sexual violence aimed at degrading or controlling the victim. Reproductive coercion also is not a criminal act in itself, but may have severe consequences for the woman whose wishes about childbearing are disregarded.

IPSV is usually perpetrated by an individual as part of a pattern of violence and control. However, while battered women are statistically more likely to experience rape and sexual assault (Russell 1990), it also happens in relationships not characterized by other forms of violence, or that may appear to be otherwise egalitarian (Black *et al.* 2011; Easteal and McOrmond-Plummer 2006).

## How common is intimate partner sexual violence?

By some estimates, as much as 60 percent of abused women are also sexually assaulted by their partners (Howard *et al.* 2003). A recent US study reports that 51.1 percent of rapes upon women are by past or present partners, and that 9.4 percent of American women have been raped by an intimate partner (Black *et al.* 2011). This is consistent with an earlier British Home Office study which found that 45 percent of all rapes were committed by present partners, with a further 11 percent by ex-partners, making IPSV the most common type of sexual assault (Myhill and Allen 2002).

## Risk factors for intimate partner sexual violence

The risk factors for IPSV described by Raquel Kennedy Bergen in *Marital Rape: New Research and Directions* (2006) are as follows:

- being physically abused
- being pregnant
- being ill or recently discharged from the hospital
- attempting to leave a partner
- being separated or divorced.

This list makes clear the connection between vulnerability of the victim and coercion by the abuser. Sexual assault becomes a means of reinforcing the abuser's power over his partner.

## The impact of intimate partner sexual violence

Despite the common assumptions that "only stranger rape is real rape" and that sexual assault is less serious when the victim and perpetrator have a prior relationship, several studies indicate that women who have been sexually assaulted by partners experience longer-lasting and more devastating effects than women raped by strangers (Easteal 1994; Finkelhor and Yllo 1985; Russell 1990). Importantly, IPSV coupled with battering is recognized as a risk factor for lethal violence (Campbell and Alford 1989).

## Lack of understanding

Although IPSV is, as we have seen, a highly prevalent form of sexual assault which accrues serious impact, widespread understanding of it lags behind other forms of sexual assault and domestic violence. Research from the 1980s up until the present indicates that many professionals in fields that have contact with survivors of IPSV are unsure about how to proceed when they encounter this issue. This may lead to IPSV survivors receiving less than adequate service (Bergen 1996; Finkelhor and Yllo 1985; Parkinson and Cowan 2008).

Practitioner and service provider ignorance may be attributed at least in part to the fact that the literature about working with sexual assault and/or domestic violence rarely gives focus to IPSV. Where it does, it often does not cover the special and discrete issues that accompany this specific form of violence against women. As Diana Russell (1990) writes, marital rape frequently has been filed under the rubric of domestic violence. Russell warns of the disservice that this does to survivors in terms of not addressing the special issues that rape by an intimate partner may carry, and promoting the false assumption that it only happens in violent relationships.

In her 1996 book *Wife Rape*, Raquel Kennedy Bergen agreed, writing that still too many service providers are uncertain as to who should take ownership of the issue of marital rape, with the result that they shunt women between agencies with little in the way of real assistance. This is problematic because, as Bergen's research respondents indicated, women want specific assistance for the sexual violence experienced from their partners. Issues of violence to women and children have been traditionally addressed in the women's movement. Yet, with regard to IPSV, problems may also exist within feminist-based organizations specifically set up to tackle domestic or sexual violence. For example, women who have experienced IPSV have been asked not to mention rape in domestic violence support groups. Sexual assault services have given IPSV survivors lower priority because there may be a mistaken belief that IPSV is not as serious as other types of rape (Bergen 1996).

Unfortunately, inequitable service provision for IPSV victims and survivors is not a thing of the past. More recent studies have indicated that survivors of IPSV continue to receive inadequate treatment (Bergen 2005, 2006; Easteal and McOrmond-Plummer 2006; Heenan 2004; Parkinson and Cowan 2008).

## Horror stories: the need for this book

Women seeking help from advocates, counseling professionals, law enforcement, religious leaders, and medical professionals may receive treatment ranging from ignorance to seeming cruelty. Indeed, accessing help can be nightmarish. One woman told us about a visit to her doctor, where she disclosed that she had been waking up to her husband sexually assaulting her. The doctor's opinion was that wake-up sex is "sexy" and that the woman should appreciate it as such. Another woman reported partner rape to the police, who suggested to her that it was really just "kinky sex" and not worth reporting— and this was a police unit with specific training in handling sexual offenses (Aphrodite Wounded 2002). Religious leaders have forbidden congregations to assist women escaping sexually violent husbands (Parkinson and Cowan 2008). Counselors may view IPSV as a mutual dysfunction rather than something a man does to control and abuse his partner, and so they offer couples counseling, which can be dangerous to women still in relationships of abuse (Easteal and McOrmond-Plummer 2006). A chronic issue with many service agencies is a reluctance to *name* IPSV as rape, sexual assault, or a crime (Heenan 2004; Parkinson and Cowan 2008).

Service responses do not need to be verbal to be harmful. Changing the subject, silence, or refusing to recognize IPSV as an issue at all can be damaging. For example, survivors of IPSV have reported that doctors commonly make no response to a disclosure of sexual assault and do not bring it up again in subsequent appointments (Parkinson and Cowan 2008).

Why do we call these responses "horror stories"? When one looks at their impact on victims and survivors of IPSV, the term seems warranted. Disbelief, minimization, or other responses that deny IPSV and its harms or its criminality serve to entrap women further. A victim silenced by a bad professional response may feel reluctant to tell somebody again. Thus, her psychological pain or the danger she may still face will thrive in this environment of silence. We have already mentioned that IPSV coupled with battery is more likely to result in fatality to the victim. For this and other reasons, it is imperative for professional helpers to provide better responses to IPSV. Women are already often afraid to mention IPSV because of issues such as shame and fear of retaliation by abusive partners. Inadequate professional responses make them more afraid. It is unacceptable for women to feel afraid to report a crime to the police, or to seek medical treatment because the *professional* might respond badly. Importantly, poor responses do not hold perpetrators responsible, ensuring that they can continue to rape and abuse unchecked.

Subsequent to publication of the book *Real Rape, Real Pain*, the authors received the following correspondence:

> When I was [age] I was in a relationship where I was constantly forced to have sex. He was very hard to leave and stalked me for a year once I did. I spoke to a counselor just this week about how I developed [illness] following this period in my life and I wondered if this was connected to the trauma. She said I wasn't really raped and surely I had consented if he was my boyfriend. She kept saying "YOU repeatedly put YOURSELF in that situation." (Easteal and McOrmond-Plummer 2010, personal communication)

We knew that a Centre Against Sexual Assault (CASA, Victoria, Australia) had done some commendable work around IPSV, and after expressing regret for the appalling response she had been given, we suggested that this woman phone CASA. Fortunately, she was willing to do so, and she later updated us with the following: "I have found some great support at CASA and through them I am surprised to discover how much the assault impacted on my life. I am also feeling empowered to find out I can take a strong stand on partner rape" (Easteal and McOrmond-Plummer 2010, personal communication).

So, horror stories may be transformed. Empowering support for somebody victimized by IPSV is obviously a much more favorable outcome than victim-blame, silence, and further endangerment. Change is happening; some professionals are getting educated about IPSV. However, the change is slow, and we believe that the present work can expedite the process.

A doctor, priest, rape crisis counselor, or other professional may be the person to whom a victim of IPSV first reaches out. When this is the case, the professional is in a position to do much good, rather than reinforcing a culture wherein IPSV survivors continue to feel that there is no redress and nobody to turn to.

# Who will benefit from reading the book?

We intend for the primary audience to be professionals who intersect with victims and survivors of IPSV, such as counselors, emergency shelter or refuge workers, victim advocates, social workers, doctors, lawyers, police, the judiciary, and clergy. A second critical group is comprised of those studying to be helping practitioners; students in social work, sociology, psychology, criminal justice, and law programs can benefit from learning about IPSV *before* they start their professional practices.

We also hope that survivors themselves, who may be seeking additional information and resources, will be empowered through reading these pages. Knowledge is power and can assist in identification and healing.

# The structure of the book

## Overview

Because we believe that there must be an integrated, multidisciplinary approach to the crime of IPSV, we have structured the material to flow logically and to draw the interest of professionals from all fields. Doctors need to know what advocates do, and therapists need to know what legal challenges their clients may face, for example.

Chapter 2 distills essential knowledge that is applicable to all professionals reading this book, and counteracts misconceptions about IPSV with facts. Chapter 3 aims to furnish sexual assault and domestic violence workers as well as practitioners from other fields with an understanding of how IPSV can differ from stand-alone sexual assault or domestic violence. Drawing on existing literature, it will also explore differing impacts in victims, and what it is about IPSV, as opposed to other domestic violence and sexual assault, that causes these different effects.

## How serious is intimate partner sexual violence?

Part 2 of the book examines the seriousness of IPSV. It is practitioner-focused, with information on important aspects of IPSV for practitioners to know about. Chapter 4, by Jocelyn C. Anderson, Jessica E. Draughon, and Jacquelyn C. Campbell, explores IPSV as an indicator of potential fatality in abusive relationships, and why it is essential for professionals to take note of clients experiencing it. In Chapter 5, Walter S. DeKeseredy highlights sexual assault that takes place after separation and divorce, the high risk of sexual assault at this time, and why it is important for service providers to know about it, with directives for appropriate intervention. Chapter 6, by Emma Williamson, explores the links between IPSV and reproductive coercion, which has the potential to change the course of a survivor's life.

## Intimate partner sexual violence and best practice service response

Part 3 of the book contains information, strategies, and recommendations for improving service delivery and preventing IPSV, as well as specific information for particular disciplines. Readers are likely to benefit from the information regardless of profession because of the need for coordinated service response.

The first four chapters of this section focus on advocacy and counseling services for IPSV survivors. In Chapter 7, rape crisis worker Isabelle Kerr provides information on dynamics for deeper understanding and describes effective strategies for counselors and advocates who are working with victims and survivors of IPSV. Jennifer Y. Levy-Peck, in the following chapter, delves into the role of various types of advocates in addressing IPSV, explaining the differences between community-based and system-based advocates and offering practical suggestions for meeting the needs of IPSV survivors in a variety of advocacy programs. As we saw above, sexual assault and domestic violence services have had difficulties with taking ownership of IPSV. In Chapter 9, sexual assault worker Di Macleod writes about the necessity of filling service provision gaps by providing cross-training for both sexual assault and domestic violence workers. Research reveals that survivors of IPSV wish for support groups, and that generic domestic violence or rape survivor groups are often not appropriate (Bergen 1996). In Chapter 10, Jennifer Y. Levy-Peck gives information on how to create and facilitate support groups for IPSV survivors.

A comprehensive discussion of IPSV should contain preventive strategies. Chapter 11 contains a discussion by Debra Parkinson and Susie Reid about prevention and its impact on social change.

Mental and physical health care providers may be the first professionals to encounter individuals affected by IPSV. Chapter 12, by Charlotte Palmer and Vanita Parekh, gives advice to medical professionals on the types of physical and psychological indicators they are likely to see in patients experiencing IPSV, and on appropriate responses and care. In Chapter 13, counselor Elizabeth Layton provides a composite of case studies to highlight the issues clients with IPSV may present to a mental health counselor or psychotherapist, the social and cultural issues to consider, and the psychological effects of this form of violence, such as self-blaming and posttraumatic symptomology. She then offers practical recommendations for therapeutic treatment.

Domestic violence programs have traditionally been reluctant to work with clergy, who are seen as having a poor track record in terms of helpfulness. Abused women who seek help from clergy tend to remain longer with the men who hurt them (Adams 1995). This may be due to a tendency for religious leaders to tell women to submit or to go home and pray, or that their very salvation depends upon remaining with the husbands who rape and otherwise abuse them (Easteal and McOrmond-Plummer 2006). Yet for many abused women, their belief system is important and they want pastoral guidance. In Chapter 14, Barbara Roberts details how religious leaders can give compassionate and helpful responses to IPSV victims who seek their help.

Many survivors of IPSV do not interact with the criminal justice system. When a survivor does reach out for justice, the response may or may not contribute to safety and healing. Although IPSV is a crime, policing practice with respect to partner rape remains largely problematic (Easteal and McOrmond-Plummer 2006; Parkinson and Cowan 2008). In Chapter 15, Police Sergeant Mike Davis draws on his extensive experience to discuss strategies for change. In Chapter 16, two sexual assault forensics experts, Vanita Parekh and Angela Williams, give instruction about the collection of evidence from IPSV survivors facing the criminal justice system. The legal process can be daunting for IPSV survivors. Chapter 17, by Patricia Easteal AM, is thus titled "Advice for Criminal Justice Staff and/or Advocates to Aid Intimate Partner Sexual Violence Survivors."

When a woman reports IPSV, it is still largely assumed she is motivated by vindictiveness toward an ex-partner. In Chapter 18, Lynn Hecht Schafran, attorney and Director of the National Judicial Education Program, explores IPSV in the criminal and family courts, and how injustices may be circumvented. She describes an educational program aimed at the judiciary but of benefit to any service professional working with IPSV survivors.

## *Reaching and assisting different populations*

Part 4 of the book focuses on specific client groups with whom professionals may interact. We begin with Chapter 19, by Marianne Winters and Isobel Morgan, who identify social justice issues for women of color and those from diverse cultural backgrounds who have experienced IPSV, and how their concerns can be respected and effectively addressed by helping professionals.

As a specific group that requires a culturally sensitive response, immigrant women sexually victimized by their partners may face additional burdens due to language barriers and other issues. In Chapter 20, Bushra Sabri, Veronica Barcelona de Mendoza, and Jacquelyn C. Campbell discuss barriers these women face in help-seeking for IPSV, and how professionals can assist in meeting their needs in a sensitive and appropriate manner.

Other groups of people who require specialized understanding are those within the Lesbian, Gay, Bisexual, Transgender, and Queer (LGBTQ) communities. For example, violence in a lesbian relationship may be assumed to be mutual, when in fact it often contains similar dynamics to abusive heterosexual relationships (Winters 2009). In Chapter 21, Janice Ristock discusses the dynamics of sexual violence in lesbian relationships and directives for service provision to this victim and survivor group.

Women who live in rural settings may face different issues with regard to IPSV than their metropolitan counterparts. For example, their isolation may be greater, and police, doctors, and others in whom they might confide may have friendships with the perpetrator (Parkinson and Cowan 2008). In Chapter 22, Debra Parkinson and Claire Zara discuss the difficulties faced by IPSV victims and survivors in rural areas. Attention is given to their special needs and to appropriate service provision.

Teenagers subjected to IPSV may experience different consequences than adults (Easteal and McOrmond-Plummer 2006). In Chapter 23, Jennifer Y. Levy-Peck explores the unique dynamics and impact of teen IPSV and identifies response strategies for sexual assault and coercion perpetrated against teens by partners.

Finally, another underserved group is the large number of women in prison who have histories of sexual assault and other abuses against them (Easteal 2001). In Chapter 24, Debbie Kilroy discusses effective approaches to helping incarcerated IPSV survivors.

## Conclusion
Chapter 25 extracts and distills highlights and recommendations from the central points made by contributors in the previous chapters.

## A note about gendered pronouns
Because most IPSV victims and survivors are female and the majority of perpetrators of IPSV are male, the relevant pronouns are generally used throughout the book, unless there is a specific reference to survivors or abusers of another gender. This is not meant to minimize or ignore the possibility of sexual coercion or assault involving male victims or female perpetrators, but it most accurately reflects the populations with which service providers will be working.

## References
Adams, C. (1995) "'I Just Raped My Wife! What Are You Going to Do About It, Pastor?' The Church and Sexual Violence." In E. Buchwald, P. Fletcher, and M. Roth (eds.) *Transforming a Rape Culture*. Minneapolis, MN: Milkweed Editions.

Aphrodite Wounded (2002) *Read the Good, Bad and Silly Responses People Make to Survivors of Partner Rape and Domestic Violence*. Available at www.books.dreambook.com/louplu/helpful_responses.html, accessed February 7, 2013.

Bergen, R.K. (1996) *Wife Rape: Understanding the Response of Survivors and Service Providers*. Thousand Oaks, CA: Sage.

Bergen, R.K. (2005) *Still a Long Way to Go: Comparing Services for Marital Rape Survivors from 1994 and 2004*. Unpublished.

Bergen, R.K. (2006) *Marital Rape: New Research and Directions*. VAWnet Applied Research Forum. Available at www.vawnet.org/assoc_files_vawnet/ar_maritalraperevised.pdf, accessed February 24, 2013.

Black, M.C., Basile, K.C., Breiding, M.J., Smith, S.G. *et al.* (2011) *The National Intimate Partner and Sexual Violence Survey (NISVS): 2010 Summary Report*. Atlanta, GA: National Center for Injury Prevention and Control, Centers for Disease Control and Prevention. Available at www.cdc.gov/violenceprevention/pdf/nisvs_executive_summary-a.pdf, accessed June 2, 2013.

Campbell, J.C. and Alford, P. (1989) "The dark consequences of marital rape." *American Journal of Nursing 89*, 946–949.

Easteal, P. (1994) *Voices of the Survivors*. North Melbourne: Spinifex Press.

Easteal, P. (2001) "Women in Australian prisons: the cycle of abuse and dysfunctional environments." *The Prison Journal 81*, 1, 87–112.

Easteal, P. and McOrmond-Plummer, L. (2006) *Real Rape, Real Pain: Help for Women Sexually Assaulted by Male Partners.* Melbourne: Hybrid Publishers.

Finkelhor, D. and Yllo, K. (1985) *License to Rape: Sexual Abuse of Wives.* New York: The Free Press.

Heenan, M. (2004) *Just "Keeping the Peace": A Reluctance to Respond to Male Partner Sexual Violence.* Melbourne: Australian Centre for the Study of Sexual Assault. Available at www.aifs.gov.au/acssa/pubs/issue/i1.html, accessed September 3, 2012.

Howard, A., Riger, S., Campbell, R., and Wasco, S. (2003) "Counseling services for battered women: a comparison of outcomes for physical and sexual assault survivors." *Journal of Interpersonal Violence 18*, 7, 717–734.

Myhill, A. and Allen, J. (2002) *Rape and Sexual Assault of Women: Findings from the British Crime Survey.* London: Home Office. Available at www.aphroditewounded. org/Myhill and Allen.pdf, accessed July 4, 2013.

Parkinson, D. and Cowan, S. (2008) *Raped by a Partner: Nowhere to Go, No-One to Tell.* Victoria: Women's Health Goulburn North East.

Russell, D. (1990) *Rape in Marriage.* Bloomington, IN: Indiana University Press.

Winters, M. (2009) "Making the Connections: Advocating for Survivors of Intimate Partner Sexual Violence." In Washington Coalition of Sexual Assault Programs (ed.) *Intimate Partner Sexual Violence: Sexual Assault in the Context of Domestic Violence.* Olympia, WA: Washington Coalition of Sexual Assault Programs. Available at www.wcsap.org/sexual-assult-context-domestic-violence, accessed February 24, 2013.

CHAPTER 2

# Preventing Secondary Wounding by Misconception

## WHAT PROFESSIONALS REALLY NEED TO KNOW ABOUT INTIMATE PARTNER SEXUAL VIOLENCE

Louise McOrmond-Plummer

## Introduction

Trauma expert Aphrodite Matsakis has written at some length about "secondary wounding" and defines it as responding to survivors of trauma with disbelief, denial, minimization, stigmatization, or refusal of help. Secondary wounding may compound the original trauma, or in some cases cause the survivors to feel even worse than the rape itself. Further, women who have survived abusive relationships experience more secondary wounding than any other group of trauma survivor (Matsakis 1992). Intimate partner sexual violence (IPSV) survivors frequently experience elements of secondary wounding, including by professionals (Easteal and McOrmond-Plummer 2006; Parkinson and Cowan 2008). At least part of the reason for this is that service providers—legal, medical, counseling, and other—are drawn from a wider society that is largely accepting of misconceptions that pass for fact about IPSV. Many of the misconceptions are based in ideas about what constitutes "real" rape, what a "good" victim does, and beliefs about women's tendency to level false accusations. In this chapter, I share some facts about IPSV that are often subject to misconception. Much of this will be explored more thoroughly in further chapters. It is important that myths are overturned so that survivors' interactions with professionals do not become occasions of secondary wounding.

# What professionals really need to know about intimate partner sexual violence

*Partner rape is real rape:* Rape, in general, is viewed as something strangers who lurk in alleyways do. A prior relationship between rapist and victim raises the specter of probable consent. What is an assault becomes diluted then by a myriad of other issues. For example, rape becomes confused with sex; it is viewed as just sex one more time with a partner with whom the woman may have been having consensual intercourse for years, and in any case, isn't the perpetrator "entitled to it" by dint of the relationship?

One of the most injurious aspects of IPSV is that, unlike the survivor of stranger rape, the survivor of partner rape gets little to no community recognition that a real crime has occurred, one that accrues real wounds (Easteal and McOrmond-Plummer 2006). It is also true that perpetrators of IPSV don't see themselves as real rapists; commonly, they believe they have a right to have sex with partners whether consent is present or not (Parkinson and Cowan 2008). Although perpetrators of IPSV may not fit common stereotypes of what a rapist is, they are still rapists. Some of them are serial rapists, having sexually assaulted multiple partners, or the same partner multiple times (Lisak and Miller 2002).

Some people who consider themselves to be against sexual violence may see it somewhat differently when the victim has had a sexual relationship with her rapist. For example, consider the (ironic) words of this man:

> I would never think of taking it by force, except from my wife. I don't think I could get it up in a rape situation. It so appalls me that I couldn't do it. I have forced myself on my wife when she has repeatedly refused me and has led me to believe I could have some and then closed up. (Hite 1982, p.761)

This bias is also found in areas where it may reasonably be least expected. For example, the president of a sexual assault service stated, "Marital rape is just not as traumatic as other types of rape. Your husband is a known entity so it's not so bad" (Bergen 1996, p.79).

However, sexual assault should not be considered as less of a crime because of the context in which it takes place. Imagine the application of such a rule to robbery, making the victim "less" robbed because (s)he knows the thief. Therefore, when dealing with a survivor of

IPSV, it is essential for the service provider to never say or imply that her assault doesn't matter or is less serious because it wasn't a stranger.

*Anyone can be raped or sexually assaulted by their partner:* While it must be acknowledged that certain factors—such as an abusive childhood, poverty, or the presence of physical violence in a relationship— may place women at greater risk for IPSV, it is very important not to stigmatize or blame victims. We should not make the mistake of thinking that a certain "type" of woman is sexually abused (Easteal and McOrmond-Plummer 2006). Factors such as widely held views about a man's entitlement to pursue and have sex using any means necessary are deeply enshrined in most cultures, and it is this mindset that many men carry into relationships, creating potential IPSV risk for their partners (Easteal and McOrmond-Plummer 2006).

*Women do not commonly lie about IPSV:* There is a popular notion that women often lie about IPSV in order to win custody cases or get back at ex-partners for leaving them, among other things. This enduring myth is generated everywhere from the courts down to the person next door. As will be seen in Chapter 18, family court personnel may treat women who allege domestic violence with skepticism and hostility; this may be worse when sexual assault is claimed. Fear of vindictive wives flooding the courts to "cry rape" has been raised as a reason for not overturning legal exemptions (Russell 1990). However, while there may be a small number of false accusations, they are not part of a larger trend. In fact, partner rape has particularly low reporting, prosecution, and conviction rates (Easteal and Feerick 2005; Easteal and Gani 2005; Heenan and Murray 2006; Kelly, Lovett, and Regan 2005; Lievore 2003). Women are not seeking redress for this crime often enough, and when they do, they are not often enough taken seriously.

*IPSV can have serious physical and psychological effects:* There is a tendency to view IPSV as less serious than other types of sexual assault, when in fact impact may be longer-lasting. As Finkelhor and Yllo write, "When you are raped by a stranger, you have to live with a frightening memory. When you are raped by your husband, you have to live with your rapist" (1985, p.138). It is also worth remembering that perpetrators who batter and rape may become lethal, as discussed in

Chapter 4. Accordingly, Evan Stark (2007) argues that, with respect to law, partner rape should be treated with greater seriousness because:

> As a result of its unique relation to personal life, sexual assault is far more likely to be repeated when it is committed by partners and almost always occurs amid other forms of violence, intimidation and control. The level of unfreedom, subordination, dependence, and betrayal associated with marital rape has no counterpart in public life. (p.388)

As described in Chapter 3, IPSV may have some differing effects when compared to other types of sexual or domestic violence, and this just means *different*, not lesser. Professionals hearing a disclosure of IPSV should remember that discounting it can add greatly to the impact (Easteal and McOrmond-Plummer 2006).

It is also necessary to consider that there may be serious impact on any children, perhaps those conceived in rape, or who have witnessed the violation of their mothers (Finkelhor and Yllo 1985).

*It's still rape if the victim remained with, returned to, or still loves the perpetrator:* It is commonly believed that a woman who continues a relationship with, and/or still professes love for, the partner who raped her was not in fact raped. People may think too that, if it was really that bad, she would have left. This is often based in ideas about the "good" victim; that is, "real" rape victim would run away screaming and call the police. She would feel nothing but revulsion for the rapist. Here, we see the intrusion of scenarios that may belong to stranger rape, which is perceived as the only truly *bona fide* rape. These have no place in a consideration of IPSV, where the dynamics are more similar to those of other forms of intimate partner violence.

It is essential for professionals to understand that there are many reasons why women remain with perpetrators. First, there may be the factors more traditionally related to domestic violence, such as fear of reprisal or financial dependency.

Or, women who have experienced IPSV may not know that they were raped because they, too, have been socialized to accept stranger rape as real rape. Even if a woman does think otherwise, she may still love her partner, because he is rarely "just a rapist"; he may also be the father to her children and still may exhibit at times the favorable characteristics she fell in love with. She may be fighting to suppress her feelings about sexual assaults in order to justify continuing the relationship.

There must be space for the woman to express these feelings and receive the message from her listener that she is not stupid or crazy for having them. It is possible for the professional to give that affirmation while still upholding that it is never acceptable for anybody to sexually assault her (Easteal and McOrmond-Plummer 2006). A woman's decision to remain with a perpetrator cannot magically turn a rape into consensual sex, and does not mean that it was not serious. Ongoing love for the perpetrator may mean it hurts all the more.

*IPSV is not a "gray area"*: As discussed in Chapter 11, it is common for professionals to see sexual assault by intimate partners as a "gray area," one which belongs in the private realm of people's bedrooms, and as such may not be considered worth the focus given to other types of sexual assault. This minimizing view implies that there are special rules for sexual partners about what is or isn't rape and what may or may not negate consent, etc. However, regardless of the context in which it occurs, rape is rape.

*IPSV is not the victim's fault:* It is common for rape victims to be blamed for what they wore, for where they walked and with whom, and for leading the perpetrator on. With IPSV, people may blame the survivor for being "frigid" or "withholding." One man was advised by his psychiatrist to rape a wife who was withholding sex (Hite 1982). Yet, Finkelhor and Yllo (1985) found that marital rape victims had not withheld sex from their partners, but were responsive when approached with respect and affection. Indeed, even if the opposite were true, this can be no justification for sexual assault. It is just a way of saying that a withholding woman is "asking for it" and should be punished accordingly. This upholds notions about male entitlement.

Survivors of IPSV may be blamed for "liking it rough," and be labeled "masochistic" (Finkelhor and Yllo 1985). Some women survive ongoing IPSV by developing the ability to respond physically, with some victims experiencing orgasm in the course of rape (Finkelhor and Yllo 1985). This may be a survivor's best-kept and most shameful secret, but it should never be construed as evidence that she liked or wanted the assault, or that it was not serious. In fact, victims of child sexual abuse or stranger rape may also experience physical arousal and orgasm. Levin and van Berlo (2004) answer the question

"Can an orgasm be induced in a subject despite their not wanting one?" by saying, "Looking at all the available evidence (see this review) the answer appears to be 'yes'..." (p.84). Regardless of what her body did, if she did not consent, she was raped.

Women who are adherents of the Bondage Discipline Sado-Masochism (BDSM) lifestyle can also claim the right not to be raped. Actual sexual assault should be recognized as quite different from fantasies or games. IPSV is not "kinky sex." It is a crime.

People may blame an IPSV survivor for ongoing sexual assault if she remained in the relationship, and she will frequently blame herself for the same. It is, of course, patronizing to a survivor to pretend she is not responsible for her choices (and it is also necessary to be careful about the word "choice" in an environment of trauma). There may be an assumption that a victim can "just leave," without taking into account the cold fact that, with domestic violence, the risks of further rape, physical violence, and even murder escalate sharply as a woman is leaving or after she has done so (Adams 2007; Bancroft 2003; see also Chapter 5).

In looking at the issue of blaming women for remaining, we must not neglect mother-blame. It's very common for people to make statements to victims of violence about whether they are "considering the children." First, perpetrators commonly denigrate their victims as mothers, and it is important that service providers do not replicate this behavior. Professionals should not presume to understand the needs of the survivor's children better than she does. Women who have survived abuse are mostly loving mothers who are deeply concerned about the impact of abuse on their children. They struggle to balance survival with their children's needs (Bancroft 2003). Where children are actually at risk, professionals are mandated to make a report to protective services. However, remember that women are often afraid to disclose abuse because they fear removal of their children. If professionals have concerns about children's safety but are not sure, they are advised to seek advice from a domestic violence advocacy service *before* making a report (Bancroft 2003).

And, while IPSV victims are blamed for the rape because they remained in the relationship, they may also be blamed because they left. For example, a religious leader may tell a victim she is being disobedient to God for seeking safety, as if the sexual assaults don't matter. One religious leader blamed the woman by creating moral equivalency between rape and the victim's behavior: "The main responses I remember are the 'Yes, but's': 'Yes, but your behaviour hasn't been perfect either.' 'Yes, but your attitude to him is wrong.' 'Yes, but you have put him under a lot of pressure'" (Easteal and McOrmond-Plummer 2006, p.119).

Or, a perpetrator who rapes an ex-partner may receive sympathy because he was upset about the end of the relationship, even in the courts. For instance, one Australian judge, presiding over a case in which a man raped his estranged wife, made the observation that "the respondent probably hoped to repair the rupture and resume living with his wife" (*DPP* v. *Cowey* 1995).

It will help if service providers operate from a belief that the perpetrator needs to be held accountable for his behavior. Professionals should also be careful of unintentionally imposing blame with questions such as "Why didn't you call the police?"

*Perpetrators have control over their actions:* A popular misconception about sexual assault is that perpetrators are "out of control." Issues such as alcohol, anger, and insecurity may play a role in IPSV. There are contributing factors, and it would be unwise to ignore them. However, perpetrators are still accountable for their behavior. An alcoholic perpetrator may stop drinking, and then he will merely be a sober perpetrator (Bancroft 2003), if he still carries a mindset of sexual entitlement.

Perpetrators themselves may excuse their behavior by saying things like, "I was too turned on to control myself." However, it really is an excuse, one that plays into popular myths about how men can't help themselves (Easteal 2001).

A client who discloses IPSV may want to understand about potential contributing factors. But first she will need to hear that no factor mitigates her being raped. Carol Adams (1995) writes, "Men who abuse and rape their partners are men who seek to control others. In being abusive they are not out of control; rather, they establish control" (p.68). The stories of survivors of IPSV certainly portray a chilling choice and control on the part of their abusers (see for example Easteal and McOrmond-Plummer 2006).

*It's still rape if the victim doesn't know what to call it:* The idea that women are "led" to call non-rape experiences rape gained currency in the 1990s with books and articles that stated that rape awareness was a product of feminist hysteria, and that "man-hating" feminists or women's groups encourage women to make false allegations (Warshaw, 1994). This implies that women don't have minds of their own.

There are many reasons why women raped by partners might be confused about whether their experiences were rape. Some of the confusion may be due to internalization of myths about what is real rape. And sometimes a victim is unwilling to name her experiences correctly. If she deeply loves her partner, the implications of labeling the experience as rape, and him as a rapist, may be frankly too painful (Russell 1990). Rape researcher Robyn Warshaw writes, "Not knowing the right label for an experience doesn't mean it didn't happen" (1994, p.xxiv).

The paradox of a survivor maintaining love for an abuser is often the most difficult aspect of IPSV for service providers to understand. It is made clearer by the well-established psychological theory of cognitive dissonance (Festinger 1957), which states that a person holding two conflicting beliefs may minimize and avoid information that enhances the conflict. Thus the two-pack-a-day smoker, while otherwise grounded in reality, may rationalize that cigarette smoking is not really bad for one's health. The IPSV survivor, on the one hand, has many reasons for wishing to believe that her partner loves her and simply has made a mistake; on the other hand, she feels deeply injured emotionally. It makes sense that the second belief, being more painful, is more subject to minimization and dismissal.

*IPSV happens in relationships that may not otherwise be violent:* Although IPSV often does coexist with physical violence, it is not always the case. There may be other forms of abuse and control such as financial or emotional abuse (Easteal and McOrmond-Plummer 2006). It may also take place as the only manifestation of control by the male partner (Easteal and McOrmond-Plummer 2006). As Diana Russell (1990) points out, it is a mistake to simply file partner rape under a general heading of domestic violence, as if it only happens in very violent relationships. When we do this, it denies the experience and voices of women who are raped but not beaten.

*It's still rape if the coercion does not include physical force:* Perpetrators of IPSV often know of methods other than force or violence to coerce their partners into sex. Consider the words of this man: "I would act like I was mad at her and she would give in. It works every time" (Hite 1982, p.776). Sex under these circumstances is not with consent and the perpetrator knows this; perhaps not in the sense that he labels it as rape, but that he has triumphed and got what he wants when she doesn't want it. Moreover, nonphysical coercive sexual assault, as will be seen later in this book, is still traumatic to its victims.

*Submission is not consent:* The stereotype of what is real rape is also based on ideas about victim behavior. For example, she must have uttered a clear "No," or have actively fought, preferably sustaining an injury to prove she didn't consent. However, consent actually means free agreement—that is, the ability to say no without fear of unpleasant consequences. Submitting because of the likelihood of a beating, or because the partner will withdraw affection, is not consent (see Chapter 4). It is also worth remembering that perpetrators of IPSV may not care if consent is present or not. They may be thinking of their own gratification above all else, or they may not actually *want* consent if they want to *rape* their partner in order to hurt, punish, or take ownership of her (Easteal and McOrmond-Plummer 2006).

*Not naming IPSV colludes in the silence around it:* Speaking specifically about rape in marriage, Carol Adams (1995) writes, "A problem inadequately named cannot be adequately addressed" (p.63). Yet, professionals may be reluctant to name intimate partner sexual assault or rape. They may fear that they are denying control to the victim, or that it will retraumatize her (Heenan 2004). Service providers may be uncomfortable with the sexual part of IPSV, or may also subscribe to stereotypes about real rape (Parkinson and Cowan 2008). Chapter 11 provides information about why naming IPSV as rape and a crime is essential to assisting a survivor and also to achieving social justice.

*IPSV is not a mutual problem:* When professionals view IPSV as a sexual dysfunction or other mutual issue between the couple, they may suggest couples' counseling. But this is not safe for women in abusive relationships. There is also the danger of victim-blame and collusion with perpetrators who may be good at manipulating counselors (Bancroft 2003). For example, I experienced beatings for talking about the violence in couples' counseling, and also blame from the counselor for provoking my batterer.

Any counseling must be predicated on holding the perpetrator accountable, and on concern for the victim's safety.

# Conclusion

I have explored some common misconceptions about IPSV that can lead to harmful or unhelpful service provider responses to survivors. It is a good idea to adopt "First, do no harm" as a motto, and remember that words and responses can hurt very deeply, even prolonging danger. The professional to whom the survivor turns for help is in a position to do so much good.

# References

Adams, C. (1995) "'I Just Raped My Wife! What Are You Going to Do About It, Pastor?' The Church and Sexual Violence." In E. Buchwald, P. Fletcher, and M. Roth (eds.) *Transforming a Rape Culture*. Minneapolis, MN: Milkweed Editions.

Adams, D. (2007) *Why Do They Kill? Men Who Murder Their Intimate Partners*. Nashville, TN: Vanderbilt University Press.

Bancroft, L. (2003) *Why Does He Do That? Inside the Minds of Angry and Controlling Men*. New York: Berkeley Publishing Group.

Bergen, R. (1996) *Wife Rape: Understanding the Response of Survivors and Service Providers*. Thousand Oaks, CA: Sage.

*DPP* v. *Cowey* (Unreported, South Australia Court of Criminal Appeal, Cox, Prior, Lander, July 18, 1995).

Easteal, P. (2001) *Less Than Equal: Women and the Australian Legal System*. Sydney: Butterworths.

Easteal, P. and Feerick, C. (2005) "Sexual assault by male partners: is the license still valid?" *Flinders Journal of Law Reform 8*, 2, 185–207.

Easteal, P. and Gani, M. (2005) "Sexual assault by male partners: a study of sentencing factors." *Southern Cross University Law Review 9*, 39–72.

Easteal, P. and McOrmond-Plummer, L. (2006) *Real Rape, Real Pain: Help for Women Sexually Assaulted by Male Partners*. Melbourne: Hybrid Publishers.

Festinger, L. (1957) *A Theory of Cognitive Dissonance*. Stanford, CA: Stanford University Press.

Finkelhor, D. and Yllo, K. (1985) *License to Rape: Sexual Abuse of Wives*. New York: The Free Press.

Heenan, M. (2004) *Just "Keeping the Peace": A Reluctance to Respond to Male Partner Sexual Violence*. Melbourne: Australian Centre for the Study of Sexual Assault. Available at www.aifs.gov.au/acssa/pubs/issue/i1.html, accessed September 3, 2012.

Heenan, M. and Murray, S. (2006) *A Study of Reported Rapes in Victoria 2000–2003*. Melbourne: Office of Women's Policy. Available at http://mams.rmit.edu.au/igzd08ddxtpwz.pdf, accessed March 17, 2013.

Hite, S. (1982) *Hite Report on Male Sexuality: How Men Feel About Love, Sex and Relationships*. New York: Ballantine Books.

Kelly, L., Lovett, J., and Regan, L. (2005) *A Gap or a Chasm? Attrition in Reported Rape Cases*. Home Office Research Study 293. London: Home Office Research, Development, and Statistics Directorate. Available at http://library.npia.police.uk/docs/hors/hors293.pdf, accessed March 16, 2013.

Levin, R. and van Berlo, W. (2004) "Sexual arousal and orgasm in subjects who experience forced or non-consensual sexual stimulation—a review." *Journal of Clinical Forensic Medicine 11*, 82–88.

Lievore, D. (2003) *Intimate Partner Sexual Assault: The Impact of Competing Demands on Victims' Decisions to Seek Criminal Justice Solutions.* Canberra: Australian Institute of Criminology. Available at www.aifs.gov.au/conferences/aifs8/lievore.pdf, accessed February 24, 2013.

Lisak, D. and Miller, P. (2002) "Repeat rape and multiple offending among undetected rapists." *Violence and Victims 17*, 1, 73–84.

Matsakis, A. (1992) *I Can't Get Over It: A Handbook for Trauma Survivors.* Oakland, CA: New Harbinger Publications, Inc.

Parkinson, D. and Cowan, S. (2008) *Raped by a Partner: Nowhere to Go, No-One to Tell.* Victoria: Women's Health Goulburn North East.

Russell, D. (1990) *Rape in Marriage.* Bloomington, IN: Indiana University Press.

Stark, E. (2007) *Coercive Control: The Entrapment of Women in Personal Life.* New York: Oxford University Press.

Warshaw, R. (1994) *I Never Called It Rape: The Ms. Report on Recognizing, Fighting and Surviving Date and Acquaintance Rape.* New York: HarperPerennial.

# CHAPTER 3

# Considering the Differences

## INTIMATE PARTNER SEXUAL VIOLENCE IN SEXUAL ASSAULT AND DOMESTIC VIOLENCE DISCOURSE

Louise McOrmond-Plummer

## Introduction

Many years ago, I became free of a dangerous man. He beat me regularly, threatened me with weapons, and pursued me with threats to my life when I sought to leave. He had other ways of subjugating and demeaning me, too. He raped me repeatedly, when his sense of ownership of me was threatened, to punish me, to force reconciliation after beating me, or just because I presumed the right to say no. At the time, avoiding or surviving the battery was a priority because this was violence that people could see, and I was afraid it would kill me. I had no place to put the "sexual stuff," no name to give it—or more properly, no name that I felt justified in giving it. I found that one could both know a thing and not know it. One bad night, I sat on my bed musing that I had been raped by my fiancé; then that thought was immediately borne away by my internalized social notions of what rape is: it's something that strangers behind park bushes do. I had no idea that, in my future, it would be the sexual violence that would be the most deeply scarring.

Fortunately, I got away. I tried to bury myself in a new life and took along the non-wisdom that horrible things were best forgotten. When my ex-partner was charged with murder, the barricade against memory and feeling that I had attempted to construct began to crumble. Most disconcertingly, memories of the *rapes* bothered me. It occurred to me that it was different, *worse* somehow, than the battery. I decided to seek information that could help me begin to process it.

This was immensely frustrating. What I found was a world of the same socialization I had experienced. In rape and domestic violence literature, as well as within agencies, intimate partner sexual violence

(IPSV) and the range of issues it carries, as distinct from general sexual assault or domestic violence, were not well defined. It was as if there was a hole in the knowledge; my experiences had only limited commonality. It left me feeling as if what happened to me was given lip-service as rape, but somehow *less* rape than any other kind. I concluded that my level of trauma must be an overreaction, but even so and much to my shame, the pain wouldn't go away.

Upon entering the university setting, I had the opportunity to study IPSV. I discovered that researchers were indeed drawing attention to partner rape, pointing out the need to be aware of the specific dynamics of it (Finkelhor and Yllo 1985; Russell 1990). I became passionate about doing something about an issue that has affected me and other women deeply.

In this chapter, I explore some distinct differences between IPSV and general sexual assault and domestic violence, based on research and survivor accounts. Anybody with a working knowledge of sexual assault and domestic violence knows that they carry some similar effects like shame, fear, and diminished self-esteem. However, a specific issue does need to be made of IPSV, because putting it under a catch-all heading and proceeding as if the same wisdom applies is neither adequate nor always appropriate, and can work to the actual detriment of help-seeking survivors (Bergen 1996; Heenan 2004). It is my hope that this chapter will be a helpful contribution to the growing body of professional knowledge not just about IPSV, but also, and most importantly, about care of the survivors of this crime.

## Problems with equating intimate partner sexual violence and general sexual assault

It is true that all types of rape are traumatic, and that in any context rape should be seen as *rape*. But common wisdoms about sexual assault are often ill-suited to IPSV survivors. Raquel Bergen (1996) writes about the insufficiency of treating IPSV survivors as generic rape survivors, with particular regard to counseling and support groups. In my own experience of membership in a generic rape survivor group, there simply wasn't the space to explore my specific issues such as ambivalent feelings for the perpetrator and the deep shame of having continued the relationship after being raped by him. I believed that to put my experiences on a par with those of the other women would offend them. This led to a deeper sense of isolation and belief that my experiences didn't matter as much as those of the other women (see more information about IPSV support groups in Chapter 10). It didn't occur to me then that a different experience was not a lesser experience.

Finkelhor and Yllo write about the "special traumas" of IPSV and tell us, "It is these special traumas that we need to understand in their full and terrible reality" (1985, p.138). Survivor Linda articulates:

> And they say marital rape is not as bad as stranger rape. I don't know. I have never been raped by a stranger. But I think being raped by your husband in your own home must be worse in some ways. At least if you're attacked by a perfect stranger it is not so personal. Your husband is the person whom you should be able to turn to for comfort, who should protect you. When it is the person you have entrusted your life to who abuses you, it isn't just physical or sexual assault, it is a betrayal of the very core of your marriage or your person, your trust. If you're not safe in your own home, next to your husband, where are you safe? (Easteal and McOrmond-Plummer 2006, p.138)

Below are some of the psychological, physical, and social response characteristics of IPSV that differ from other sexual assault contexts:

- *Longer-lasting trauma:* There's a common notion that IPSV doesn't have as bad an impact as sexual assault by a stranger. In fact, research reveals that the trauma can be longer lasting. Effects may be prolonged by lack of recognition and ability to share the pain, the breach of trust involved, and vulnerability to further rape. Survivors of IPSV may be afraid of the perpetrator and the recurrence of sexual assault for a very long time after. Further, survivors of IPSV are more than twice as likely to be diagnosed with depression or anxiety as survivors not raped in this context (Easteal 1994; Finkelhor and Yllo 1985; Plichta and Falik 2001).

- *Higher levels of physical injury:* Generally, most rapes do not involve additional physical injury, but those that do are likely to be partner rape (Myhill and Allen 2002). This is another reason for "challenging enduring stereotypes suggesting spousal sexual assaults are less violent and less serious" (Stermac, Del Bove, and Addison 2001, p.1218).

- *The incidence of multiple rapes:* Although IPSV can be a one-time-only offense, survivors of IPSV suffer the highest frequency of multiple rapes, with some women reporting being raped more than 20 times (Finkelhor and Yllo 1985; Myhill and Allen 2002).

- *Higher levels of anal and oral rape:* Partner perpetrators commonly use these forms of assault to humiliate, punish, and take "full" ownership of their partners (Finkelhor and Yllo 1985).

- *Higher levels of victim-blame and rape-supportive attitudes:* Rape in marriage is viewed socially as less serious and the victim as more responsible than in other contexts. This perception changes somewhat if the couple is separated, but even these cases still tend to be viewed as less serious than other types of sexual assault (Ewoldt, Monson, and Langhinrichsen-Rohling 2000). IPSV victims are a group singularly prone to being advised by church, family, or friends that they should be grateful that the rapist is a good father, and that it's their duty to submit to him (Parkinson and Cowan 2008). In effect, these responses tell women to put up with rape. It's hard to imagine this suggestion being given to other rape victims, and it leads to further endangerment of IPSV victims who may conclude that this advice is correct.

- *Safety issues:* The IPSV survivor may need a place of refuge, court orders, and assistance with legal or custody matters.

- *Difficulty defining the act(s) as sexual assault:* Women, like many people in our communities, are socialized to see rape as involving nonconsensual sex between two strangers. Additionally, there may be reluctance to define a partner the victim loves as a "rapist." Some women may become more aware of a rape having occurred when the abuse moves from activity they consider "normal," such as vaginal intercourse, to acts they perceive as more deviant, such as anal sex (Bergen 1996). However, some women, even if their victimization does conform to more stereotypically violent notions of rape, may still be confused. Summer was violently beaten and raped orally, anally, and vaginally at knifepoint by her ex-partner, and yet speaks of "the shame of feeling 'half-raped'" (Easteal and McOrmond-Plummer 2006, p.44). Like many women,

Summer got plenty of social help in her inability to call the act rape:

> My secondary-wounding was riddled with insinuations that it just "couldn't have been that bad" that because I chose to stay in an unhealthy relationship, in a relationship that I had been warned repeatedly to get out of, that that somehow was me asking for "more of the same." I've also been told in no uncertain terms that had I decided to report, that it would not be considered rape. (Easteal and McOrmond-Plummer 2006, p.180)

- *A general climate of sexual assault/abuse:* Women living with IPSV may face a host of behaviors other than penile rape that would not be acceptable if committed by strangers, such as their breasts being mauled, being forced to touch the perpetrator sexually, and degrading name-calling (Easteal and McOrmond-Plummer 2006).

- *Less likely to seek agency, medical, or police help than other groups of rape survivors:* This may be due to factors such as an inability to label the assault(s) as rape, or a crime, and presents a challenge to professionals in terms of how to encourage women to come forward (Mahoney 1999).

- *Financial dependency on the rapist:* Women with children who are permitted no money or employment of their own may feel that there is no escape.

- *Genuine and deep love of the rapist:* For some women, the fact that the partner who sexually assaults them may be an otherwise good or loving partner seems to outweigh the assaults. Outside of a context of abuse, women may still enjoy sex with the same partners who are abusing them. Of course, this may be due to stringent coping mechanisms, such as denial, that some women put into place in order to submerge their pain and continue the relationship (Bergen 1996; Finkelhor and Yllo 1985). Whatever the case, women need to have those feelings heard and understood, and at the same time to hear that it is never okay for anybody to sexually assault them.

## Problems with equating intimate partner sexual violence and general domestic violence

There has been a trend in domestic violence discourse to view IPSV as simply another abuse. Yet, Bergen's study reveals that most women who were battered as well as raped by their partners considered rape to be the most significant issue. She adds that, "When treated as battered women, the wounds left by the sexual abuse often go unaddressed" (Bergen 1996, p.89). To be sure, all domestic violence, be it physical, emotional, sexual, or otherwise, usually is aimed at control and subjugation. Battery is a serious issue with serious consequences, and I have already said that, in my violent relationship, it seemed the most frightening and physically dangerous issue. But sexual assault attacks a woman's psyche in different ways, and I'm going to share parts of my story in an attempt to illustrate some of these differences.

In my experience, the battery was aimed at getting me to do what I was told or hurting me for not doing so, but the rape had a far nastier and more contemptuous message. It was more calculated to inflict psychological harm than the battery. My rapist-partner would say ugly things to me in the course of rape, sometimes thrusting in my body in an exaggerated way as if to emphasize his power over me and to make the experience as dirty and humiliating as possible. He intended rape as an ultimate insult, and that is how I experienced it. And the outcome could be different: I was apt to be less defiant after rape than after battery. One night, I began to pack his clothes, telling him to get out. He slapped and punched me for exercising this autonomy. This alone did not make me back down; that came after he raped me and said he would do it again and again throughout the night until I changed my mind or until he couldn't get an erection anymore. I cried and I broke—a usual response that did not even need to involve the threat of more to come. If battery was terrifying, rape made me almost childlike in the fragility I felt. I was so *sad* that somebody who said he loved me wanted to do this to me. And my partner liked inducing that fragility and its pursuant compliance. This man knew that the use of rape possessed, controlled, and finally conquered me in ways that battery couldn't.

The *shame* in being raped was particularly bad. I felt physically sick with it. While I was ashamed of being battered—certainly in terms of the blame it accrued from others—the shame of being raped was more deeply excoriating. I didn't think I would ever tell anybody because then they'd know I was "dirty" for being raped as well as "stupid" for being beaten. Much more than the battery, the rape seemed like an attack on my very womanhood, which I came to feel was disgusting.

These are some of the ways in which rape was different than battery for me, and while my story is not intended to be definitive for all women, neither is it unique. Domestic violence workers and other helping professionals can immeasurably aid women when they are prepared to lift IPSV out of general domestic violence discourse, and acknowledge that it has special wounds that need tending and, like other forms of rape, is nothing for a woman to be ashamed of.

Another serious problem in subsuming IPSV under the heading of domestic violence is that it may foster the assumption that rape only happens in battering relationships. While rape is indeed more likely to occur in very violent and physically dangerous relationships (Russell 1990), it does occur also in relationships not characterized by other violence. Natalie says:

> There was absolutely no indication in the seven years of our relationship that he could be violent, and I know he adored me. I simply couldn't reconcile the Sean who attacked me with the Sean that I had known all those years. (Easteal and McOrmond-Plummer 2006, p.111)

Researchers have remarked on the difficulty of finding a large enough study sample of women who have experienced rape without battery or other forms of violence (Bennice *et al.* 2003). However, in the years of operating my website, Aphrodite Wounded, I have had numerous emails from women who are almost apologetic because they were raped but not beaten "like so many other women." I have observed that these women are often immensely confused about whether they deserve to call their experiences rape. Yet they are certainly hurting and deserving of support. These women are also suffering from the social myth that a woman must be badly beaten to prove she didn't consent to rape.

Women who don't identify as domestic violence victims because they haven't been beaten, or whose sexual assaults are more coercive than physically violent (i.e. the perpetrator withdraws affection or verbally badgers to get what he wants), will continue to fall through the cracks when IPSV is not clearly defined and given a prominence of its own. It is already problematic enough that even IPSV survivors

INTIMATE PARTNER SEXUAL VIOLENCE

who did experience physical violence sometimes feel that the rape will not be understood.

Let us now look at some specific differences between battery and IPSV:

- *Potential fatality:* Research establishes that women who are being raped as well as battered are in greater danger of being killed than women who are battered only. In one study, 75 percent of women who survived attempted murder by their partner were also raped (Adams 2007; Campbell and Alford 1989). Screening women for life-threatening issues is an important part of shelter intake; viewing IPSV in this light may save lives.

- *Deliberately inflicted pregnancy:* Violent men may rape to impregnate their partners in order to force them to remain in or return to the relationship. Research reveals that when women become pregnant by rape, partners are most frequently the perpetrators. Pregnancy related to partner rape is also associated with fewer live births and poor maternal outcomes (Easteal and McOrmond-Plummer 2006; Holmes *et al.* 1996; McFarlane 2007).

- *Deliberately inflicted STD:* IPSV has been positively correlated with the spread of HIV/AIDS. Abusive men force their partners into unprotected sex to infect them with sexually transmitted diseases to prevent the women from seeing other men (Wilson 1997).

- *Psychological effects:* Women who have been raped as well as battered may suffer greater damage to self-esteem and body issues—and this effect has been measured as separable from battery (Shields and Hanneke 1983). Battered and raped women who consider the sexual assault(s) by their partners worse than the battery develop posttraumatic stress disorder (PTSD) at more than twice the rate of women who consider the battery the worst issue they faced (Bennice *et al.* 2003). Further, relationship sexual abuse, especially when combined with physical abuse, is shown to present a greater risk of developing complex PTSD (Roth *et al.* 1997).

# Different issues among subgroups of intimate partner sexual violence survivors

In thinking about the distinct issues that IPSV survivors face, we should not neglect determinant factors that may have a bearing on different IPSV survivors' reactions. Other chapters in this book refer to issues for specific groups. In general, some factors to consider are:

- *The age of the survivor:* Teenage survivors of IPSV experience some different effects from their adult counterparts. For example, teenage rape survivors are more prone to self-injury and risk-taking behaviors, and may have fewer social and legal options (Easteal and McOrmond-Plummer 2006).

- *The levels of violence involved:* Women who have been beaten in the course of IPSV generally experience higher levels of PTSD than women whose assaults involved less physically violent coercion—especially when the violence involves more "extreme" types of violence such as beating or choking (Roth *et al.* 1997; Russell 1990). In my experience, the presence of physical violence made it seem so much more likely to become lethal, and knowing that one could have been killed does take some coming to terms with. The trauma generated by the fact that my abuser's violence might have killed me (exacerbated by the fact that he did eventually commit a murder) was, along with rape, a whole other issue to deal with. This still gives me pause to acknowledge my good fortune compared to the women who are not here because their partners actually murdered them. This is not to say, however, that sexual assaults which do not contain the stereotypical element of physical violence do not have impact (e.g. see Chapter 4); such assaults are still painful violations and may be more confusing to the victim. Further, Russell's study found that, while 70 percent of the IPSV survivors interviewed said they were "extremely upset" by threats of a physical nature, a larger proportion of the women (83%) were "extremely upset" by a partner's threats to leave or withdraw his love (1990).

- *Duration and frequency of the assaults:* Women who have experienced multiple rapes are three times more likely to experience long-term impact from IPSV, and this figure climbs the longer the rapes go on (Russell 1990). Nevertheless, it is necessary to bear in mind that one incident can still comprise a profound shock and trauma (Easteal and McOrmond-Plummer 2006).

- *Type of assault:* Completed penile-vaginal penetration is found to be the most distressing type of sexual assault, having greater impact than attempted rape or other forms such as anal or oral rape (Russell 1990).

Naturally, it is most important for research to be done and disseminated so that professional people have a handle on what they may encounter in survivors of IPSV. However, it is also important to listen to each woman's description of how she feels and what she needs. It is not appropriate on the front lines to compare one survivor's pain to another. While this may be self-evident to some professionals, it still bears stating because IPSV and its harms are so frequently minimized by wider society, professionals included, when compared to other types of rape.

## To conclude

IPSV is sexual assault and domestic violence—"both/and" rather than "either/or"—with some distinct features, the recognition of which are crucial if survivors are to be aided effectively. I close with an appeal to professionals to please educate yourselves about these differences so that you can assist victims and survivors of IPSV in a way tailored to them. Women's lives may depend on it. I cannot overstate the danger or at very least the pain of feeling as if what happened doesn't count even when it is hurting badly. We can all do much better.

## References

Adams, D. (2007) *Why Do They Kill? Men Who Murder Their Intimate Partners.* Nashville, TN: Vanderbilt University Press.

Bennice, J.A., Resick, P.A., Mechanic, M., and Astin, M. (2003) "The relative effects of intimate partner physical and sexual violence on post-traumatic stress disorder symptomatology." *Violence and Victims 18*, 87–94.

Bergen, R. (1996) *Wife Rape: Understanding the Response of Survivors and Service Providers.* Thousand Oaks, CA: Sage.

Campbell, J.C. and Alford, P. (1989) "The dark consequences of marital rape." *American Journal of Nursing 89*, 946–949.

Easteal, P. (1994) *Voices of the Survivors.* North Melbourne: Spinifex Press.

Easteal, P. and McOrmond-Plummer, L. (2006) *Real Rape, Real Pain: Help for Women Sexually Assaulted by Male Partners.* Melbourne: Hybrid Publishers.

Ewoldt, C., Monson, C.M., and Langhinrichsen-Rohling, J. (2000) "Attributions about rape in a continuum of dissolving marital relationships." *Journal of Interpersonal Violence 15,* 1175–1182.

Finkelhor, D. and Yllo, K. (1985) *License to Rape: Sexual Abuse of Wives.* New York: The Free Press.

Heenan, M. (2004) "Just 'Keeping the Peace': A Reluctance to Respond to Male Partner Sexual Violence." *Australian Centre for the Study of Sexual Assault 1.* Available at www.aifs.gov.au/acssa/pubs/issue/i1.html, accessed September 3, 2012.

Holmes, M.M., Resnick, H.S., Kilpatrick, D.G., and Best, C.L. (1996) "Rape-related pregnancy: estimates and descriptive characteristics from a national sample of women." *American Journal of Obstetrics and Gynecology 175,* 2, 320–325.

Mahoney, P. (1999) "High chronicity and low rates of help-seeking among wife rape survivors in a nonclinical sample: implications for research and practice." *Violence Against Women 5,* 993–1016.

McFarlane, J. (2007) "Pregnancy following partner rape: what we know and what we need to know." *Trauma, Violence and Abuse 8,* 127–134.

Myhill, A. and Allen, J. (2002) *Rape and Sexual Assault of Women: Findings from the British Crime Survey.* London: Home Office. Available at www.aphroditewounded. org/Myhill and Allen.pdf, accessed July 4, 2013.

Parkinson, D. and Cowan, S. (2008) *Raped by a Partner: Nowhere to Go, No-One to Tell.* Victoria: Women's Health Goulburn North East.

Plichta, S.B. and Falik, M. (2001) "Prevalence of violence and its implications for women's health." *Women's Health Issues 11,* 244–258.

Roth, S., Newman, E., Pelcovitz, D., van der Kolk, B., and Mandel, F.S. (1997) "Complex PTSD in victims exposed to sexual and physical abuse: results from the DSM-IV field trial for posttraumatic stress disorder." *Journal of Traumatic Stress 10,* 539–555.

Russell, D. (1990) *Rape in Marriage.* Bloomington, IN: Indiana University Press.

Shields, N. and Hanneke, C. (1983) "Battered Wives' Reactions to Marital Rape." In R. Gelles, G. Hotaling, M. Straus, and D. Finkelhor (eds.) *The Dark Side of Families: Current Family Violence Research.* Thousand Oaks, CA: Sage Publications, Inc.

Stermac, L., Del Bove, G., and Addison, M. (2001) "Violence, injury, and presentation patterns in spousal sexual assaults." *Violence Against Women 7,* 1218–1233.

Wilson, K. (1997) *When Violence Begins at Home: A Comprehensive Guide to Understanding and Ending Domestic Abuse.* Alameda, CA: Hunter House.

## PART 2

# How Serious Is Intimate Partner Sexual Violence?

CHAPTER 4

# Fatality and Health Risks Associated with Intimate Partner Sexual Violence

Jocelyn C. Anderson, Jessica E. Draughon, and Jacquelyn C. Campbell

## Intimate partner sexual violence and fatality risk

Almost 10 percent of all adult US women have experienced sexual violence by an intimate partner during their lifetime (Black et al. 2011). This is compared to the one in six (16.67%) of women who have experienced sexual violence, perpetrated by anyone, in their lifetime (Tjaden and Thoennes 2006). However, Tjaden and Thoennes (2006) found that 20.2 percent of those reporting sexual victimization, or one in five, were assaulted by a current or former intimate partner, while the more recent Centers for Disease Control (CDC) National Intimate Partner and Sexual Violence Survey (Black et al. 2011) found that 51.1 percent of rape of women was perpetrated by an intimate partner or ex-partner. Sexual violence by an intimate partner often does not occur in isolation. In 2011, 4.4 percent of US women reported only forced sex, 8.7 percent reported both forced sex and physical violence, and a further 12.5 percent experienced forced sex, physical violence, and stalking from a current or former intimate partner (Black et al. 2011).

Intimate partner sexual violence (IPSV) may be a sign of increasing overall violence in the relationship. IPSV was observed more often in relationships where the abuse had been occurring over a longer period of time (Dutton et al. 2005). In a recent study validating a severity assessment tool, sexual aggression was more often present in intimate partner violence (IPV) relationships that were classified as "severe cases" than "nonsevere cases" (Echeburúa et al. 2009). Women who experienced IPSV more often perceived that there was a "higher threat" from their intimate partner (Dutton et al. 2005). IPSV is also associated with myriad mental and physical health sequelae (Campbell et al. 2002), sometimes leading to lifelong deficits including HIV (Campbell et al. 2008), or even homicide.

A recent review of the literature found that IPSV is a significant predictor of intimate partner homicide (Campbell *et al.* 2007). Over two thirds of a sample of women who had survived an attempted homicide had experienced prior physical or sexual abuse by their intimate partner (Nicolaidis *et al.* 2003). In a comparison of lethal versus non-lethal IPV in the UK, sexual violence was observed in the lethal cases, but not the non-lethal cases (Dobash *et al.* 2007). IPSV was also significantly associated with intimate partner homicide among abused women in a national US study (Campbell *et al.* 2003).

## The varied forms of intimate partner sexual violence

IPSV can take many different forms, and has been the subject of much discussion, research, and reconceptualization. There is a continuum of sexual contact ranging from mutually wanted or desired at one end, to physically forced rape or sexual assault at the other extreme, with threats, implied threats, or verbal coercion on the sexual violence end of the continuum. For example, a woman may have been forced once and never actually physically forced again because the "lesson" has already been taught. In the middle, there are situations where one partner may not wish to engage in sexual contact, but this contact occurs anyway. A woman may always submit, for example, because in her culture or religion saying no to her husband sexually is not an option.

The majority of sexual coercion literature definitions include rape as the most extreme case of coercion. Appropriately differentiating between cases of coerced sex along the continuum from mutually desired sexual contact to rape entails understanding what is culturally acceptable in the particular individual's eyes. Furthermore, the experience of one form of sexual coercion is not necessarily better or worse than another. For example, many would argue that physically forced sex is more traumatic than verbally coerced sex; however, in a recent study, women who had experienced sexual coercion were more similar in their scores on the Trauma Symptoms Inventory to women who had experienced rape or attempted rape than to women who had not experienced any form of victimization (Broach and Petretic 2006).

## Verbal coercion

Some differentiate "sexual coercion" from "sexual aggression" or "sexual assault" as the use of words versus the use of physical force respectively (DeGue and DiLillo 2005). We will address verbal coercion as two separate classes: (a) pressure and (b) threats. Both may be either implied or explicit.

### CASE STUDY: PRESSURE

Vania is an 18-year-old college student who has been dating her current boyfriend for two months. She relates the story of their first intercourse. She didn't want to have sex with him, but he "was insistent." He "kept saying he loved me, so why didn't I want to have sex with him? He said that if I didn't have sex with him, he'd get it from someone else, so we had sex."

Most adults are familiar with the phrase "you would if you loved me," whether they've heard it themselves, been warned about it while maturing, or used it themselves in order to obtain sex (DeGue and DiLillo 2005). This is not to say that a discussion between adults where the male partner expresses a desire for sexual contact when it is not desired by the female constitutes a case of coerced sex. From a research and clinical perspective, verbal pressuring is present when the discussion moves from a statement or two of desire to repeated attempts at obtaining the sexual contact, possibly including false promises, lies, bribes, or insistent unwanted pressuring. In the above case study, some would say that the intercourse was consensual. However, consent was obtained under duress; the sexual contact was still unwanted. Some use the term "coercive sex" for such a scenario; others would call it "pressured sex." For the purpose of the present work, it is important that professionals understand that pressure such as that described in the case study above may constitute a very real threat to a woman, and that sexual contact using such methods is not consensual.

Conversely, what may be considered verbal pressuring for sex by one person will be considered a normal component of a sexual relationship by another. For example, some people who experienced what was considered coercion (by an outside interviewer) constructed it as a socially acceptable experience (Marston 2005). There is further confusion in terms of the "sexual contract" which has been discussed as being part of dating relationships. This may involve *willingly* participating in *unwanted* consensual sex within the confines of a dating partnership (Broach and Petretic 2006). There are also issues of gender with this terminology, with some considering the example above coercive if a male is exerting the pressure because of inherent power differentials in sexual negotiations between men and women, while if it is a female who is being verbally insistent (even with false promises, bribes, or lies) this may not be considered coercve.

## CASE STUDY: THREATS

Judy is a 35-year-old woman who has been married to her husband for the past ten years. She submits to sexual contact with him almost every night even though she is not desirous of intercourse. When asked why she does this, Judy relates the story of their first night together after their honeymoon. She had lovingly refused sex. Her husband became angry and started cursing, pulled out a shotgun, loaded it, and placed it under the bed. Judy understood this to mean that if she did not comply with his wishes in bed, her husband would shoot her.

A threat does not have to be explicit to be effective. The abused partner is made aware of the threat of consequences, implicit in noncompliance with the abusive partner's demands, requests, or anticipated wants (Dutton and Goodman 2005). These threats may include physical or psychological harm. Threats may be to tangibles such as finances, job, family pets, or children, or to intangibles, such as humiliation, rejection, or loss of relationship. Again, there may be gender differences in what is perceived as abusive based on whether a male or female is doing the threatening and contextual factors of the relationship. In their reconceptualization of coercion in IPV, Dutton and Goodman (2005) state that, to be coercive, communication of a demand as well as a credible threat must occur. Taking the example of IPSV, once the demand for sex as well as threat of consequences have been communicated, the abused partner may feel that "going along" may be easier than resisting—it does not mean the sexual contact was desired (Dutton and Goodman 2005).

It may be difficult to fully differentiate between verbal pressuring and threats, as both are considered forms of verbal coercion by some experts in the field (DeGue and DiLillo 2005). Others feel that pressuring should be labeled as such and the term coercion be reserved for actual threats of physical or sexual assault, as this is more consistent with the dictionary definition of coercion: "to compel by force, intimidation, or authority." According to this definition, if the setting were one of extreme gender power differentials, the authority provision would allow for coercion to be verbal pressure, as would the case where a woman has been hit by the man before or the gun is under the bed, and therefore any verbal threat carries an implied threat of physical assault.

## CASE STUDY: PHYSICAL FORCE

Elise is a 40-year-old woman who has been living with her partner for the past 18 years. She has come to the hospital to have a forensic exam. When asked what happened, she states, "He did it again." Elise relates that she and her partner were drinking the night before and, after she fell asleep on the couch, she woke up to him having vaginal sex with her. She states that this has happened several times in the past.

Physical force is often what comes to mind when people think of IPSV or sexual violence of any kind. A recent study found that IPSV including physical force is associated with physical violence in the overall relationship (VanderLaan and Vasey 2009). Sexual violence, including physical force, can range from being shoved or hit to the use of a weapon or threatening with a weapon. This includes rape, as rape is by definition nonconsensual, whereas consent may be obtained under duress in coerced sex. Some would say that the case above does not constitute physical force; however, Elise was unable to give consent, which does constitute rape. If individuals are unable to give consent due to their mental state, intoxication, or age, then they are, by definition, unable to engage in consensual sex. A woman does not need to have bruises on her body to have experienced physically forced sex. However, the conceptualization of coercive sex should not be broadened to the point where it includes unwanted sex where one partner "goes along with it" because the other really wants it and is perhaps insistent. And maybe it is easier to go along, but she is not intoxicated, is not below the age of consent, is not in a powerless position in society, and the other partner does not threaten, and has not been violent to her before; she is not afraid of him, and there is no gun under the bed. This is perhaps pressured sex but not coerced.

## Physical and mental health consequences and a need for a multidisciplinary response

IPV has been linked to a number of negative physical and mental health consequences. Increases in acute and chronic medical issues including headache, back pain, gynecological conditions (i.e. pelvic pain, vaginal bleeding), and sexually transmitted infections have been reported in the literature among women experiencing physical and sexual abuse (Campbell *et al.* 2002; Ellsberg *et al.* 2008; Tjaden and Thoennes 2006; Wingood, Diclemente, and Raj 2000). In comparing women who experienced physical violence to women who also reported sexual violence, gynecologic, central nervous system, and chronic stress disorders were reported with higher frequency among those who experienced sexual violence.

As the health consequences span a continuum of acute and chronic disorders, vague to specific complaints and disorders, and the reluctance of women to voluntarily disclose for fear of embarrassment and being further victimized by system responses, identifying women based on symptoms presents a significant challenge. A multidisciplinary approach to identifying and responding to the needs of women who have experienced IPSV is necessary. Collaboration among a wide variety of professionals who encounter women during or after disclosure, including forensic medical providers such as sexual assault nurse examiners, law enforcement, and mental health and crisis professionals, is necessary to improve outcomes for these women.

### Intimate partner sexual violence and HIV risk

One health consequence that has been closely linked and widely considered in connection with IPSV is HIV. In samples of women living with HIV, IPV is often reported at higher rates, while women experiencing IPV have also shown more frequent risk factors for HIV acquisition (Campbell *et al.* 2008; Gielen *et al.* 2007). Theoretical models explaining this risk include both biological and behavioral factors (Campbell *et al.* 2013; Dunkle *et al.* 2004). Women in abusive relationships often have less control over their sexual health, including sexual practices, condom use, and birth control (Miller *et al.* 2010, 2011). Physically forced sex and the presence of other sexually transmitted infections may also lead to increases in genital injuries and inflammation, which increases the likelihood of seroconversion in women who are exposed to HIV (Campbell *et al.* 2013).

The behavioral risks of both women and their partners have been examined as risk factors for HIV acquisition. Women in unsafe relationships report mental health disorders including posttraumatic stress disorder (PTSD), depression, and substance use that may increase their risk for HIV exposure (Ellsberg *et al.* 2008). Individual sexual risk behaviors including casual sex, concurrent partners, and exchange sex are more common in women who have experienced IPV than women who have not (Cole, Logan, and Shannon 2007; Stockman *et al.* 2013). Women in violent relationships have also reported that their partners had increased HIV risk with concurrent partners, inconsistent condom use, and intravenous drug use.

While HIV treatment has improved dramatically in the past decades, HIV still contributes to the morbidity and mortality of women globally. In some areas of the world where both violence against women and HIV are highly prevalent, HIV rates in women are growing at an alarming rate (United Nations Joint Programme on HIV/AIDS (UNAIDS) 2012). Interventions to address the joint epidemics of HIV and violence are greatly needed in order to address these complex biopsychosocial issues. Sexual violence among intimate partners not only increases risk for HIV acquisition, but has also been shown to affect HIV treatment, decreasing adherence and increasing missed clinic visits (Schafer *et al.* 2012).

## The Danger Assessment

In addition to providing and documenting direct medical care for women who disclose abuse, further assessment of the abusive behavior and risk for homicide can be conducted using the Danger Assessment (DA) (Campbell *et al.* 2004). This assessment can be used by health care providers, law enforcement, and victim advocates. The DA takes approximately ten minutes to complete. It is a self-report scale, so it does not require staff time. Women often underestimate their risk of lethality or near lethality (Nicolaidis *et al.* 2003) despite the presence of known risk factors. The DA is an excellent tool to create that awareness. A calendar should be provided to the patient for her to identify the approximate dates of assault and to help the woman cut through her normal tendency to minimize the abuse. The DA can be used in its original format of a calendar and 20 yes/no risk factors, and is available for free at the website (www.dangerassessment.org). There is also an online training module available, completion of which is required to use the weighted scoring for the DA, which results in four levels of danger: variable, increased, severe, and extreme. At severe and extreme danger levels, women should be assisted in getting immediate help in safety planning, either from the police or from a domestic violence advocate or agency. Even without having done the DA training, a provider can use a rough cut-off of ten or more yes answers on the DA to identify abused women at high risk. The DA includes an item specific to IPSV as well as other known risk factors for intimate partner homicide.

## Conclusion

In conclusion, there is a continuum of IPSV encompassing the use of physical violence at one end, threats and sexual coercion somewhere in the middle, and finally at the other end of the spectrum, verbally pressured sex that may end up in unwilling sex and an unhappy relationship but not necessarily an abusive one. A co-occurring continuum is that of fatality risk from IPV. Unfortunately, these continuums do not parallel each other neatly. Although it is important for providers to be aware of sexually coercive acts which can result in mental health sequelae such as PTSD, it is physically forced sex which is a risk factor for intimate partner homicide.

Health care providers need to screen all patients not only for IPV and psychological abuse but forced sex as well. If the woman says yes to the question "does your partner ever force you into sex?" or "does your partner ever force you into sexual activities you do not want to participate in?" (from the Abuse Assessment Screen [AAS], www.nnvawi.org) then the provider can assess the degree and nature of the forced acts. Often a woman will answer that she is unsure whether or not he has forced her into sex, and when asked to elaborate will describe verbally coerced acts or pressured sex which can help the provider understand the nature and degree of the coercion.

If possible, comprehensive medicolegal care should be provided after sexual violence. At the very least, a thorough head-to-toe exam and documentation of the incident as well as any visible injuries will provide a paper trail if the patient decides to pursue legal action. At most, it may provide evidence leading to incarceration of the perpetrator, removing him/her at least temporarily as a threat to the patient's safety (please see Chapter 16 for more information about forensic medical evaluation).

Finally, if a woman discloses that her current or former intimate partner has physically forced her to have sex, then she already has one risk factor for intimate partner homicide. The DA can assist the provider in helping women more accurately assess their risk for being killed or almost killed by this partner and thereby inform their choices about getting help to end the violence in their relationships.

# References

Black, M.C., Basile, K.C., Breiding, M.J., Smith, S.G. *et al.* (2011) *The National Intimate Partner and Sexual Violence Survey (NISVS): 2010 Summary Report.* Atlanta, GA: National Center for Injury Prevention and Control, Centers for Disease Control and Prevention. Available at www.cdc.gov/ViolencePrevention/pdf/NISVS_Executive_Summary-a.pdf, accessed February 13, 2013.

Broach, J.L. and Petretic, P.A. (2006) "Beyond traditional definitions of assault: expanding our focus to include sexually coercive experiences." *Journal of Family Violence 21*, 8, 477–486. doi:10.1007/s10896-006-9045-z

Campbell, J.C., Baty, M.L., Ghandour, R. M., Stockman, J.K., Francisco, L., and Wagman, J. (2008) "The intersection of intimate partner violence against women and HIV/AIDS: a review." *International Journal of Injury Control and Safety Promotion 15*, 4, 221–231. doi:10.1080/17457300802423224

Campbell, J.C., Glass, N., Sharps, P.W., Laughon, K., and Bloom, T. (2007) "Intimate partner homicide: review and implications of research and policy." *Trauma, Violence & Abuse 8*, 3, 246–269. doi:10.1177/1524838007303505

Campbell, J.C., Lucea, M.B., Stockman, J.K., and Draughon, J.E. (2013) "Forced sex and HIV risk in violent relationships." *American Journal of Reproductive Immunology 69*, 1, 41–44. (Special Issue: Sexual Violence and HIV Transmission.)

Campbell, J.C., Snow Jones, A., Dienemann, J., Kub, J. *et al.* (2002) "Intimate partner violence and physical health consequences." *Archives of Internal Medicine 162*, 1157–1163.

Campbell, J.C., Torres, S., McKenna, L.S., Sheridan, D.J., and Landenburger, K. (2004) "Nursing Care of Survivors of Intimate Partner Violence." In J. Humphreys and J.C. Campbell (eds.) *Family Violence and Nursing Practice.* Philadelphia: Lippincott Williams & Wilkins.

Campbell, J.C., Webster, D., Koziol-McLain, J., Block, C.R. *et al.* (2003) "Risk factors for femicide-suicide in abusive relationships: results from a multisite case control study." *American Journal of Public Health 93*, 7, 1089–1097. Available at www.ncbi.nlm.nih.gov/pubmed/16494130, accessed February 13, 2013.

Cole, J., Logan, T.K., and Shannon, L. (2007) "Risky sexual behavior among women with protective orders against violent male partners." *AIDS and Behavior 11*, 1, 103–112.

DeGue, S. and DiLillo, D. (2005) "'You would if you loved me': toward an improved conceptual and etiological understanding of nonphysical male sexual coercion." *Aggression and Violent Behavior 10*, 4, 513–532. doi:10.1016/j.avb.2004.09.001

Dobash, R.E., Dobash, R.P., Cavanagh, K., and Medina-Ariza, J. (2007) "Lethal and nonlethal violence against an intimate female partner: comparing male murderers to nonlethal abusers." *Violence Against Women 13*(4), 329–353. doi:10.1177/1077801207299204

Dunkle, K.L., Jewkes, R.K., Brown, H.C., Gray, G.G. *et al.* (2004) "Gender-based violence, relationship power, and risk of HIV infection in women attending antenatal clinics in South Africa." *Lancet 363*, 9419, 1415–1421.

Dutton, M.A. and Goodman, L.A. (2005) "Coercion in intimate partner violence: toward a new conceptualization." *Sex Roles 52*, 11–12, 743–756. doi:10.1007/s11199-005-4196-6

Dutton, M.A., Kaltman, S., Goodman, L.A., Weinfurt, K. *et al.* (2005) "Patterns of intimate partner violence: correlates and outcomes." *Violence and Victims 20*, 5, 483–497. Available at www.ncbi.nlm.nih.gov/pubmed/16248486, accessed February 13, 2013.

Echeburúa, E., Fernández-Montalvo, J., De Corral, P., and López-Goñi, J.J. (2009) "Assessing risk markers in intimate partner femicide and severe violence: a new assessment instrument." *Journal of Interpersonal Violence 24*, 6, 925–939. doi:10.1177/0886260508319370

Ellsberg, M., Jansen, H.A., Heise, L., Watts, C.H. *et al.* (2008) "Intimate partner violence and women's physical and mental health in the WHO multi-country study on women's health and domestic violence: an observational study." *Lancet 371*, 9619, 1165–1172.

Gielen, A.C., Ghandour, R.M., Burke, J.G., Mahoney, P., McDonnell, K.A., and O'Campo, P. (2007) "HIV/AIDS and intimate partner violence: intersecting women's health issues in the United States." *Trauma, Violence & Abuse 8*, 2, 178–198.

Marston, C. (2005) "What is heterosexual coercion? Interpreting narratives from young people in Mexico City." *Sociology of Health & Illness 27*, 1, 68–91. doi:10.1111/j.1467-9566.2005.00432.x

Miller, E., Decker, M.R., McCauley, H.L., Tancredi, D.J. *et al.* (2011) "A family planning clinic partner violence intervention to reduce risk associated with reproductive coercion." *Contraception 83*, 3, 274–280.

Miller, E., Decker, M.R., Raj, A., Reed, E. *et al.* (2010) "Intimate partner violence and health care-seeking patterns among female users of urban adolescent clinics." *Maternal and Child Health Journal 14*, 6, 910–917.

Nicolaidis, C., Curry, M.A., Ulrich, Y., Sharps, P. *et al.* (2003) "Could we have known? A qualitative analysis of data from women who survived an attempted homicide by an intimate partner." *Journal of General Internal Medicine 18*, 10, 788–794. doi:10.1046/j.1525-1497.2003.21202.x

Schafer, K.R., Brant, J., Gupta, S., Thorpe, J. *et al.* (2012) "Intimate partner violence: a predictor of worse HIV outcomes and engagement in care." *AIDS Patient Care and STDs 26*, 6, 356–365. doi:10.1089/apc.2011.0409

Stockman, J.K., Lucea, M.B., Draughon, J.E., Sabri, B. *et al.* (2012) "Intimate partner violence and HIV risk factors among African-American and African-Caribbean women in clinic-based settings." *AIDS Care 25*, 4, 472–480.

Tjaden, P. and Thoennes, N. (2006) *Extent, Nature, and Consequences of Rape Victimization: Findings from the National Violence Against Women Survey.* Washington, DC: US Department of Justice, National Institute of Justice. Available at www. ncjrs.gov/pdffiles1/nij/210346.pdf, accessed February 16, 2013.

United Nations Joint Programme on HIV/AIDS (UNAIDS) (2012) *Global Report: UNAIDS Report on the Global AIDS Epidemic 2010.* Geneva: United Nations. Available at www.unhcr.org/refworld/docid/4cfca9c62.html, accessed February 14, 2013.

VanderLaan, D.P. and Vasey, P.L. (2009) "Patterns of sexual coercion in heterosexual and non-heterosexual men and women." *Archives of Sexual Behavior 38*, 6, 987–999. doi:10.1007/s10508-009-9480-z

Wingood, G.M., Diclemente, R.J., and Raj, A. (2000) "Identifying the prevalence and correlates of STDs among women residing in rural domestic violence shelters." *Women & Health 30*, 4, 15–26.

CHAPTER 5

# Separation/Divorce Sexual Assault

Walter S. DeKeseredy

There is a wealth of social scientific knowledge about the extent, distribution, sources, and outcomes of male-to-female sexual assaults perpetrated by boyfriends, "hook-up partners," spouses, and cohabiting partners. However, much less is known about the plight of women who make "dangerous exits" from violent or sexist men (DeKeseredy and Schwartz 2009). Still, as we enter the second decade in this new millennium, a growing body of empirical and theoretical work is being accumulated on separation/divorce sexual assault. The main objective of this chapter is to review the North American social scientific literature on this problem and to suggest new directions in research and policy.

## Definition of separation/divorce

Contrary to popular belief, a couple does not have to live apart to be separated or divorced. Nonetheless, most surveys that address marital rape (Black *et al.* 2011; Finkelhor and Yllo 1985; Tjaden and Thoennes 2000), as well as the majority of surveys of nonsexual types of woman abuse, seem to define separation and divorce this way. Assaults that occur during the process of exiting—when a woman decides to leave her partner, or when she makes an unsuccessful attempt to leave a relationship—are typically ignored. Brownridge (2009, p.56), for example, focuses on "post-separation violence," which he conceives as "any type of violence perpetrated by a former married or cohabiting male partner subsequent to the moment of physical separation." This approach to understanding the abuse of separated/divorced women is common, but highly problematic for several reasons.

Many women are attacked when they first state they want to leave or when they try to leave the "house of horrors" (Sev'er 2002). Of the 43 rural Ohio women interviewed by DeKeseredy and Schwartz (2009),

74 percent were sexually assaulted when they expressed a desire to leave. Forty-nine percent were sexually abused while they were trying to leave or while they were leaving, and 33 percent were victimized after they left. These data reveal that studies limited to focusing on events occurring after women depart greatly underestimate the rate of separation/divorce sexual assault and other variants of male-to-female abuse.

Many men are fanatically determined to prevent their spouses or live-in partners from leaving and will use violence "to keep them in their place" (Russell 1990). Therefore, Mahoney (1991) and others (e.g. DeKeseredy 2011) use the term "separation assault." It is defined as:

> ...the attack on the woman's body and volition in which her partner seeks to prevent her from leaving, retaliate for the separation, or force her to return. It aims at overbearing her will as to where and with whom she will live, and coercing her in order to enforce connection in a relationship. It is an attempt to gain, retain, or regain power in a relationship, or to punish the woman for ending the relationship. It often takes place over time. (Mahoney 1991, pp.65–66)

Another key point to mull over when defining separation/divorce is that a woman's decision to leave a relationship may be long and complex. One reason for this is that many women have a well-founded fear of being killed (Johnson and Dawson 2011). In fact, some studies show that separated women have five to six times the risk of being murdered than other women (Brownridge 2009; DeKeseredy and Schwartz 2009; Gartner, Dawson, and Crawford 1999; Wilson and Daly 1994). It is not surprising, then, that scores of Evan Stark's (2007) clients told him that "they were never more frightened than in the days, weeks, or months after they moved out" (p.116).

Also, a woman may feel simultaneously oppressed and trapped by an inability to leave a relationship right now. This could be because of insufficient funds to house and feed her and her children. Keep in mind what this woman from a small Ohio town told DeKeseredy and Schwartz (2009, p.21) about a friend who was permanently trapped in a violent relationship:

> I went down and done some wallpapering for her. And she's in her eighties and she was talking to me and of course her and her husband know my husband real well and she says, "Susan, let me tell you." She says, "If you can get out, get out. You're still young enough." She says,

"I'm sitting here waiting to die." She says, "I'm too old to get out," and she says she takes abuse every day.

Some women resist their partners' patriarchal practices by emotionally exiting them. Emotional exiting is a woman's denial or restriction of sexual relations and other intimate exchanges (Ellis and DeKeseredy 1997). Emotionally exiting a relationship can be just as dangerous as physically or legally exiting because it, too, increases the likelihood of male violence and sexual abuse (Block and DeKeseredy 2007).

A woman does not have to be legally tied to a man to be assaulted (Bergen 1996; Block and DeKeseredy 2007). Actually, cohabiting men are at least twice as likely to beat female intimates as are married men, with some studies revealing four times more likely (Brownridge and Halli 2001). As Campbell (1989, p.336) points out, "a marriage license probably does not change the dynamics of sexual abuse within an ongoing intimate relationship…"

In sum, based on an in-depth review of the extant literature, "separation and divorce" here means physically, legally, or emotionally exiting a marital or cohabiting relationship (DeKeseredy and Schwartz 2009). This chapter focuses on woman-initiated exits because "they are the decisions that challenge male hegemony the most" (Sev'er 1997, p.567).

## The need for a broad definition of separation/divorce sexual assault

Although dated, Liz Kelly's (1988) conceptualization of sexual violence as a continuum is still useful today. Walklate and Brown (2012, p.490) note:

> Kelly's continuum alerts us to the frequency of sexual violence's occurrence as common rather than rare and to the high levels of unreported incidence of such violence. Also key to this continuum is the idea that sexual violence arises out of the normal routines of everyday life, the purpose of which is to exert control…either by extremes of violence or by "sexual innuendo."

Kelly's concept also sensitizes us to the fact women experience a broad range of sexual assaults that do not involve penetration, such as unwanted acts when they were drunk or high, or when they were unable to give consent (Bachar and Koss 2001; DeKeseredy 2011; Meloy and Miller 2011). Also, married and cohabiting women experience threats that can result in painful unwanted sex and "blackmail rapes" (Russell 1990). Below is what happened to Carrie, a rural Ohio woman interviewed by DeKeseredy *et al.* (2006, p.239). She was clearly unable to consent and her experience is a glaring example of what Sanday (1990) refers to as using alcohol to "work a yes out":

> I agreed to meet with him to discuss visitation and child support for our daughter and I wanted to go to a public place after everything he had done because it wasn't just sexual, it was mental, physical. And I showed up there. I had a couple of friends who were sitting throughout keeping an eye on me. Ordered the drink, got up to use the bathroom, drank my drink, and that was pretty much the last thing I remembered until the next morning when I woke up with a killer headache and my daughter crying in her crib... He was in bed next to me... I had strangulation marks around my neck. I had marks around my wrists and an open wound on my face and he had obviously had sex. (p.113)

Broad definitions of separation/divorce sexual assault are essential for other reasons. Many women have unwanted sex that occurs "out of obligation" (Bergen 1996), sexual relations stemming from ex-partners' threats of fighting for sole custody of children, and other sexual acts that do not involve the use of threats or force. One of DeKeseredy and Schwartz's (2009, p.24) interviewees spoke about unwanted sex that occurs out of women's sense of obligation:

> ...I see many, many, many women submitting to men, submitting to what they, their men, want them to be. I have had many, many discussions, over a hundred, women saying to me, my boyfriend wants to have sex, but I don't want to have sex, but I am going to do it anyway to please him. And so, I consider that unwanted sex, because, yes, these women are consenting, but they don't know any other out. They have no other option. And that is what I find sad. And there is so much peer influence about being cool, about being heterosexual, you know?

As is the case with focusing only on post-separation/divorce abuse, ignoring the aforementioned hurtful behaviors exacerbates the problem of underreporting and ultimately underestimates the extent of sexual assault (DeKeseredy and Schwartz 2013). Moreover, in sharp contrast to what Kelly (1988, 2012) continues to call for, narrow, legalistic definitions create a hierarchy of abuse or violence when, in fact, no behavior is automatically more injurious than another (DeKeseredy and Schwartz 2013). Feminist scholars, activists, and practitioners have long stated that we need to listen closely to women's voices (Mahoney 1991).

## Separation/divorce sexual assault: research and theory

Empirical and theoretical work on many variants of woman abuse has mushroomed over the past 40 years. Brown and Walklate (2012) edited Routledge's *Handbook on Sexual Violence*, resulting in an anthology of 516 pages and 23 chapters. Yet, the words separation and divorce are not in the book's index. This is largely due to the fact that researchers around the world have devoted very little attention to separation/divorce sexual assault compared to other sexual "intimate intrusions" (Stanko 1985). The limited North American work now available tells us many things about sexual assaults that occur during and after exiting marital/cohabiting relationships.

The offering by DeKeseredy and colleagues guided the first US qualitative study of separation/divorce sexual assault in rural communities (see DeKeseredy and Schwartz 2009). Before then, all studies that touched on this harm were done in urban areas. Listed below are some of their major findings:

- Eight percent of the wife rape survivors in Russell's (1990) survey were assaulted after their marriages ended and 7 percent were raped just before separation.

- Seventeen percent of the divorced women interviewed by Kurz (1995) reported that their ex-husbands forced them to have sex.

- Twenty percent of the 40 wife-rape survivors interviewed by Bergen (1996) were raped after separation/divorce.

- Two thirds of the women in Finkelhor and Yllo's (1985) interview sample (n = 50) were raped in the last days of a relationship, either after previous separations, or when they were trying to leave a relationship.

- Slightly more than six percent of the total number of rape survivors (n = 288) who participated in the US National Violence Against Women Survey stated that they were raped after the relationship ended (Tjaden and Thoennes 2000).

- The Chicago Women's Health Risk Study found that abused women in violent relationships reported more forced sex than did women who leave such relationships (Block and DeKeseredy 2007).

Would researchers obtain similar, lower, or higher estimates if they surveyed or interviewed men? To date, there are no scientifically valid answers to this question. So far, all of the data on separation/divorce sexual assault are derived from women. Research on male perpetrators is much needed.

Where are separation/divorce sexual assaults most likely to occur? Using 1992–2009 National Crime Victimization Survey (NCVS) data, Rennison, DeKeseredy, and Dragiewicz (2012) found that rural divorced/separated women are at higher risk of being sexually assaulted than their urban and suburban counterparts. Their project is also the first one in North America to closely examine the characteristics of men who sexually assault their ex-partners. It is not surprising that male peer support was a constant theme among their respondents' stories because it is strongly associated with other types of woman abuse, such as date rape, campus party rape, nonpartner rape in rural South Africa, and wife beating (Armstrong, Hamilton, and Sweeney 2006; Bowker 1983; DeKeseredy and Schwartz 1998, 2013; Jewkes et al. 2006).

Seventy-nine percent of the interviewees said that their partners strongly believed that men should be in charge and control of domestic household settings. Additionally, almost all of the respondents said they were raped during or after separation/divorce because their partners wanted to show them "who was in charge."

Almost two thirds of the estranged partners (65%) of the women in this study viewed pornography, and 30 percent of the interviewees reported that pornography was involved in sexually abusive events they experienced. Since the consumption of pornography is often a secretive event, this may well be an underestimate of its use by abusers (Bergen and Bogle 2000; DeKeseredy and Schwartz 2013). These findings support Jensen's (2007) claim that some violent men use "pornography as a training manual for abuse" (Bergen and Bogle 2000, p.231).

Male partners' possession of firearms and their illegal drug use were two other common themes respondents identified. More than half of the women said that male offenders had guns, and some of them threatened to use them. More than 65 percent of the women said that their partners used illegal drugs and that their consumption of these substances contributed to abusive conduct. One interviewee who desperately wanted to leave her partner said:

> He quit drinking for a while and switched addictions and started doing cocaine. He started shooting cocaine with his insulin needles. He's also an insulin dependent diabetic, as well as a chronic alcoholic. He'd come home and force me to have sex with him, and it was like sleeping with a brewery. I would sit in the living room afterwards and he'd be passed out. And I'd think about how I could get away with killing him. I mean it was getting really bad… I couldn't, like, escape him… (DeKeseredy and Schwartz 2009, p.78)

DeKeseredy and Schwartz found that most of the women interviewed experienced multiple forms of other types of abuse, including physical violence and psychological abuse. Certainly, their study supports Lewis' (2003, p.31) assertion that "in many rural communities, there are hidden crimes, unspoken crimes, that are often hushed and ignored, crimes of sexual violence that require sensitivity and understanding to promote safety and justice."

The small amount of data presented in this chapter and elsewhere shows that leaving or trying to leave a marital/cohabiting relationship increases women's chances of being sexually assaulted, especially if they are connected to patriarchal or abusive men. Nonetheless, there is still much we do not know about the problem of separation/divorce sexual assault. Obviously, more empirical and theoretical work is required. It is also necessary to develop policies and practices that meet the unique needs of women who are victimized by the men who will not let them leave and by men whom they have left.

## Future directions

One of the first social scientific steps required is gathering data from men to more precisely determine what motivates them to be abusive (DeKeseredy, Rogness, and Schwartz 2004; Jewkes *et al.* 2006). Of course, we learn much from asking the women who know these men best. Nevertheless, such information does not obviate the need for direct research on men. As Scully (1990, p.4) puts it, there are problems in depending completely on female partners to report on male sexual abusers because "they do not share the reality of sexually violent men.

Such insight is acquired through invading and critically examining the social constructions of men who rape."

A large-scale representative sample survey of separation/divorce sexual assault that includes men and women would be especially useful. Previous quantitative studies reviewed earlier were not specifically designed to generate rich data on separation/divorce sexual assault. More qualitative work, too, is warmly welcomed because quantitative methods alone cannot adequately describe the complexities of separation/divorce sexual assault and community responses to it (DeKeseredy and Schwartz 2008). Regardless of what techniques are used, there are certain groups of men and women at the margins of mainstream studies that need to be included in future research. Some examples are refugees/immigrants, public housing tenants, and people with physical and psychological disabilities.

Little is known about sexual assaults directed at women who terminate dating relationships. Women in university/college dating relationships and those heavily involved in the "hook-up culture" are at very high risk of being sexually assaulted, and thus it is logical to assume that many who exit casual or more serious relationships are equally, if not more, vulnerable.

What is to be done about separation/divorce sexual assault? It would take an entire chapter to properly answer this question. Be that as it may, a few effective suggestions are provided here. For instance, more subsidized housing is essential because many women who escape abusive men cannot afford to rent an apartment or other housing (Davies 2011; Renzetti 2011; Tutty 2006). Subsidized transportation would also be very helpful, especially in rural areas. More government funds should be used to pay the transportation costs of rural advocates who spend much time on the road in their efforts to save lives (DeKeseredy and Schwartz 2009).

Last, but certainly not least, as Purdon (2003, p.49) contends, "More support and more opportunities for retraining or additional education are needed for abused women so they can find the work that will lead to long-term financial security and independence." Nevertheless, policy makers should not assume that women who get jobs as a result of state-sponsored education and job training programs will automatically be safe. Some estranged partners engage in "patriarchal terrorism" (Johnson 1995) to humiliate their ex-partners and to make them lose their jobs (Raphael 2001; Renzetti 2011; Sokoloff and Dupont 2005). Hence, it is crucial that policies be created that guarantee abused women the ability to collect disability pay if they cannot work due to injuries sustained from their ex-partners' abusive behaviors. Legislation is also required to prohibit employers from firing women who are being stalked or assaulted at work (Brandwein 1999; DeKeseredy and Schwartz 2009).

Advocates and counselors are another professional group whose clients can benefit from attention to the danger of separation/divorce sexual assault (see Chapter 8 for information about safety planning by advocates).

The policies proposed here constitute just the tip of the iceberg. Above all, it cannot be emphasized enough that too often separation/ divorce does not end sexual assault and other forms of woman abuse. Therefore, it is necessary to develop solutions that meet the unique needs of women who are brutalized by men who will not let them leave and men whom they have left. If, as Bergen (1996) found, victims of marital rape do not receive proper assistance, we can only assume that survivors of separation/divorce sexual assault are given even less.

# References

Armstrong, E.A., Hamilton, L., and Sweeney, B. (2006) "Sexual assault on campus: a multilevel integrative approach to party rape." *Social Problems 53*, 483–499.

Bachar, K. and Koss, M.P. (2001) "From Prevalence to Prevention: Closing the Gap Between What We Know About Rape and What We Do." In C.M. Renzetti, J.L. Edleson, and R.K. Bergen (eds.) *Sourcebook on Violence Against Women*. Thousand Oaks, CA: Sage.

Bergen, R.K. (1996) *Wife Rape: Understanding the Response of Survivors and Service Providers*. Thousand Oaks, CA: Sage.

Bergen, R.K. and Bogle, K.A. (2000) "Exploring the connection between pornography and sexual violence." *Violence and Victims 15*, 227–234.

Black, M.C., Basile, K.C., Breiding, M.J., Smith, S.G. *et al.* (2011) *The National Intimate Partner and Sexual Violence Survey (NISVS): 2010 Summary Report*. Atlanta, GA: National Center for Injury Prevention and Control, Centers for Disease Control and Prevention.

Block, C.R. and DeKeseredy, W.S. (2007) "Forced sex & leaving intimate relationships: results of the Chicago Women's Health Risk Study." *Women's Health and Urban Life 6*, 6–24.

Bowker, L.H. (1983) *Beating Wife-Beating*. Lexington, MA: Lexington Books.

Brandwein, R.A. (1999) "Family Violence, Women, and Welfare." In R.A. Brandwein (eds.) *Battered Women, Children, and Welfare Reform: The Ties that Bind*. Thousand Oaks, CA: Sage.

Brown, J. and Walklate, S. (eds.) (2012) *Handbook on Sexual Violence*. London: Sage.

Brownridge, D.A. (2009) *Violence against Women: Vulnerable Populations*. New York: Routledge.

Brownridge, D.A. and Halli, S.A. (2001) *Explaining Violence Against Women in Canada*. Lanham, MD: Lexington Books.

Campbell, J.C. (1989) "Women's response to sexual abuse in intimate relationships." *Health Care for Women International 10*, 335–346.

Davies, J. (2011) "Personal Reflection." In C.M. Renzetti, J.L. Edleson, and R.K. Bergen (eds.) *Sourcebook on Violence Against Women*, Second Edition. Thousand Oaks, CA: Sage.

DeKeseredy, W.S. (2011) *Violence Against Women: Myths, Facts, Controversies*. Toronto: University of Toronto Press.

DeKeseredy, W.S. and Schwartz, M.D. (1998) *Woman Abuse on Campus: Results from the Canadian National Survey*. Thousand Oaks, CA: Sage.

DeKeseredy, W.S. and Schwartz, M.D. (2008) "Separation/divorce sexual assault in rural Ohio: survivors' perceptions." *Journal of Prevention and Intervention in the Community 36*, 1–15.

DeKeseredy, W.S. and Schwartz, M.D. (2009) *Dangerous Exits: Escaping Abusive Relationships in Rural America*. New Brunswick, NJ: Rutgers University Press.

DeKeseredy, W.S. and Schwartz, M.D. (2013) *Male Peer Support and Violence Against Women: The History and Verification of a Theory*. Boston: Northeastern University Press.

DeKeseredy, W.S., Rogness, M., and Schwartz, M.D. (2004) "Separation/divorce sexual assault: the current state of social scientific knowledge." *Aggression and Violent Behavior 9*, 675–691.

DeKeseredy, W.S., Schwartz, M.D., Fagen, D. and Hall, M. (2006) "Separation/divorce sexual assault: the contribution of male peer support." *Feminist Criminology 1*, 228–250.

Ellis, D. and DeKeseredy, W.S. (1997) "Rethinking estrangement, interventions, and intimate femicide." *Violence Against Women 3*, 590–609.

Finkelhor, D. and Yllo, K. (1985) *License to Rape: Sexual Abuse of Wives*. New York: Holt, Rinehart and Winston.

Gartner, R., Dawson, M., and Crawford, M. (1999) "Women killing: intimate femicide in Ontario, 1974–1994." *Resources for Feminist Research 26*, 151–173.

Jensen, R. (2007) *Getting Off: Pornography and the End of Masculinity*. Cambridge, MA: South End Press.

Jewkes, R., Dunkle, K., Koss, M.P., Levin, J.B. *et al.* (2006) "Rape perpetration by young, rural South African men: prevalence, patterns, and risk factors." *Social Science and Medicine 63*, 2949–2961.

Johnson, H. and Dawson, M. (2011) *Violence Against Women in Canada: Research and Policy Perspectives*. Toronto: University of Toronto Press.

Johnson, M.P. (1995) "Patriarchal violence and common couple violence: two forms of violence against women." *Journal of Marriage and the Family 57*, 283–294.

Kelly, L. (1988) *Surviving Sexual Violence*. Minneapolis, MN: University of Minnesota Press.

Kelly, L. (2012) "Preface." In J. Brown and S. Walklate (eds.) *Handbook of Sexual Violence*. London: Routledge.

Kurz, D. (1995) *For Richer, For Poorer: Mothers Confront Divorce*. New York: Routledge.

Lewis, S.H. (2003) *Unspoken Crimes: Sexual Assault in Rural America*. Enola, PA: National Sexual Violence Resource Center.

Mahoney, M.R. (1991) "Legal issues of battered women: redefining the issue of separation." *Michigan Law Review 90*, 1–94.

Meloy, M.L. and Miller, S.L. (2011) *The Victimization of Women*. New York: Oxford University Press.

Purdon, C. (2003) *Woman Abuse and Ontario Works in a Rural Community: Rural Women Speak Out About Their Experiences with Ontario Works*. Ottawa: Status of Women Canada.

Raphael, J. (2001) "Domestic Violence as a Welfare-to-Work Barrier: Research and Theoretical Issues." In C.M. Renzetti, J.L. Edleson, and R.K. Bergen (eds.) *Sourcebook on Violence Against Women*. Thousand Oaks, CA: Sage.

Rennison, C.M., DeKeseredy, W.S., and Dragiewicz, M. (2012) "Urban, suburban, and rural variations in separation/divorce rape/sexual assault: results from the National Crime Victimization Survey." *Feminist Criminology*. Available at http://fcx.sagepub.com, accessed February 3, 2012.

Renzetti, C.M. (2011) "Economic Issues and Intimate Partner Violence." In C.M. Renzetti, J.L. Edleson, and R.K. Bergen (eds.) *Sourcebook on Violence Against Women*, Second Edition. Thousand Oaks, CA: Sage.

Russell, D.E.H. (1990) *Rape in Marriage*. New York: Macmillan.

Sanday, P.R. (1990) *Fraternity Gang Rape*. New York: New York University Press.

Scully, D. (1990) *Understanding Sexual Violence: A Study of Convicted Rapists*. Boston: Unwin Hyman.

Sev'er, A. (1997) "Recent or imminent separation and intimate violence against women: a conceptual overview and some Canadian examples." *Violence Against Women 3*, 566–589.

Sev'er, A. (2002) *Fleeing the House of Horrors: Women Who Have Left Abusive Partners*. Toronto: University of Toronto Press.

Sokoloff, N. and Dupont, I. (2005) "Domestic violence at the intersection of race, class, and gender." *Violence Against Women 11*, 38–64.

Stanko, E.A. (1985) *Intimate Intrusions: Women's Experience of Male Violence*. London: Routledge & Kegan Paul.

Stark, E. (2007) *Coercive Control: How Men Entrap Women in Personal Life*. New York: Oxford University Press.

Tjaden, P. and Thoennes, N. (2000) *Extent, Nature and Consequences of Intimate Partner Violence: Findings from the National Violence Against Women Survey*. Washington, DC: US Department of Justice.

Tutty, L.M. (2006) *Effective Practices in Sheltering Women Leaving Violence in Intimate Relationships*. Toronto: YWCA Canada.

Walklate, S. and Brown, J. (2012) "Conclusion: Taking Stock—Plus ça change, plus c'est meme chose?' In J. Brown and S. Walklate (eds.) *Handbook on Sexual Violence*. London: Routledge.

Wilson, M. and Daly, M. (1994) *Spousal Homicide*. Ottawa: Canadian Centre for Justice Statistics.

# CHAPTER 6

# Reproductive Coercion

Emma Williamson

## Introduction

This chapter is concerned with exploring the issue of reproductive coercion in the context of violence against women and girls (VAWG). By locating a discussion of reproductive coercion within the current debates about coercion and control more generally, this chapter will look at the ways in which those addressing sexual violence, reproductive health, and wider gender inequality can benefit from the theoretical perspective offered by the theory of coercive control. This chapter also includes the voices of victims/survivors of abuse, who for many years have told researchers, service providers, and activists that for them it is the nonphysical impacts of abuse—the cumulative impact of ongoing coercion and control—that cause the greatest damage to their sense of self. Whilst this discussion of coercion and control is considered within both the domestic and sexual violence literature, these factors are very rarely considered together.

Reproductive coercion usually concerns the ways in which decisions about reproduction are made and how the context of VAWG might influence these decisions. Much of the literature within the reproductive coercion field comes from concerns that interventions for improving the health outcomes for women in relation to reproductive health, particularly within developing countries, are undermined by VAWG (Jewkes and Abrahams 2002; Jewkes et al. 2001; Wood and Jewkes 1997). This includes sexual and domestic violence and abuse, as well as more subtle forms of coercion, whether that be pressure on girls to engage in sexual activity or a reluctance by male partners to use condoms. Located within a wider debate about women's choices, this chapter will consider how negotiations about sexual activity are made in heterosexual relationships between men and women, and how this in itself impacts on women's choices, regardless of whether abuse is present. This chapter will contribute to our understanding of how practitioners and activists in the field of reproduction can understand

and challenge the ways in which women's choices are shaped by gendered inequalities.

## Women's experiences

Returning to the testimonies of women whom I interviewed as part of the research which I conducted for my Ph.D. (Williamson 2000), I am struck by the way in which women who have experienced abuse struggle to account for the ongoing, and what could be described as "low level" attacks on their confidence and self-esteem. I have described previously (Williamson 2010) how women have to negotiate the "unreality" of their abusive situations in order to survive, and in so doing learn that, in the short term at least, life is easier and safer if you acquiesce to the demands of your abusive partner, albeit with acts of resistance. Women survivors talk constantly about "giving in to keep the peace" or "walking on eggshells." Evan Stark, in his 2007 work *Coercive Control*, suggests that often these seemingly insignificant events focus on undermining women in relation to their actions associated with traditionally feminine roles such as caring, cleaning, shopping, and mothering. In relation to reproductive coercion, and the impact of gender on women's sexuality, this is particularly relevant.

Within my own research, four out of the ten women who were interviewed talked explicitly about physical sexual abuse within their adult intimate relationships. Others described engaging in sexual activity to keep the peace. Not surprisingly, women found talking about this issue the most difficult, personal, and upsetting. In most cases, issues of sexual violence emerged when women spoke of how the abuse they experienced had affected their reproductive choices, and in particular when discussing the violence they experienced when they were pregnant.

A case study based on our research illustrates these issues. Amy was in her mid-forties when I spoke to her. She described herself as a white, educated, middle-class, professional woman. Amy had two grown children, and had been in an abusive relationship for 23 years. Amy was interviewed (untaped at her request) in her home, several years after the end of the abusive relationship and several years after her abusive husband had died. Despite the fact that her husband had died some time ago, the impact of her experiences of abuse was still evident. Amy talked at length about how the abuse she experienced throughout her 23-year marriage impacted on her reproductive choices. She had been physically and psychologically abused for many years including throughout both her pregnancies.

Amy also talked about a particularly traumatic time when she fell pregnant after being raped by her husband and made the difficult decision to have a secret termination. Amy felt that the abuse was already affecting her two children and didn't want to bring another child into the relationship, a decision made more difficult by her husband's (and to a lesser extent her own) Catholic religious beliefs. Having made this decision, Amy secretly terminated the pregnancy, an experience she described as traumatic and lonely. Afterwards Amy began to use contraception against the wishes of her husband, a strategy which engendered great fear and anxiety as she constantly worried that her husband would find out.

Within Amy's story we can see how the sexual violence she experienced and the impact this had on her reproductive options was part of a wider pattern of coercion and control. This control made it difficult for her to make safe decisions about contraception, an issue which was difficult for Amy to articulate, as the act of intercourse which might result in pregnancy was itself outside her control. This raises questions about the ability of women in abusive and controlling relationships to negotiate on any subject, let alone those related to reproduction and sex.

In more recent research (Williamson and Abrahams 2010) evaluating the effectiveness of a UK-based intervention program intended to help women identify and address their experiences of domestic violence and abuse (Craven 2008), a large number of the women who participated identified sexual coercion as part of their experiences and a major cause of disagreement within relationships. In answer to a question about how often they disagreed with their partner about sexual activities, among 14 women six stated that they "often" disagreed, two that they sometimes disagreed, three rarely disagreed, and three reported "never." When asked about areas of disagreement in *previous* intimate relationships, ten (out of 22) women said they would often disagree about sexual activities (45%), eight stated sometimes (37%), and only four stated never (18%). When dealing with these disagreements with partners, 15 women said they would avoid the topic or change the subject and 17 (out of 22 respondents) said that they would normally give in to keep the peace (Williamson and Abrahams 2010).

These data suggest a number of issues. When still in an abusive relationship, women find it difficult to acknowledge the ways in which they may feel coerced into engaging in sexual activities. They are more able to acknowledge this coercion when asked about previous relationships. This begs the question whether women see this type of sexual coercion as a "normal" part of women's heterosexuality. It identifies how women negotiate their safety through giving in to demands from their partners, in a range of areas of their lives including sexual activity, in order to "keep the peace." This suggests that women internalize coercion within their intimate relationships, which in turn impacts on all of their choices, including those related to their sexual and reproductive lives.

## Understanding reproductive coercion

Coining the phrase "reproductive coercion," Elizabeth Miller's work has examined the different ways in which health outcomes for women are impacted by the coercion they experience. In an editorial for the journal *Contraception* in 2010, Miller outlines a definition of reproductive coercion as including "explicit male behaviors to promote pregnancy (unwanted by the woman)…birth control sabotage (interference with contraception) and/or pregnancy coercion, such as telling a woman not to use contraception and threatening to leave her if she doesn't get pregnant" (Miller, Levenson, and Silverman 2010, p.457). On the basis of research evidence, Miller identifies the ways in which those providing sexual health and reproductive services need to address the issue of coercion and abuse within their intervention strategies.

However, the notion of "reproductive coercion" is often problematic, like many of the terms used to describe the experiences of women and girls in relationships where control and coercion is present. By focusing on reproductive health outcomes, this body of literature often fails to fully engage with the domestic and sexual violence literature, and vice versa. As such, the ways in which sexual coercion, sexual violence, and all gendered coercion impact on women's views of their right to make reproductive choices are not always integrated in theory and practice. (See Chapter 8, p.107 for promising practices regarding interventions to link advocacy and reproductive health concerns.)

Also of concern are the ways in which sexual violence within domestically abusive intimate relationships are often annexed and considered in isolation rather than as part of an ongoing and systematic pattern of abuse. Thus in service provision, some issues are addressed whilst others are marginalized and silenced. Given the examples above and the difficulty for women of identifying and naming sexual coercion, this lack of voice and recognition within service provision is worrisome. Also of concern in relation to reproductive coercion, particularly within a UK context, is the apparent split between services for those experiencing domestic or sexual violence. Within the UK, the historic developments of the rape crisis and domestic violence refuge movements has resulted in a separation which might not be useful for service users. Such divisions are also likely within the health field.

Ann Blanc (2001) describes three specific ways in which power in sexual relationships is linked to sexual and reproductive health: "(1) directly; (2) through its relationship with violence between partners; and (3) through its influence on the use of health services" (p.190). We need to examine reproductive coercion within the context of wider abusive relationships and coercive control. This analysis also raises questions about how we bring together our understanding of the reproductive impacts of abuse on women from sometimes divergent literatures. From women's experiences, it seems important to consider reproductive coercion within a wider context of gendered coercion, whether within individual relationships, or in the wider society through gendered norms and expectations.

## Sexual violence, coercion, and reproductive health

Research identifying the high prevalence rates of sexual coercion within intimate relationships is important in understanding the context within which any discussion of reproductive choice takes place. Identifying the scale of the problem in different countries highlights how aspects of sexual coercion, rather than being rare, appear to be integrally linked to women's experiences of intimate relationships. Some of these studies focus specifically on young women's experiences (see Chapter 23). Whilst these experiences are not necessarily isolated to young women only, they highlight the ways in which sexual coercion and force are significant for heterosexual women from early on in their sexually active lives. This literature also demonstrates how these early experiences subsequently impact on women's sexual experiences and reproductive choices later in life.

Evans (2000) examined power and negotiations in young women's choices about sex and contraception. Their findings, particularly those related to women making "choices" to please their partners rather than themselves, suggests that the power imbalances between men and women prevent honest communication within heterosexual intimate sexual relationships.

A recent UK-based survey of young people's experiences of domestic violence and abuse (Barter *et al.* 2009) found that sexual violence and coercion was an issue too for young girls. Whilst this research was not concerned directly with reproductive coercion, it highlights the prevalence of coercion in teen dating relationships within the UK. This is important, as such research is often focused on so-called developing countries where it is assumed that the economic position of women (and men) contributes to limited options for women. As both this and the previous study illustrate, even within societies where women are purported to have equality sanctioned in law, coercion is still rife and a part of a large number of women's sexual experiences.

Maharaj and Munthree (2007) conducted research in South Africa which focused on coercion within first sexual encounters and its impact on reproductive health outcomes. Experiencing sexual coercion in one's first sexual encounter was linked to having less control over subsequent sexual encounters as well as reducing women's confidence in negotiating condom use with their current partner. In addition, a higher percentage of those women who reported being coerced into first sexual encounters reported ever being pregnant and having fallen pregnant at an earlier age. The study authors reported that "of the women who had experienced pregnancy before the age of 15, more of them had been coerced at first sex" (Maharaj and Munthree 2007, pp.236–237).

Recent research in Egypt found that despite "relatively low" rates of sexual coercion in relation to global statistics and other statistics from Egypt, "husband's control [of his partner] was significantly associated with forced intercourse during a woman's lifetime" (Kaplan, Khawaja, and Linos 2011, p.1465).

All of these studies highlight the ways in which, irrespective of country and therefore legal protections or social expectations, coercion plays an important part in many women's experiences of sex with men. Whether in initial sexual encounters or established partnerships, many women feel pressured and coerced into engaging in sexual activity irrespective of their own desires. This is an important issue in its own right, irrespective of the wider health and reproductive consequences of coercion, which will be addressed shortly. Whilst in many cases women do not identify their experience as sexual violence or rape, large numbers of women are reporting feeling coerced and/or threatened into sexual encounters. The seemingly widespread nature of coercion implies that women globally face difficult decisions about whether and when to have sex and how to negotiate safe refusals. It also raises questions about men's perceptions of entitlement and access to women's bodies which need to be addressed.

Within this context, it is not surprising that women struggle to take control of their reproductive health in order to achieve better health outcomes. Research suggests that there is a range of consequences for women's reproductive health related to intimate heterosexual partnerships, sometimes irrespective of whether those relationships might be considered abusive and/or coercive. This includes birth control sabotage (Miller *et al.* 2011; Thiel de Bocanegra *et al.* 2010), additional risk of HIV/AIDS (Fox *et al.* 2007), unwanted pregnancies (Miller *et al.* 2007), and women's use of abortion services (Silverman *et al.* 2010).

## Discussion

All of the research identified above makes clear the impact of gendered coercion on the reproductive and sexual health experiences of women. Whilst it is important to recognize the ways in which coercion and control impact on these areas of women's lives, this body of literature does not identify how or why these sites of intervention (reproductive and/or sexual health services) differ from other women-only interventions where issues of gendered inequality and abuse are raised and addressed with women. It could be argued therefore that "reproductive coercion" is not a specific phenomenon but better understood as part of the wider gendered coercion and control which women experience, particularly within heterosexual relationships.

Moore, Frohwirth, and Miller (2010), in their study of male reproductive control of women, report that "reproductive control was present in violent as well as non-violent relationships" (p.1737), which they suggest supports the use of reproductive services as an intervention site. I would argue that, whilst identifying sites for interventions with women is important, this finding suggests that the coercion and control of women is much more widespread and accepted, both by individual women and wider society, than accounting for a specific phenomenon in its own right. Whilst the ways in which these impacts are experienced might differ across different contexts, the use of coercion, centered around the gendered expectations of women in their sexual lives, serves to control women, as outlined by Evan Stark, both individually and as a group. Stark describes the ways in which the use of coercion and control to limit women's liberty or personhood is often focused on specifically gendered roles. Given that reproduction and sexual health are inherently gendered, it is not surprising that many women experience coercion in these aspects of their lives.

The danger in discussing reproductive coercion in isolation is the focus on individual women/patients rather than the wider systemic gender inequality which affects women. By continuing to focus on women and not men, this approach may perpetuate the idea that it is women who take responsibility for sexual and reproductive matters irrespective of the fact that the evidence suggests that women are not in control of their own sexual encounters.

Thinking about reproductive or sexual coercion within this wider framework is useful for a number of reasons. Stark (2007) identifies the ways in which the domestic violence movement in particular has stalled somewhat and would serve women better if it refocused its efforts to challenge the ways in which women are prevented from obtaining full personhood. In this respect, the challenge facing those providing interventions for women within the sexual and reproductive health contexts is to also engage with this process and recognize that reproductive and sexual coercion are examples of the ways in which women are prevented from taking custody of their own potential as human beings. Such a stance requires service providers to challenge the inequality (including inequality in opportunities to fulfilling personhood and liberty) which gives men leverage to manipulate women, and particularly young women, in relation to reproductive and sexual experiences.

## Practitioner strategies

Whilst there are some concerns that focusing on women as agents of change diminishes the responsibility attached to the actions of male perpetrators of gender-based violence, given that reproductive health settings are conducive to interventions with women, it is important that such services consider the impact of their interventions. There are a number of initiatives which provide guidance to practitioners in how to address some of the specific issues which have been raised in this chapter. These include, in the US, the Futures Without Violence guidance on addressing reproductive and sexual coercion (Chamberlain and Levenson 2012) and the Washington Coalition of Sexual Assault Programs and Washington State Coalition Against Domestic Violence's (2013) *Toolkit for Working with Pregnant and Parenting Survivors: Practice Guidelines for Professionals.* The DAPHNE-funded guidance on a range of interventions within primary health and maternity services across Europe provides additional strategies (Bacchus *et al.* 2012). These approaches recognize a range of factors which practitioners and policy makers need to address, including: 1) clinical leadership in order for effective implementation, including use of domestic violence champions, 2) both a top-down and bottom-up approach which marries the organizational objectives with front-line practice, 3) appropriate and ongoing training and supervision for clinical staff, 4) effective multi-agency collaboration which recognizes the role of specialist domestic and sexual violence services, and 5) the inclusion of service users in the evaluation of interventions to ensure that the needs of victims/survivors are being met.

On a practical level, it is crucial that interventions are provided in a nonjudgmental way which does not blame women for the abuse they experience. Providing a supportive environment for women to explore their options and be referred, if appropriate, to specialist domestic and sexual violence services is central to any effective intervention.

## Conclusion

There is no doubt that interventions that help women recognize how they might be limited from full personhood through the subtle ways in which they are coerced and controlled are useful. The reproductive coercion literature identifies a number of specific sexual and reproductive health sites where issues of sexual and other coercion can be raised with women, and services, where they exist, provided. Such services, however, need to be fully integrated with those services which for a number of decades have provided shelter, support, and safety for women experiencing sexual and/or domestic violence. It also needs to be recognized that the rights of women, in relation to sexual freedom and reproductive choices, differ globally. Rape in marriage is still not defined as illegal in many countries, and rape is considered an adulterous act by the female victim in others. These two examples of state-sponsored gendered control are extreme, but should be considered alongside the more subtle forms of control which serve to influence women's sexual and reproductive decisions, such as the ways in which women who experience abuse are both blamed for the failure to protect their children within that relationship, and blamed for leaving.

# References

Bacchus, L., Bewley, S., Fernandez, C., Hellbernd, H. *et al.* (2012) *Health Sector Responses to Domestic Violence in Europe: A Comparison of Promising Intervention Models in Maternity and Primary Care Settings.* London: London School of Hygiene & Tropical Medicine. Available at http://diverhse.eu and http://diverhse.org, accessed July 29, 2012.

Barter, C., McCarry, M., Berridge, D., and Evans, K. (2009) *Partner Exploitation and Violence in Teenage Intimate Relationships: Executive Summary.* London: National Society for the Prevention of Cruelty to Children. Available at www.nspcc.org.uk/inform/research/findings/partner_exploitation_and_violence_wda68092.html, accessed March 17, 2013.

Blanc, A.K. (2001) "The effect of power in sexual relationships on sexual and reproductive health: an examination of the evidence." *Studies in Family Planning* 32, 3, 189–213.

Chamberlain, L. and Levenson, R. (2012) *Addressing Intimate Partner Violence, Reproductive and Sexual Coercion: A Guide for Obstetric, Gynecologic and Reproductive Health Care Settings,* Second Edition. San Francisco, CA: Futures Without Violence. Available at www.futureswithoutviolence.org/userfiles/file/HealthCare/reproguidelines_low_res_FINAL.pdf, accessed August 2, 2012.

Craven, P. (2008) *Living with the Dominator: A Book About the Freedom Programme.* Knighton, Powys, UK: Freedom Publishing.

Evans, A. (2000) "Power and negotiation: young women's choices about sex and contraception." *Journal of Population Research 17,* 2, 143–162.

Fox, A.M., Jackson, S.S., Hansen, N.B., Gasa, N., Crewe, M., and Sikkema, K.J. (2007) "In their own voices: a qualitative study of women's risk for intimate partner violence and HIV in South Africa." *Violence Against Women 13,* 6, 583–602.

Jewkes, R.K. and Abrahams, N. (2002) "The epidemiology of rape and sexual coercion in South Africa: an overview." *Social Science and Medicine 55,* 1231–1244.

Jewkes, R.K., Vundule, C., Maforah, F., and Jordaan, E. (2001) "Relationship dynamics and teenage pregnancy in South Africa." *Social Science and Medicine 52,* 733–744.

Kaplan, R.L., Khawaja, M., and Linos, N. (2011) "Husband's control and sexual coercion within marriage: findings from a population-based survey in Egypt." *Violence Against Women 17,* 11, 1465–1479.

Maharaj, P. and Munthree, C. (2007) "Coerced first sexual intercourse and selected reproductive health outcomes among young women in Kwazulu-Natal, South Africa." *Journal of Biosocial Science 39,* 231–244.

Miller, E., Decker, M.R., McCauley, H.L., Tancredi, D.J. *et al.* (2011) "A family planning clinic partner violence intervention to reduce risk associated with reproductive coercion." *Contraception 83*, 274–280.

Miller, E., Decker, M.R., Reed, E., Raj, A. *et al.* (2007) "Male partner pregnancy-promoting behaviors and adolescent partner violence: findings from a qualitative study with adolescent females." *Ambulatory Pediatrics 7*, 5, 360–366.

Miller, E., Levenson, R., and Silverman, J.G. (2010) "Reproductive coercion: connecting the dots between partner violence and unintended pregnancy." *Contraception 81*, 457–459.

Moore, A.M., Frohwirth, L., and Miller, E. (2010) "Male reproductive control of women who have experienced intimate partner violence in the United States." *Social Science and Medicine 70*, 1737–1744.

Silverman, J.G., Decker, M.R., McCauley, H.L., Gupta, J. *et al.* (2010) "Male perpetration of intimate partner violence and involvement in abortions and abortion-related conflict." *Research and Practice 100*, 8, 1415–1417.

Stark, E. (2007) *Coercive Control*. Oxford: Oxford University Press.

Thiel de Bocanegra, H., Rostovtseva, D.P., Khera, S., and Godhwani, N. (2010) "Birth control sabotage and forced sex: experiences reported by women in domestic violence shelters." *Violence Against Women 16*, 5, 601–612.

Washington Coalition of Sexual Assault Programs and Washington State Coalition Against Domestic Violence (2013) *Toolkit for Working with Pregnant and Parenting Survivors: Practice Guidelines for Professionals: An Integrated Approach to Intimate Partner Violence and Reproductive and Sexual Coercion.* Available at: www.pregnantsurvivors.org, accessed September 1, 2013.

Williamson, E. (2000) *Domestic Violence and Health, The Response of the Medical Profession.* Bristol: Policy Press.

Williamson, E. (2010) "Living in the world of the domestic violence perpetrator: Negotiating the unreality of coercive control." *Violence Against Women 16*, 1412-1423.

Williamson, E. and Abrahams, H. (2010) *Evaluation of the Bristol Freedom Programme.* Bristol: University of Bristol.

Wood, K. and Jewkes, R.K. (1997) "Violence, rape, and sexual coercion: everyday love in a South African township." *Gender and Development 5*, 2, 41–46.

# PART 3

# Intimate Partner Sexual Violence and Best Practice Service Response

CHAPTER 7

# Counseling and Advocacy Perspectives on Intimate Partner Sexual Violence

Isabelle Kerr

*All the perpetrator asks is that the bystander do nothing. He appeals to the universal desire to see, hear and speak no evil. The victim, on the contrary, asks the bystander to share the burden of the pain. The victim demands action, engagement and remembering. (Herman 1992, p.7)*

For many years, violence against women has often been categorized and "pigeonholed" as if each form is separate and exists apart from the others. Even for those of us who work in the field, domestic abuse is sometimes seen as something separate from rape or sexual assault. But with more work being done to recognize that intimate partner sexual violence (IPSV) is a very useful weapon in the abuser's arsenal, we can now give survivors permission to speak about a difficult and often confusing aspect of domestic abuse.

Many counseling and advocacy services offer support to survivors of domestic abuse, and some focus specifically on this issue. However, in order to support survivors in identifying all of the issues and abuses they have been living with, we ourselves need to be open to recognizing the full impact of all forms of domestic abuse, not just the punch, kick, slap, or the controlling behavior, but the very complex nature of intimate partner sexual violence.

There is a real danger that, as counselors or advocates, we will view intimate partner sexual violence as only forced or at least as unwilling sex, that in order for it to come under the category of "domestic abuse" it should be an act that a woman does not seek out, does not enjoy, and participates in only under extreme pressure. If we are unable to see further than this limited definition of IPSV, how can a survivor begin to analyze the intricate complexities of this sexual abuse?

Intimate partner sexual violence is part of that continuum of gender-based violence that is accepted worldwide, but until we define and identify IPSV in all its forms as a very real aspect of domestic abuse and part of that continuum, we will continue to ignore the "nonphysical" aspects of the abuse and validate only its more extreme forms.

How we frame sexual violence determines how we respond to it. If our frame of reference is that we expect force and resistance, we will have difficulty in understanding sexual coercion. Figures for stranger rape—around eight percent in the UK (Myhill and Allen 2002)—have remained static for a number of years, yet as a society we still carry a picture of a rapist in our heads, a picture that portrays him in a dark and probably lonely place, at night, possibly disguised or at least with his face covered. He will leap out at us; we will be fighting him off with every last ounce of our strength, and, with force, he will rape us. Against this collective acceptance of the "stranger rapist" as our greatest threat, we may find it hard to identify a loving husband/ partner and father as a rapist.

As difficult as it is for many women to name overt sexual force as rape, it is also difficult for helping professionals to understand the nature and variety of IPSV. Rape is one of a range of behaviors that an abuser will use to control and dominate his partner. If we accept that a man is okay about abusing his partner physically or psychologically, why is it difficult for us to make that leap, to realize that he possibly will not hesitate to abuse his partner sexually as well?

As workers, we also need to consider the language we use when we talk about all forms of domestic abuse. Language is important and can reveal much about how comfortable we ourselves feel about an issue. In the UK, a woman is murdered by her partner or ex-partner every three to four days (UK Home Office 2012), but what we often see in newspaper headlines is "Domestic abuse kills two women a week," as if domestic abuse is a disembodied entity with a life of its own. As well as keeping perpetrators of partner murder invisible, we also de-gender other forms of male violence against women. An example of this is that we commonly use the term "violent relationship." This terminology serves only to misguide us and give the subtle impression that the abuse is a two-way street. If we are to form any kind of understanding of the nature of domestic abuse, we must have an understanding predicated on the view that it is not the relationship that is violent, it is the perpetrator: he brings violence and abuse into the relationship.

Any kind of abusive behavior within a relationship is a betrayal of trust, but there is another dimension to intimate partner sexual violence, an added betrayal of the intimacy and closeness that exists between a couple who have shared a sexual bond as an expression of their love and commitment to one another. In that relationship, consent will have been given many times, and sexual contact will have been welcomed and perhaps initiated more than once. The question for many survivors will often be, where is that line, the line of consent, and when is it crossed? When does a willing, consensual sexual act become rape?

For some women, the answer to that question is unclear or even completely unknown, and that is why survivors often struggle to name the sexual violence perpetrated against them. What survivors do know, and do identify, is the trauma that they are experiencing. This often manifests itself in poor mental health and well-being, in self-medicating with drugs or alcohol, or in a range of self-harming behaviors that may then lead to the blame for the abuse being shifted to the woman and sympathy being directed at the perpetrator.

It is also important that we challenge the myth that lack of injury is evidence that no rape occurred—how do you name sexual acts that are performed under pressure or the use of sex as appeasement? In Scotland under the new Sexual Offences (Scotland) Act 2009, any sexual act must be carried out with the consent and "free agreement" of both parties. We could argue that appeasement, coercive, or pressurized sex is not "free agreement" as clearly laid out in the Act. However, the question would then be, how do we prove this in a court of law? And of course many women don't want to involve the police: they are ashamed, they may not want their family and friends to know, their partner's job may be at risk, they may lose their home or their family, or social services may become involved, creating the added fear of losing their children. Law enforcement being involved is not always the answer; women often say that they don't want police involved nor do they want the relationship to end—they just want the abuse to stop. In this case the victim advocate, whose role it is to support the survivor through the justice process, may be deemed to be redundant, but a role in risk assessment and safety planning may be possible.

So how can we provide services to survivors who are living with, or have lived with, an abusive partner?

## We look at our own understanding of the issue

In order to provide a service that meets the need of survivors, we need to fully understand the level of trauma and conditioning that the survivor has undergone. Without this understanding, we will not effectively support the woman.

Our analysis of intimate partner sexual violence often exists only on the surface. We may think of forced sex as only an extension of the physical violence, and not be aware of the coercive and controlling way that sexual violence can be used to abuse. The type of sexual coercion that survivors more often identify is forced sex as it exists within our framework of understanding rape. It's physical; it's forced. If we do not recognize the sexual violence aspect of the relationship in all its forms, we are in danger of missing a significant trauma indicator. We use language like "coercive and controlling behavior," but we need to deconstruct these phrases in order to fully understand the impact of the abuse they are describing.

*Appeasement sex*—This is a strategy that survivors often use to manage the abuser. It may be used to forestall physical abuse, to ensure that the survivor and her children have money for food or clothing, or so that the bills get paid. Women will rarely, if ever, see this as relating to sexual violence in any way, as the woman will often initiate the sexual act and may be physically satisfied by it. Also, many women would argue that this is a gray area as most of us will use appeasement sex at some point in our relationships. However, I would argue that when appeasement sex becomes a conscious strategy for avoiding abusive consequences, it can then be clearly placed on that spectrum of abusive behavior.

*Pressure sex*—This sexual activity is unwanted but necessary to "meet his needs." This may involve acts which the woman finds distasteful but she will comply to ensure that her partner is satisfied. Again, this may be used to reduce the risk of physical or verbal abuse or to ensure that financial commitments are met. Pressure sex may also involve the use of pornography (Easteal and McOrmond-Plummer 2008).

*Pornography*—Pornography is a significant feature in intimate partner sexual violence. In the 2009 survey by the Rape Crisis Centre in Glasgow, Scotland, mentioned above, almost half of respondents (48%), answered yes when asked the question, "Has your partner or ex-partner ever asked or forced you to watch pornography?" Survivors also commented that their partners often expected or forced them to "act out" the scenes they had viewed in the pornography.

*Coercive control*—This is a pattern of behavior that women experience as "ongoing" rather than "repeated," which means that it is not one act, such as hitting, that is repeated regularly, but a range of behaviors designed to be cumulative in effect, thus controlling every aspect of the woman's life. This can include a woman's use of appeasement sex as a coping or survival strategy. Coercive control does not have to be severe, as Evan Stark states:

> ...the main means men use to establish control is the microregulation of everyday behaviors associated with stereotypic female roles, such as how women dress, cook, clean, socialize, care for their children, or perform sexually... These dynamics give coercive control a role in sexual politics that distinguishes it from all other crimes. (2009, p.5)

The main indicators that sex is part of coercive control are that it is ongoing, it is routine, and it is cumulative in its effect.

*Traumatic bonding*—Traumatic bonding, or Stockholm Syndrome, is another coping strategy used by the survivor. She may attach to the positive behavior of the abuser: the "occasional indulgences" as identified in Biderman's "Chart of Coercion" (Biderman and Zimmer 1961). These "indulgences" may simply be that the woman does not have to perform sexual acts for him or that the sex will be directed at meeting her needs and not his. The survivor can become so attuned to her abuser's behavior and thoughts that she begins to think as he does and knows almost instinctively how to appease and manage his moods. As the survivor's safety is completely controlled by the abuser, it is often extremely difficult for that survivor to identify her "safe space" where she can begin to process the trauma.

## We work within a "trauma model"

To meet the needs of survivors we must understand, and through our own understanding help inform the survivor that her responses to the domestic abuse she has been experiencing are a normal response to trauma. We should feel comfortable talking to the woman about how that trauma is manifesting itself. Is she taking prescription medication, perhaps for depression, anxiety, or inability to sleep? Is she using alcohol as a coping mechanism or perhaps nonprescription drugs to self-medicate? Does she find it difficult to leave her home because of her levels of anxiety or perhaps because of obsessive thoughts or compulsive behavior? All of these point to a normal response to trauma. However, as a society we often look to the woman to allocate blame—"She's neurotic," or "She's a drunk"—thus missing the root cause of the behavior and the person responsible.

## We recognize that home may not be safe

What should be the woman's safe place, her home, may not in fact be safe for her. For a survivor of IPSV, her home may be a place of entrapment, where she is caught within a pattern of abuse from the person that society would like to believe should be protecting and nurturing her. If we are using Herman's (1992) three-stage model of recovery from trauma, establishing safety can be difficult, as a woman may have no place she can call "safe." She may feel safe within the counseling room, and this may be invaluable, as it may be the only time and space she has that is her own. But if we aim to support the woman to create a place of safety inside herself, we may have to recognize that it might not be possible, as she may need to maintain that state of "unsafety"—a state of hypervigilance, that keeps her alert to the abuser's actions, demands, or presence. In addition, it is worth recognizing that any work on integrating the abuse into the survivor's life experiences is undermined by the fact that the experiences may be ongoing (if she is still in the relationship). Therefore, as support workers or counselors, we must maintain a "holding pattern" of offering support while the survivor looks at her options.

We recognize that many women will have been raped by their partners over and over again. If we accept that in a war zone a woman who is the victim of multiple rapes can experience posttraumatic stress disorder, it follows that a woman who is raped many times by her partner or ex-partner would not be exempt from trauma, especially when she is being repeatedly raped by the person who is supposed to care for and protect her. Contrary to popular belief, rape by a partner is not less traumatic than rape by a stranger but more so as, among other factors, the chance of revictimization after stranger rape is low, whereas the chance of revictimization and consequently retraumatization after partner rape is high (Tjaden and Thoennes 2006).

INTIMATE PARTNER SEXUAL VIOLENCE

# We don't ask, "Why doesn't she leave?"

We recognize, and accept, that a woman has the right to make a decision about whether she stays with or leaves her partner. We recognize the effects that forced sex, pressure sex, and appeasement sex can have on a woman's self-esteem and sense of self-worth. We also recognize the cumulative effect that coercive control has on survivors and accept that leaving is a process, not an event. We also recognize that separation does not always mean safety (see Chapter 5).

If a woman does manage to leave the abuser, the focus may still be very firmly on her behavior. For example, if the woman continues to be coerced by her partner and has contact with him after legal protection has been put in place (variously identified as injunctions, barring orders, restraining orders, nonharassment orders, domestic violence orders, or apprehended violence orders), she may be the one who is judged and accused of breaching the order. Yet again, his behavior becomes invisible. Protection orders are very positive and can save women and children's lives, but only if they are properly enforced. One of the challenges is that if the perpetrator does not obey the order, he can only be dealt with *after* the breach, which means that the woman—and possibly her children—may be retraumatized. Unless the perpetrator is taken into custody, this can happen over and over again. If the woman then takes her partner back, she will often be blamed and her behavior judged, not his. She may be continuing to see him, reducing the risk by managing the situation, keeping herself safe by knowing where the perpetrator is, and using tried and trusted coping strategies to keep herself and her children safe.

# We look at our own role in this process

It is our role to give the survivor space and support. It may be the only support she has, as she may be isolated from family and friends. But we must remember that we are the facilitators. It is not our role to advise, suggest, or direct, but only to give safe space and sometimes to ask the right questions so that the woman can, through the process of exploration, reach her own decisions. If our fundamental role is to empower, we must always be aware of our own position in the support relationship. We, as counselors or support workers, are in a position of safety and power. We are working with a woman who has possibly been controlled by her partner for a considerable time.

Her way of remaining safe may be by doing as she is told. Consequently, she may ask for advice or direction. It can be very tempting to tell the woman what to do because we want her to be safe. However, we must maintain strict boundaries at all times, remembering that we are not the experts: the woman is the expert in her own situation. She has been living with this man and/or she knows him pretty well. Our role is to help empower her to look at her options and choose the one that is best for her and has the best chance of keeping her, and her children, safe.

## We must separate our experiences from those of our clients

If we are survivors ourselves, we must explore how we feel and discuss with our supervisor. As service providers/survivors, it can be easy to think that we know exactly what the survivor is feeling, what her experiences have been, and how she can escape the abuse. This can never be the case, as not only is every woman's experience of abuse different, but her coping strategies, her survival techniques, her way of managing the situation, will all be her own, developed to respond to the demands and caprices of her abuser. And of course each abuser is different, including the level of violence he is willing to use should the woman attempt to leave him.

## We must ask ourselves, "Are there any barriers to accessing our service?"

One major barrier is that some agencies will demand that a woman has separated from the abuser before she can access support or advocacy services. If your service has this policy, perhaps revisiting the reason for reaching that decision would be useful. A counselor or advocate who is working with a survivor who is still living with her partner may find that it is extremely difficult to support the survivor when we know she will be returning to the abuser after our counseling or advocacy appointment. A survivor may want our support to get free from the abuser; she may need our help in the practical aspects of her life such as housing or finance, and yet be reluctant to talk about the detail of the abuse she has experienced. It is useful to consider Maslow's hierarchy of needs (1943): if a survivor has no means of financial support, no way to ensure that she has food and shelter for herself and her children, she will not be in a safe place to talk about her support needs. The practical considerations must take precedence.

Other barriers may also exist. Is your organization a "9 to 5" set-up? This may prove inaccessible for survivors who are in paid employment. Do you have adequate language support, including for deaf women? How easy is it to reach your service? Do you have private, confidential space to speak to clients or patients? For many agencies this consideration of barriers may seem too much like going back to basics, but sometimes the simplest detail can make the difference between someone being able to access a service or not. Aesthetics are also important, as one survivor showed in a rape crisis feedback form:

> My legs were shaking as I was coming up the stairs. I didn't know what to expect. I could hardly ring the bell and then I came in and it was lovely and you had the lamps on and it smelled so nice. You've got the rooms just lovely. I felt so welcomed. (Rape survivor 2011)

## We must listen, take seriously, and believe

To a counselor or support worker, this may seem obvious, but it cannot be stressed enough that we must always be ready to challenge ourselves, because we may find it hard to believe some of what a survivor is saying. Our default position must be, "Just because a woman's story is unbelievable doesn't mean that it's not to be believed." It can be difficult to listen to a woman talking about the abuse she has experienced— the humiliation, the degrading acts that she has been subjected to. It may be easier for us to dismiss the story as exaggeration, but that's only because it will make us feel a bit better. It's more likely that the survivor will be minimizing her experiences or may be keeping some facts from you because she is too ashamed of what happened. She is testing you to see what your response will be before she tells the whole story or because she is trying to protect you from the full horror of her experience.

Providing a support service for survivors of any form of gender-based violence is always a work in progress. As service providers, we must ask women for their opinions and suggestions on how the service can be improved. Some of those suggestions will not be practical as we all struggle with the vagaries of government funding, space, and health and safety regulations, but it is important that we ask, listen, and improve when we can. For most survivors, the overriding need is for a safe place to speak and be heard. The main thing we must show is our commitment to breaking the silence. For many women, your service will be the first time that they have been given a voice and listened to.

> *Thank you, thank you, thank you for letting me talk. (Rape crisis service user, Scotland 2012)*

# References

Biderman, A. and Zimmer, H. (1961) *The Manipulation of Human Behavior*. New York: John Wiley & Sons, Inc.

Easteal, P. and McOrmond-Plummer, L. (2008) *Real Rape, Real Pain: Help for Women Sexually Assaulted by Male Partners*. Melbourne: Hybrid Publishers.

Glasgow Rape Crisis Centre (2009) *Intimate Partner Sexual Violence—20 Years On*. Glasgow: Glasgow Rape Crisis Centre. Available at www.rapecrisiscentre-glasgow.co.uk, accessed December 1, 2012.

Herman, J. (1992) *Trauma and Recovery: From Domestic Abuse to Political Terror*. New York: Basic Books.

Johnson, M. (2008) *A Typology of Domestic Violence: Intimate Terrorism, Violent Resistance, and Situational Couple Violence*. Boston, MA: Northeastern University Press.

Maslow, A. (1943) "A theory of human motivation." *Psychological Review 50*, 370–396.

Myhill, A. and Allen, J. (2002) *Rape and Sexual Assault of Women: Findings from the British Crime Survey*. London: Home Office. Available at www.aphroditewounded.org/Myhill and Allen.pdf, accessed July 4, 2013.

Stark, E. (2009) *Coercive Control: The Entrapment of Rape Victimization: Women in Personal Life*. New York: Oxford University Press.

Tjaden, P. and Thoennes, N. (2006) *Extent, Nature, and Consequences of Rape Victimization: Findings from the National Violence Against Women Survey*. Washington, DC: National Institute of Justice. Available at www.ncjrs.gov/pdffiles1/nl/210346.pdf, accessed February 16, 2013.

UK Home Office (2012) *Homicides, Firearm Offences and Intimate Violence 2010/11: Supplementary Volume 2 to Crime in England and Wales 2010/11*. Available at www.homeoffice.gov.uk/publications/science-research-statistics/research-statistics/crime-research/hosb0212, accessed December 30, 2012.

CHAPTER 8

# The Role of the Advocate in Addressing Intimate Partner Sexual Violence

Jennifer Y. Levy-Peck

Advocates, who are trained workers who assist victims of crime, are a critical part of the multidisciplinary approach to addressing intimate partner sexual violence (IPSV). They may be community-based advocates, who are employed by domestic violence or sexual assault agencies, or system-based advocates, who work out of a public agency such as a prosecutor's office or a law enforcement agency. Advocacy services have been shown to reduce rates of revictimization, increase social support and the ability to access resources, and enhance quality of life (Wathan and MacMillan 2003).

## Understanding the difference between system-based and community-based advocates

System-based advocates have a specific role, which is generally to assist the victim so as to enhance the efficient investigation and prosecution of the criminal case. They can be extremely valuable in clarifying and conveying information to individuals who have been victimized and who are willing to go forward with a court case. System-based advocates have access to prosecutors and investigators and can often help victims to feel less alone and frightened as they navigate the unfamiliar systems they encounter. Lonsway and Archambault of End Violence Against Women International offer clear explanations of the value of both system-based and community-based advocates, and draw an important distinction: "System-based advocates typically never qualify for counseling privilege, so their private communications with victims—and their written records documenting services—can never be guaranteed to remain confidential" (Lonsway and Archambault 2007, p.5).

Community-based advocates offer a range of support services to survivors of domestic and sexual violence, most commonly working within nonprofit agencies. They can assist with crisis intervention, safety planning, temporary shelter, emotional support, legal information, and accompaniment to medical, investigative, and court proceedings. They also assist in arranging medical care and offer information and referrals to those who have been victimized. Community-based advocacy programs often provide support groups for survivors and prevention services for schools and the community. They do not press survivors to take certain actions, such as following through with prosecution of the abuser, but rather help them to explore all their options and to make informed decisions (Office for Victims of Crime 2011).

While both community-based and system-based advocates may accompany women to forensic exams immediately after a sexual assault and maintain contact throughout any involvement with the criminal justice system, community-based advocates may also begin working with survivors many years after IPSV occurs and have off-and-on contact with clients over a period of years. For example, a woman may have been sexually assaulted by a boyfriend as a teenager, and she may not seek advocacy services until she is in her early thirties and having sexual intimacy problems with her husband. She may return again when her own children are teenagers and she is experiencing anxiety about their entering the dating world.

## Differences between domestic violence and sexual assault advocacy

Even when domestic violence and sexual assault services are housed within the same agency, there are differences in the services provided by the advocates within each program. Shelter or refuge housing is a major component of many domestic violence programs; advocates working in these settings offer crisis intervention to the shelter residents and their children, and many agencies offer a range of community-based services as well. Therefore, domestic violence advocates are often well prepared to assist survivors with safety planning, housing needs, financial issues, child-centered concerns, protection orders, and a host of other practical and emotional concerns.

Sexual assault advocacy programs usually offer medical and legal advocacy. Personnel are normally well versed in trauma response, and these programs may have strong relationships with mental health providers to whom they refer clients, or the sexual assault program may actually employ therapists as well as advocates. In the US, the Centers for Disease Control and Prevention (CDC) funds a range of sexual assault prevention efforts (CDC 2012), which has strengthened sexual assault programs' focus on prevention activities, often with teens.

## Advocates as agents of change

Most advocacy agencies work not only to assist individual survivors, but also (particularly in the case of community-based programs) to improve the system response to those who have been abused. Throughout this book, authors describe the difficulties women face when they call the police, see a health care provider, seek solace from clergy, or reach out for justice from the courts. Advocacy agencies build relationships with the various service providers in a community and address the barriers to humane and effective intervention. They are committed to social change in order to reduce or eliminate abusive behaviors in the first place, and to reduce the revictimization that can occur when survivors are treated with disrespect or disbelief (Stop Violence Against Women 2010).

## The unique approach of advocates

Advocates have a different role than other helping professionals. For example, a mental health therapist might work with a survivor on changing her perceptions and behaviors, with improved mood and social functioning as goals. An advocate would focus on empowerment of the survivor (increasing her belief in her own efficacy), as well as offering practical assistance and resources. An advocate might provide transportation, help a survivor to locate childcare, conduct a support group, go to the doctor with a survivor, explain medical or legal procedures, or explore the dangers inherent in certain courses of action (Stop Violence Against Women 2010).

## Challenges in intimate partner sexual violence advocacy

Most community-based advocates working with IPSV survivors are working within an agency or program whose focus is either domestic violence or sexual assault. Even those advocates working in agencies that provide both kinds of services generally specialize in one or the other of these forms of victimization. A recurring theme in this book is the need to address the intersection of domestic violence and sexual assault, which is where IPSV is located. IPSV survivors may not raise the issue of sexual victimization with a domestic violence advocate, and may not be able to have their safety or economic needs addressed by a sexual assault advocate. Therefore, advocates in rape crisis centers may need to work collaboratively with domestic violence agencies for safety and financial resources, while domestic violence advocates may need to improve their understanding of sexual assault issues and their comfort in discussing these concerns.

Both sexual assault and domestic violence agencies need to be intentionally welcoming to IPSV survivors, who otherwise may feel out of place. This can be accomplished by including information about IPSV in agency brochures and on their websites, by advertising and conducting IPSV-specific support groups, and by mentioning IPSV in community presentations and prevention programs. A simple method for informing clients that IPSV is addressed by advocates is to have posters, bookmarks, or other materials on the topic visible in waiting rooms and to distribute these materials in the community with the agency contact information on them. The Washington Coalition of Sexual Assault Programs (WCSAP 2010a) offers a selection of printable posters, bookmarks, and brochures in seven languages, and the Futures Without Violence's (2012) safety cards address partner sexual and reproductive coercion in English and Spanish.

# Opportunities for intimate partner sexual violence advocacy

## Understanding the intersections

Because advocacy for violence against women is a product of the movements to address sexual and domestic violence, the field offers a unique blend of individual assistance and social justice work (The Advocates for Human Rights 2009). Advocates typically work hard to incorporate cultural competency into their approach (Beyond Diversity Resource Center 2010) so that they are equipped to understand the intersections of other oppressions (such as racism and poverty) with gender-based violence (see Chapter 19).

IPSV advocacy should include outreach to lesbian, gay, bisexual, and transgender individuals and to survivors throughout the lifespan, from young teens to elders. Programs can form partnerships with other programs that address the needs of groups such as immigrant survivors and seek to employ bilingual and bicultural advocates to work in culturally specific communities to reduce barriers to accessing advocacy services.

## *Offering sensitive support to survivors*

Advocates help survivors to cope with and overcome their victimization, rather than focusing on individual pathology, which can all too often feel like victim-blaming. Because IPSV victimization is fraught with shame and stigma, an advocate may be the first person who seems to truly listen to and believe an individual who has been sexually abused by a partner.

Advocacy programs typically maintain lists of mental health therapists and substance abuse treatment providers, and can assist survivors with referrals for treatment. Some programs have therapists on staff, or can pay for therapy services for clients. Many survivors are concerned about their children's reactions to the IPSV itself or to its consequences, such as living in a shelter or observing their mother's emotional pain. Advocacy programs can assist by helping clients locate appropriate therapeutic services for their children.

Sometimes a survivor may see the suggestion of therapy for herself or her children as a criticism that reinforces the abuser's taunts that she is "crazy" or a poor mother (see Chapter 13). An advocate's knowledgeable, compassionate reframing of the value of therapy for the aftermath of trauma can reduce the barrier of stigma and help clients know what to expect:

> Once the conversation about therapy begins, survivors…will have many questions. These can range from the practical, such as "How do I pay for this?" to more emotional concerns, like "What am I going to have to share?" While these questions (and answers) will differ for each situation, the advocate can be a sounding board, helping survivors clarify their needs and providing options to consider. (WCSAP 2010b, p.16)

## Enhancing safety for survivors and their children

Advocates can offer safety planning assistance regardless of whether survivors wish to leave the relationship. As we saw in Chapter 5, leaving the abuser does not always guarantee safety, and in fact it may exacerbate risk significantly. Advocates respect survivors' wishes with regard to the relationship, and can work on strategies to increase safety regardless of the living situation (Davies 2008).

One component of safety planning is addressing the overlap of IPSV and stalking. Advocates can provide relevant information. One in six women in the US has been stalked in her lifetime, and two-thirds of female stalking victims are stalked by a current or former intimate partner (Black *et al.* 2011). The Center for Problem-Oriented Policing (2013) provides a clear guide to stalking dangers and relevant responses.

Advocates can also acquaint IPSV survivors with any systems in place to notify crime victims of the release of an incarcerated offender. Protection orders requiring the offender to stay away from the victim, while not an infallible shield, may be useful. Some jurisdictions in the US offer sexual assault protection orders that can help women or teens who may not qualify for domestic violence protection orders— for example, with an ex-partner from a short-term dating relationship.

In extreme cases, survivors may need to protect their identity and location on an ongoing basis. Many survivors will benefit from assistance in the safe use of technology, and advocates can find up-to-date resources from the National Sexual Violence Resource Center (2013).

## Making intimate partner sexual violence on campus visible

Advocacy programs on college campuses may not fully address sexual assault that takes place within an ongoing coercive and abusive relationship, although a high proportion of offenders are boyfriends or ex-boyfriends of victims—23.7 percent for completed rapes and 14.5 percent for attempted rapes (Fisher, Cullen, and Turner 2000). Lisak and Miller (2002) offer a chilling view of the lack of appropriate response to "undetected rapists" on campus, whose actions may be dismissed by campus officials as "misunderstandings." In fact, of the 120 self-admitted rapists they studied, 38.3 percent also admitted to intimate partner physical violence. The recent focus on adolescent relationship abuse (see Chapter 23) should be expanded to emphasize the seriousness of IPSV directed at college students. The new Campus Sexual Violence Elimination Act in the US may prompt more effective responses to sexual violence and offer opportunities for advocates to provide information about best practices in IPSV prevention and response (Clery Center 2012). The Act requires institutions of higher education to more effectively address victims' rights in their response to sexual assault, and mandates specific outreach and prevention activities on campus.

## Offering extended medical advocacy and enhancing trauma-informed medical care

### Connecting intimate partner sexual violence survivors with harm-reduction resources for reproductive health

In Chapter 6, Emma Williamson describes the impact of reproductive coercion on women's lives and the need for a harm-reduction approach by medical practitioners. Advocates can be a crucial link between survivors and sensitive, timely medical intervention to enhance contraceptive options, offer survivors more control over reproductive choices, and prevent or treat sexually transmitted infections. In Washington State, sexual assault and domestic violence advocacy agencies have been involved in a pilot program to create multidisciplinary linkages addressing reproductive coercion (WCSAP 2013). Key interventions include educating advocates about emergency contraception (EC), and training them to offer information about EC and birth control methods that are less likely to be detected by abusive partners to all clients, early in the advocacy relationship. Advocates are also encouraged to offer informed referrals to medical providers who have been trained on these issues. The safety cards developed by Futures Without Violence are an easy-to-use resource for initiating conversations about IPSV and reproductive health with advocacy clients (Chamberlain and Levenson 2012).

### Facilitating ongoing medical care for survivors

Because IPSV is associated with a host of medical issues across the lifespan (Campbell and Soeken 1999; see also Chapter 4), medical advocacy for survivors must go beyond accompaniment to the forensic exam. For example, advocates have the opportunity to connect IPSV survivors with trauma-informed medical and support care during pregnancy, childbirth, and the postpartum period. Cross-training with doulas (who offer support during labor and childbirth), midwives, childbirth educators, and obstetricians can enhance survivors' access to appropriate care during life events that contribute to stress and vulnerability (A Safe Passage 2008).

### Providing strategies for survivors when they are patients

Advocates can normalize survivors' fears of medical procedures and encounters and teach strategies to reduce the trauma triggers in those situations. For example, Pandora's Project (2010) offers downloadable cards that survivors can take to appointments with the doctor or dentist that include statements such as: "I am a survivor of sexual assault. Oftentimes I find my experiences difficult to talk about, and some medical procedures are very triggering. I would be more comfortable with a female in the room."

### Enhancing health care responses to survivors

Advocates can also work with medical professionals to help develop trauma-informed services.

> It is important to note that providing trauma-informed services does not mean service providers must determine exactly what has happened to an individual. Rather, organizations and providers should examine the way in which they conduct business and make modifications based upon an understanding of how a trauma survivor might perceive what is happening. (WCSAP 2012, p.1)

As an example of enhancing trauma-informed services, an advocate could encourage providers of gynecological services to ask their patients about anything that might raise anxiety during a medical exam and then to modify the exam accordingly if possible. Advocates could explain the value of telling patients in advance if the provider is going to touch their body. It is not necessary for the doctor or nurse to ask or to know if the patient is an IPSV survivor, but these simple actions will make survivors more comfortable and may benefit other patients as well.

Facilitating patient access to advocacy services helps both the health care provider and the survivor. For example, an advocate may respond to a call from a nurse to whom a patient has disclosed IPSV by meeting with the woman at the medical clinic rather than expecting her to evade her abuser and find her way to the advocacy office. These types of requests from medical staff are most likely to increase in the US now that "screening and counseling for interpersonal and domestic violence" is required to be covered by health plans approved through the Affordable Care Act (Health Resources and Services Administration 2012).

## Supporting clients through the legal process

While only a very small minority of IPSV survivors ever participate in the prosecution of sexual assault, many more women will be involved in the criminal justice system because of domestic violence charges, or in the civil legal system because of the need for protection orders or custody determinations. For those survivors who do wish to report sexual assault to the police and move forward with prosecution, advocates offer vital support (Lonsway and Archambault 2007). For all the reasons described throughout this book (see especially Chapter 2), IPSV survivors may very likely encounter disbelief, disrespect, and victim-blaming from professionals (see Chapters 16 and 17). For example, the police investigation can be extremely traumatic for survivors, and a firm and fearless advocate can make all the difference, as described by the Women's Justice Center (2010).

## Building awareness

Advocates routinely reach out to law enforcement, prosecutors, mental health professionals, and health care providers by providing and accepting referrals, participating in multidisciplinary teams, and engaging in cross-training. System-based advocates have daily contact with law enforcement and/or prosecution professionals. Thus, advocates are well situated to offer training and resources on the topic of IPSV. A multidisciplinary approach is critical, and rallying other professionals to increase awareness and skills in working with survivors is within the routine scope of services for community-based advocacy agencies. Advocates also see the enhancement of community awareness as a necessary function in preventing domestic and sexual violence and in supporting survivors.

## Specific recommendations for advocates

- Work to increase your own knowledge and that of your colleagues on the topic of IPSV and the needs of survivors.

- Learn as much as you can about the roles of other professionals in dealing with this issue. In other words, read this entire book!

- Participate in or lead multidisciplinary cross-training on IPSV.

- Ensure that the materials and resources your agency presents to survivors and community members include specific information about IPSV.

- Offer culturally sensitive IPSV information, including resources on same-sex IPSV and teen relationship abuse.

- If your background and training is in domestic violence advocacy, seek additional information and training on sexual assault issues and resources.

- Be sure that you are knowledgeable and comfortable in talking about sexual concerns and behaviors with survivors.

- If your background and training is in sexual assault advocacy, partner with domestic violence advocates to ensure that survivors have shelter options and safety planning resources.

- Ask about IPSV (current and past) when conducting intake interviews.

- Be alert to the reproductive health needs of IPSV survivors, such as emergency contraception or birth control that is less likely to be detected by an abusive partner.

- Be aware that medical advocacy for IPSV survivors may include a wider range of issues than simply accompaniment to a forensic exam (e.g., they may need additional support for obstetric appointments during pregnancy).

- Explore the specific legal advocacy needs of IPSV survivors and be prepared to explain both domestic violence and sexual assault statutes.

- Consider offering specialized advocacy services such as an IPSV support group.

# References

A Safe Passage (2008) *Supporting Women Survivors of Abuse Through the Childbearing Year.* London, Ontario: A Safe Passage. Available at www.asafepassage.info/women.shtml, accessed March 4, 2013.

Beyond Diversity Resource Center (2010) *Cultural Competency Technical Assistance Project Year Two Final Report.* Mt. Laurel, NJ: Beyond Diversity Resource Center. Available at www.rightcode.net/development/beyonddiversity/articlefiles/report2.pdf, accessed February 28, 2013.

Black, M.C., Basile, K.C., Breiding, M.J., Smith, S.G. *et al.* (2011) *The National Intimate Partner and Sexual Violence Survey (NISVS): 2010 Summary Report.* Atlanta, GA: National Center for Injury Prevention and Control, Centers for Disease Control and Prevention. Available at www.cdc.gov/violenceprevention/pdf/nisvs_executive_summary-a.pdf, accessed June 2, 2013.

Campbell, J. and Soeken, K. (1999) "Forced sex and intimate partner violence: effects on women's risk and women's health." *Violence Against Women 5,* 9, 1017–1035.

Center for Problem-Oriented Policing (2013) *Guide No. 22: Stalking.* Madison, WI: Center for Problem-Oriented Policing. Available at www.popcenter.org/problems/stalking, accessed March 8, 2013.

Centers for Disease Control and Prevention (2012) *Rape Prevention and Education (RPE) Program.* Washington, DC: Centers for Disease Control and Prevention. Available at www.cdc.gov/violenceprevention/rpe/index.html, accessed March 7, 2013.

Chamberlain, L. and Levenson, R. (2012) *Addressing Intimate Partner Violence, Reproductive and Sexual Coercion: A Guide for Obstetric, Gynecologic and Reproductive Health Care Settings,* Second Edition. Washington, DC: American College of Obstetricians and Gynecologists; San Francisco, CA: Futures Without Violence. Available at www.acog.org/About_ACOG/ACOG_Departments/Health_Care_for_Underserved_Women/~/media/Departments/Violence%20Against%20Women/Reproguidelines.pdf, accessed February 28, 2013.

Clery Center (2012) *The Campus Sexual Violence Elimination (SaVE) Act.* Wayne, PA: Clery Center. Available at http://clerycenter.org/campus-sexual-violence-elimination-save-act, accessed August 18, 2013.

Davies, J. (2008) *When Battered Women Stay…Advocacy Beyond Leaving.* Harrisburg, PA: National Resource Center on Domestic Violence. Available at http://new.vawnet.org/Assoc_Files_VAWnet/BCS20_Staying.pdf, accessed March 8, 2013.

Fisher, B., Cullen, F., and Turner, M. (2000) *The Sexual Victimization of College Women.* Washington, DC: US Department of Justice. Available at www.ncjrs.gov/pdffiles1/nij/182369.pdf, accessed March 2, 2013.

Futures Without Violence (2012) *Safety Cards: Did You Know Your Relationship Affects Your Health?* San Francisco, CA: Futures Without Violence. Available at https://secure3.convio.net/fvpf/site/Ecommerce/1272612598?store_id=1241, accessed March 1, 2013.

Health Resources and Services Administration (2012) *Women's Preventive Services: Required Health Plan Coverage Guidelines.* Washington, DC: US Department of Health and Human Services. Available at www.hrsa.gov/womensguidelines, accessed March 16, 2013.

Lisak, D. and Miller, P. (2002) "Repeat rape and multiple offending among undetected rapists." *Violence and Victims 17*, 1, 73–83.

Lonsway, K. and Archambault, J. (2007) "Advocates and Law Enforcement: Oil and Water?" *SATI e-News, December 7, 2007* Addy, WA: Sexual Assault Training and Investigations. Available at www.mysati.com/enews/enews_html_Dec2007.htm#practices, accessed February 6, 2013.

National Sexual Violence Resource Center (2013) *Internet Safety Online Resource Collection.* Enola, PA: National Sexual Violence Resource Center. Available at www.nsvrc.org/projects/internet-safety-online-resource-collection, accessed on March 4, 2013.

Office for Victims of Crime (2011) *SART Toolkit: Advocates.* Washington, DC: Department of Justice. Available at http://ovc.ncjrs.gov/sartkit/develop/team-advocate-c.html, accessed February 2, 2013.

Pandora's Project (2010) *Quick Info Cards for Rape & Sexual Abuse Survivors.* Minneapolis, MN: Pandora's Project. Available at www.pandys.org/quickinfocards.html, accessed March 2, 2013.

Stop Violence Against Women (2010) *Sexual Assault Advocacy.* Minneapolis, MN: The Advocates for Human Rights. Available at www.stopvaw.org/sexual_assault_advocacy_program, accessed March 9, 2013.

The Advocates for Human Rights (2009) *Sexual Assault Advocacy Programs.* Minneapolis, MN: The Advocates for Human Rights. Available at www.stopvaw.org/sexual_assault_advocacy_program, accessed January 15, 2013.

Washington Coalition of Sexual Assault Programs (2010a) *IPSV Posters, Brochures, Bookmarks.* Olympia, WA: Washington Coalition of Sexual Assault Programs. Available at www.wcsap.org/ipsv-resources-publications, accessed March 12, 2013.

Washington Coalition of Sexual Assault Programs (2010b) *What Advocates Need to Know About Therapy.* Olympia, WA: Washington Coalition of Sexual Assault Programs. Available at www.wcsap.org/sites/www.wcsap.org/files/uploads/documents/WhatAdvocatesNeedtoKnowaboutTherapy2010.pdf, accessed March 8, 2013.

Washington Coalition of Sexual Assault Programs (2012) *Creating Trauma-Informed Services: A Guide for Sexual Assault Programs and Their System Partners.* Olympia, WA: Washington Coalition of Sexual Assault Programs. Available at www.wcsap.org/creating-trauma-informed-services, accessed March 16, 2013.

Washington Coalition of Sexual Assault Programs (2013) *Our Projects: Pregnant and Parenting Women and Teens Project.* Olympia, WA: Washington Coalition of Sexual Assault Programs. Available at www.wcsap.org/our-projects, accessed March 1, 2013.

Wathan, N. and MacMillan, H. (2003) "Interventions for violence against women." *Journal of the American Medical Association 289*, 5, 589–600.

Women's Justice Center (2010) *Advocating for Victims of Sex Crimes During the Police Investigation.* Santa Rosa, CA: Women's Justice Center. Available at www.justicewomen.com/handbook/advocatingsexcrimes.html, accessed March 6, 2013.

CHAPTER 9

# Real not Rare

## CROSS-TRAINING FOR SEXUAL ASSAULT AND DOMESTIC VIOLENCE WORKERS TO UNDERSTAND, RECOGNIZE, AND RESPOND TO INTIMATE PARTNER SEXUAL VIOLENCE

Di Macleod

## Note about language

Statistics and research demonstrate that the majority of intimate partner sexual violence (IPSV) is perpetrated by men against women. Therefore, in this chapter, in order to reflect the reality, the word survivor is gendered female and offender is gendered male.

## What is intimate partner sexual violence?

As previous chapters have explained, IPSV has become an internationally recognized term for sexual violence occurring in a broad range of intimate relationships including married, unmarried, dating, heterosexual, and same-sex relationships (Winters 2008). IPSV is defined as any form of unwanted sexual activity with a current or former intimate partner that is without consent or due to use of force, intimidation, or threat (direct or implied). IPSV may be experienced with or without the presence of physical violence in the relationship.

In order to illustrate some of the behaviors that constitute domestic violence, variations of the *Power and Control Wheel* developed by the Duluth Domestic Abuse Intervention Project are often used. However, the sexual violence component within domestic violence, which may be experienced with or without physical violence, is often described in general terms rather than as specific behaviors. The sexual violence component needs to be "unpacked" enough for women to consider a range of sexually abusive behaviors that might be occurring and actually be able to name these as IPSV. These behaviors can be visually represented in the spokes of a specific IPSV power and control wheel to assist in identification. See Figure 9.1.

*Figure 9.1 IPSV Power and Control Wheel*

# Why has intimate partner sexual violence been invisible?

## *Society's reluctance to acknowledge the issue*

The general community subscribes to the myths of stranger rape and is not comfortable acknowledging that sexual violence could be committed by an intimate partner. Despite the frequency, the majority of women's unwanted sexual experiences are not considered as rape (Easteal and McOrmond-Plummer 2006; Heenan 2004; Winters 2008).

## History of service development

In Australia, the sexual violence and domestic violence systems, policy, and service responses have developed as separate sectors, despite significant overlap in these fields. Services are often funded by different government departments with different measures, outcomes, and frameworks. This separation is largely true in the US as well, although the majority of sexual assault and domestic violence programs are co-located within the same multi-service agency (Patterson 2009). This development has created a silo effect and resulted in a segmentation of experiences along the continuum of violence.

Historically, the focus of refuge and domestic violence services has been to provide crisis support, rather than ongoing counseling, to women living with or escaping from domestic violence. Therefore, if sexual violence is disclosed in these services, women will most likely be referred on to sexual violence services for counseling.

## Duality of the issue

IPSV is not often specifically addressed as a dual issue by both the domestic violence and sexual violence sectors. Easteal and McOrmond-Plummer (2006) assert that IPSV is not either/or but *both* domestic *and* sexual violence. The reality is that IPSV exists in the overlap of the two issues. Unfortunately, to date, this overlap has not resulted in dual service provision; instead, it has often produced a gap where both the domestic violence and sexual violence sectors have believed that the other will address the issue. Instead of dual service provision, there appears to be double the silence and double the denial surrounding IPSV, which renders it invisible and creates additional barriers to help-seeking for survivors.

## Lack of ownership

Numerous researchers have remarked on the lack of ownership in addressing IPSV at both a policy and service delivery level (Bennice *et al.* 2003; Bergen 1996; Mahoney and Williams 1998). Since there has been no consistent leadership shown by either sector, Bergen (Washington Coalition of Sexual Assault Programs 2007) contends that it is necessary for both domestic and sexual violence sectors to take ownership of IPSV and collectively work to address it.

## Failure to identify and name

It has been my experience, having worked in both the domestic and sexual violence sectors, that if a woman seeks support at a sexual violence service, she has already managed to name her experience as "rape" or "sexual assault" or "sexual violence." However, if a woman seeks help from a domestic violence service, she is more likely to focus on the visible and more recognized aspects of the violence committed against her and may not discuss the sexual violence component. This may be because she does not feel safe enough to disclose, has not identified IPSV as such, or is not asked. This is supported by Parkinson (2008), who states that often, even when the physical violence is revealed, the sexual violence is not.

Workers may not be as comfortable exploring whether sexual violence has occurred as they are in exploring the dimensions of physical and psychological violence. This absence from routine work practice can help to maintain IPSV as a non-issue (Macleod 2009).

We can begin to address these gaps at a service delivery level through increasing worker awareness. One way to do this is by providing specialist training to build the knowledge and skill base in the area of IPSV.

# What training is available?

In Australia, nationally recognized, accredited training exists in the area of domestic violence but there is no equivalent in the area of adult sexual violence. Therefore, sexual violence workers have access and opportunity to build knowledge, skills, and competencies in domestic violence, but workers do not have the same opportunities in relation to sexual violence. Unfortunately, there is no nationally recognized, accredited training specific to IPSV for workers from any vocation to undertake as part of their professional development.

Within the US, multidisciplinary training opportunities on the topic of IPSV have recently been developed. The Washington Coalition of Sexual Assault Programs (WCSAP) has created online courses and a "train-the-trainer" guide, and has co-sponsored in-person training opportunities both within the state and at national conferences (WCSAP 2012). The National Judicial Education Program's (NJEP) online course for judges has been embraced by advocates and other professionals as well as judges (see Chapter 17), and the National

Sexual Violence Resource Center (NSVRC) offers an online course on "marital rape" (NSVRC 2010). Because training programs for domestic violence and sexual assault workers vary across the country, consistent inclusion of these relatively new resources in basic advocacy training is not standard.

In relation to the UK there is no specific IPSV training available in England, Ireland or Wales. However, Scotland does have a website featuring national training resources on violence against women. See http://www.womenssupportproject.co.uk/vawtraining/. Although IPSV is not covered separately it is covered within the DV and SV module.

Both "Real not Rare" and the WCSAP courses are able to be adapted for professionals internationally who wish to educate themselves further about understanding and responding to IPSV.

## Why is training important?

Training is important in any profession, and is particularly important in this area of service delivery where worker intervention can have a major impact on the safety, wellbeing, and lives of help-seekers.

### Intimate partner sexual violence is a common issue

IPSV might be rarely discussed but it is not rare (Mahoney and Williams 1998). IPSV is real and has serious impacts for those who experience it.

Research shows that IPSV is more common than most people realize, with one study of community counseling services finding that approximately 15 percent of married or cohabiting women and as many as 60 percent of battered women are raped at least once by their partners (Howard *et al.* 2003). It is also estimated that 10–15 percent of all rapes are committed by partners or ex-partners (Easteal 1994; Finkelhor and Yllo 1985; Russell 1990). In a more recent British Home Office study on violence to women, 45 percent of respondents reported the rape had been committed by present partners, with a further 11 percent committed by ex-partners (Myhill and Allen 2002).

These statistics require further reflection, particularly in relation to the diagram of slightly overlapping circles that is often used to visually represent the intersection of domestic and sexual violence. Based on the research and statistics, the reality of IPSV could be more accurately depicted with a much bigger overlap in the domestic violence area (see Figure 9.2). Since the overlap is substantial, a significant percentage of women seeking help from domestic violence services will be affected. Therefore, workers in the domestic violence sector must acknowledge and be appropriately trained to work within this reality.

*Figure 9.2 The intersection of intimate partner sexual violence*

## To make the invisible visible

Those who experience IPSV often have difficulty identifying their experience as rape or sexual violence. There are many situations where women would not consent to sexual activity if they had a free choice. However, they are unlikely to define and name their experiences as sexual violence. Whilst some survivors may acknowledge that the experience was unwanted, most do not view it as criminal (Heenan 2004). The shame experienced by IPSV survivors may keep them from speaking out, so it is important for workers to recognize the issue and ask sensitively about IPSV (Parkinson 2008).

Sometimes a disclosure will be spontaneous rather than part of a planned process (Lievore 2005). Therefore, it is also important for workers to be competent in appropriate strategies for responding in a variety of situations. The fact remains that women are less likely to disclose unless specifically asked, and workers are unlikely to ask unless they are confident in doing so. Training can provide workers with the skills to ask, listen, and respond to what they hear.

## *There is an identified need*

The need for specific training on IPSV to build on knowledge, skills, and confidence for a range of stakeholders has been identified as essential (Bergen 2006; Duncan and Western 2011; Heenan 2004; Parkinson 2008). Understanding, recognizing, and responding to IPSV need to be integrated into both domestic and sexual violence sectors, and not be viewed as optional "add ons" but as central to the work being undertaken in both sectors on a daily basis.

## *To close the gaps*

As long as gaps exist in training and professional development, there will likely be corresponding gaps in service delivery. Consider this from the survivor perspective. If domestic violence services view IPSV as a rape issue and sexual violence services view it as a domestic violence issue, where does that leave survivors? If the behavior perpetrated against them has no name, then what are they seeking assistance for, and to whom should they turn for support (Macleod 2009)? To ensure that fewer women fall through the gaps, it is critical that both domestic and sexual violence sectors address IPSV in the work they do.

## *To increase knowledge and understanding*

There is insufficient knowledge and understanding of IPSV across the domestic and sexual violence sectors. Bergen (2005) notes that workers often don't know how to ask about, talk about, respond to, and educate others about IPSV. Even where domestic violence and sexual violence agencies are combined or co-located, this does not necessarily mean issues will be integrated and that the issue of IPSV will be recognized and understood. Specialized training can enhance understanding, knowledge, and effective responses.

## *To achieve better outcomes for survivors*

Easteal and McOrmond-Plummer (2006) found that a number of women who sought support felt that their experience was somehow different and did not fit the agenda of either a domestic violence or a sexual violence service. Cross-sector training of workers can have a positive collective impact to ensure that a survivor of IPSV will be met with the safest, most appropriate, and most effective response from the first professional encountered, whether that person is working in a domestic violence or sexual violence agency. It is vital that workers in both these sectors are able to recognize and respond appropriately to IPSV to ensure safer outcomes for survivors.

## To acknowledge repeat victimization and potential lethality

In relation to sexual violence, cohabiting women are more likely to be assaulted by a partner than by strangers or any other known male (Lievore 2002). Survivors who have intimate relationships with offenders are at high risk of repeat victimization (Coumarelos and Allen 1999; Lievore 2002). In Russell's (1990) study, 64 percent of IPSV survivors had been sexually assaulted by their partners multiple times in the course of the relationship.

Furthermore, there is significant research linking IPSV and homicide (Bennice et al. 2003; Bergen 1996; Campbell et al. 2007; Dobash and Dobash 2009). The reality is that women are more likely to be killed by male partners who both physically and sexually assault them than by those who only use physical violence. Therefore, recognizing the seriousness of IPSV as a risk factor for lethality is a critical piece of information for all service providers. This means worker identification and effective responses to IPSV could actually save lives (see Chapter 4 for more about IPSV and fatality).

## Development of intimate partner sexual violence training

In Australia in 2000, key stakeholders in the refuge and domestic violence field were consulted in relation to their training requirements. The same year, I developed an innovative cross-sector training program on understanding and responding to sexual violence within the context of domestic violence. This program was designed to strengthen the foundation of refuge and domestic violence services by building the capacity of their workers to recognize and effectively respond to IPSV in the course of their professional practice.

The original program, informed by ongoing research and practice, has now evolved into a two-day program re-named "Real not Rare—a cross-sectoral training program to recognize and respond to intimate partner sexual violence." The program uses adult learning principles and experiential learning styles employing a range of training methods, including PowerPoint information, case studies, small group exercises, role plays, DVD presentations, and guest presentations.

## Reflecting elements of good practice

The "Real not Rare" program has been listed in the promising practice database on the Australian Centre for the Study of Sexual Assault website and also reflects many of the elements of good practice as defined by the Australian Domestic and Family Violence Clearinghouse (2011). If this program is used as a model elsewhere, it is crucial to include the following best practice elements to encourage high standards in service provision across the sector.

## Principles and definitions

At the commencement of training, a clear definition of IPSV is provided (Winters 2008) and who may be considered an intimate partner is further defined. The cornerstone of the program is the principle that everyone has a right to be safe at home and in the community. Other principles that underpin the program are that:

- societal inequalities contribute to violence against women
- IPSV is unacceptable in any form
- IPSV is a violation of human rights
- IPSV is about gaining and maintaining power and control in an intimate relationship
- many acts of IPSV are criminal
- the offender is responsible for the violence and its consequences
- the survivor is never to blame
- the first priority of any response is the physical and emotional safety of the survivor.

## Recognition of cultural diversity and other diverse needs within the community

Social and cultural diversity are considered to help workers better understand additional barriers and impact faced by some survivors. The program prepares participants to recognize the varying needs of survivors from different cultural backgrounds, in same-sex relationships, of varying physical and intellectual ability, and with generational and age differences.

In order to recognize other complex needs, the intersection between violence against women and other social problems is also explored. Intersecting issues covered include alcohol and other drug abuse, mental health, criminalization, and homelessness.

## Represents innovation or a practice benchmark

When first listed on the Good Practice database, the program was a new initiative and remains an innovative training program.

## Potential for adoption or development

The program demonstrates a capacity for replication (i.e. other services/organizations could adapt/re-model the program for their use in a range of settings).

## A clearly defined conceptual framework

Elements of the conceptual framework include context, incidence, risk, impacts, and responses. The program explores the historical context of violence against women, including domestic violence, sexual violence, and IPSV. The differences and similarities between domestic and sexual violence are compared and contrasted in relation to incidence, risk, strategies, legislation, resources, and funding.

Societal mythology around IPSV—which seeks to blame the victim, excuse the offender, and minimize the seriousness of the crime—is dispelled using current research and available statistics. The varying impacts on diverse survivors are explored, and appropriate, effective strategies for responding are presented.

## Clearly defined aims and objectives, which focus on safety and violence reduction

The aim of this program is to develop effective responses to IPSV; enhancing women's physical and emotional safety is the central focus.

## Informed by consultative processes

The program was developed after consultation; over time, continued program development has been supported by ongoing consultative processes.

## Skilled, supported, and supervised workforce

The National Council to Reduce Violence Against Women and Their Children (2009) reiterates the need to strengthen and skill the workforce to effectively respond to the complex needs of women who are victims of violence. This training program provides an opportunity for knowledge and skills-based education that can positively affect the worker, the organization, and the client group. Participants are encouraged to reflect on their current practice, engage in role-plays, and work through case studies in small groups to build skill and confidence in their ability to respond.

## Monitoring and meaningful evaluation

Although there has been no funding for an external evaluation, participant feedback on process and content, combined with ongoing consultation and monitoring of research and practice, has contributed to program development and continuous improvement.

## Good governance, planning, and policy development

The program acknowledges that good practice is supported by good infrastructure. Participants reflect on what they have learned and work in groups to compile a good practice checklist to take back to their respective organizations for consideration and application.

## *Multi-agency service collaboration and coordinated management*

Past training has provided a platform for shared understanding and a catalyst for further collaboration. This has resulted in creative practices to maximize and share resources, to further training, to creating reciprocal outreach between domestic violence and sexual violence services, and to encouraging joint work on specific IPSV resources. A more formal, coordinated approach has been taken up by some services that have undertaken training, and a Memorandum of Agreement and protocols for referral and case management have subsequently been developed. These strategies can help to narrow the gaps in effectively responding to survivors of IPSV.

## Conclusion

Regardless of which support agency is approached, the first door must be the right door for survivors of violence (National Council to Reduce Violence Against Women and Their Children 2009). By not being trained to understand IPSV, explicitly name the problem, and provide effective responses, domestic violence and sexual violence services are contributing to the invisibility of IPSV, creating barriers, and jeopardizing safety for survivors. Seeking help is difficult, but if the service accessed doesn't see the issue as part of their core business these survivors are likely to fall through the safety nets of the very services that were created to assist them (Macleod 2009).

Cross-sector training is not the solution to addressing IPSV; it is simply a beginning at the grass roots level. Domestic violence services, women's refuges, and sexual violence services have to work hard to end the silo effect of funding and service provision in relation to IPSV. This may be achieved through ongoing development and collaboration to elevate the issue and enhance policy, programs, practice, and integration at all levels within government systems and community agencies. Certainly, acknowledging the issue, and undergoing training to ensure we have the skills to respond within both the domestic and sexual violence sectors, the very place where IPSV overlaps, is an essential starting point.

# References

Australian Domestic and Family Violence Clearinghouse (2011) *Elements of Good Practice.* Sydney: Australian Domestic & Family Violence Clearinghouse. Available at www.adfvc.unsw.edu.au/elementsofgoodpractice.htm, accessed April 4, 2012.

Bennice, J.A., Resick, P.A., Mechanic, M., and Astin, M. (2003) "The relative effects of intimate partner physical and sexual violence on PTSD symptomatology." *Violence and Victims 18*, 1, 87–94.

Bergen, R.K. (1996) *Wife Rape: Understanding the Response of Survivors and Service Providers.* Thousand Oaks, CA: Sage.

Bergen, R.K. (2005) *Still a Long Way to Go: Comparing Services for Marital Rape Survivors from 1994 and 2004.* Unpublished.

Campbell, J., Glass, N., Sharps, P., Laughon, K. *et al.* (2007) "Intimate partner homicide: review and implications of research and policy." *Trauma, Violence and Abuse 8*, 3, 246–269.

Coumarelos, C. and Allen, J. (1999) "Predicting women's responses to violence: the 1996 Women's Safety Survey." Crime and Justice Bulletin, *Contemporary Issues in Crime and Justice 47*, Sydney: NSW Bureau of Crime Statistics and Research.

Dobash, R. and Dobash. R. (2009) "The Murder in Britain Study: broadening the analysis of men who murder an intimate woman partner." *Proceedings of Domestic-Related Homicide: Keynote Papers from the 2008 International Conference on Homicide.* Canberra: Australian Institute of Criminology, pp.9–24. Available at www.aic.gov.au/documents/C/C/3/%7BCC334155-D9E6-4635-84FB-32A81C3A3C69%7Drpp104_001.pdf, accessed March 6, 2012.

Duncan, J. and Western, D. (2011) *Addressing "The Ultimate Insult": Responding to Women Experiencing Intimate Partner Sexual Violence.* Stakeholder Paper 10., Sydney: Australian Domestic & Family Violence Clearinghouse. Available at www.adfvc.unsw.edu.au/documents/Stakeholder_Paper_10.pdf, accessed March 20, 2013.

Easteal, P. (1994) *Voices of the Survivors.* Melbourne: Spinifex Press.

Easteal, P. and McOrmond-Plummer, L. (2006) *Real Rape, Real Pain: Help for Women Sexually Assaulted by Male Partners.* Melbourne: Hybrid.

Finkelhor, D. and Yllo, K. (1985) *License to Rape: Sexual Abuse of Wives.* New York: The Free Press.

Heenan, M. (2004) "Just keeping the peace: a reluctance to respond to male partner sexual violence." *ACSSA Issues 1*, March. Melbourne: Australian Centre for the Study of Sexual Assault.

Howard, A., Riger, S., Campbell, R., and Wasco, S. (2003) "Counseling services for battered women: a comparison of outcomes for physical and sexual assault survivors." *Journal of Interpersonal Violence 18*, 7, 717–734.

Lievore, D. (2002) *Intimate Partner Sexual Assault: The Impact of Competing Demands on Victims' Decisions to Seek Criminal Justice Solutions.* Canberra: Australian Institute of Criminology.

Lievore, D. (2005) *No Longer Silent: A Study of Women's Help-Seeking Decisions and Service Responses to Sexual Assault.* Canberra: Australian Institute of Criminology.

Macleod, D. (2009) "Facing the reality of IPSV." *QCDFVR Reader 8*, 2, 11–14.

Mahoney, P. and Williams, L. (1998) "Sexual Assault in Marriage: Prevalence, Consequences and Treatment for Wife Rape." In J. Jasinski and L. M. Williams (eds.) *Partner Violence: A Comprehensive Review of 20 Years of Research.* Thousand Oaks, CA: Sage.

Myhill, A. and Allen, J. (2002) *Rape and Sexual Assault of Women: Findings from the British Crime Survey.* London: Home Office. Available at www.aphroditewounded. org/Myhill and Allen.pdf, accessed July 4, 2013.

National Council to Reduce Violence Against Women and Their Children (2009) *Time for Action: The National Council's Plan for Australia to Reduce Violence Against Women and Their Children, 2009–2021.* Canberra: Commonwealth of Australia.

National Sexual Violence Resource Center (2010) *Marital Rape* Available at www. nsvrc.org/elearning/7501, accessed January 26, 2013.

Parkinson, D. (2008) *Raped by a Partner: Nowhere to Go; No-One to Tell.* Wangaratta, Victoria: Women's Health Goulburn North East.

Patterson, D. (2009) *The Effectiveness of Sexual Assault Services in Multi-Service Agencies.* VAWnet Applied Research Forum. Available at www.vawnet.org/Assoc_Files_ VAWnet/AR_DualPrograms.pdf, accessed January 27, 2013.

Russell, D. (1990) *Rape in Marriage* (revised edition). Bloomington, IN: Indiana University Press.

Washington Coalition of Sexual Assault Programs (2007) "Interview with Raquel Kennedy Bergen." *Research and Advocacy Digest 9*, 2, 3–6.

Washington Coalition of Sexual Assault Programs (2012) *Intimate Partner Sexual Violence.* Olympia, WA: Washington Coalition of Sexual Assault Programs. Available at www.wcsap.org/intimate-partner-sexual-violence, accessed January 25, 2013.

Winters, M. (2008) "Making the connections: advocating for survivors of intimate partner sexual violence." *Connections 10*, 1, 10–14.

CHAPTER 10

# Forming and Facilitating Support Groups for Survivors of Intimate Partner Sexual Violence

Jennifer Y. Levy-Peck

## Why special intimate partner sexual violence support groups?

Psychoeducational support groups offer a powerful combination of healing factors: knowledge and acceptance. A psychoeducational group, led by a trained facilitator, offers information and a chance to connect with others who share a common problem or issue. Most survivors of intimate partner violence or sexual violence, and particularly intimate partner sexual violence (IPSV) survivors, feel isolated and confused. They need accurate information and a safe environment to explore their experiences and feelings. While individual advocacy and counseling are important services, support groups offer a unique experience of camaraderie and connection.

I remember the first domestic violence support group I facilitated, more than 30 years ago. After several weeks of meeting together, one brave participant stated that she had come close to killing herself in the past because of her despair over the violence in her home. She asked, tentatively, if anyone else had ever felt that way. Slowly, every woman in the group raised her hand. Each had felt like she was "going crazy," and each believed her suicidal feelings were a sign of personal weakness. Learning that deep despair in the aftermath of partner violence was a common experience created a sense of hope and opened a pathway to healing.

Creating a psychoeducational support group specifically for survivors of IPSV, when possible, can fill a major need. IPSV survivors often feel out of place in both domestic violence and sexual assault advocacy programs (see Chapters 3 and 9). Neither seems tailored to the needs of individuals who have been sexually assaulted by an intimate partner. IPSV survivors participating in general sexual assault groups may encounter survivors of other types of rape who cannot understand the nature of the bond between the survivor and the abuser. Those survivors who are still enmeshed in abusive relationships may feel judged by other group members who never had an ongoing relationship with the individuals who assaulted them. IPSV survivors in domestic violence groups may not have the opportunity to deal with the shame, disgust, and betrayal of being sexually assaulted by a partner. Issues such as regaining sexual pleasure or dealing with sexual trauma triggers are not generally part of the curriculum of domestic violence support groups, yet IPSV survivors may crave information about such topics.

> Nowhere was it more apparent that wife rape survivors felt misunderstood than in support groups. Most did not feel comfortable sharing their experiences with battered women in a group setting because they felt "different" than others... They expressed a sense that their problem was somehow different, and more embarrassing than that of the other women in the group, and they did not feel comfortable sharing their experiences of sexual violence. (Bergen 1996, p.91)

As useful as an IPSV-specific support group may be, it might not be practical to start one. In small advocacy agencies or rural areas, for example, there may not be enough resources or a sufficient number of identified IPSV survivors to get a group off the ground. Under those circumstances, it makes sense to incorporate information and activities related to IPSV into general support groups for domestic violence or sexual assault survivors.

> If the self-identified marital-rape victims are not numerous enough to form their own group, they can be integrated into groups of other rape victims or of battered women, with whom they undoubtedly share a great deal. But marital-rape victims have much to say to one another, and the formation of groups will not only help the group members themselves, but also contribute to community consciousness raising about the problem of marital rape within the community. (Finkelhor and Yllo 1985, p.192)

IPSV support groups should be included in a range of services for survivors. In *Marital Rape: A Call to Advocacy*, the Battered Women's Justice Project states, "The ideal program for survivors of marital rape would provide individual counseling as well as a support group specifically for marital rape survivors" (n.d., p.11). Individual advocacy and counseling are needed to help survivors with the array of issues created by sexual violence within a relationship. Support groups will be most useful when participants have additional resources tailored to their unique needs.

## Evaluating the need

Before deciding to start an IPSV support group, advocacy agencies should conduct a formal or informal needs assessment. Asking questions and identifying IPSV as an important issue can help raise awareness of the problem and increase commitment to the idea of offering targeted services. Advocates may ask colleagues in their own organization whether they have any current or past clients who would be good candidates for an IPSV support group. They can then expand this inquiry to other service providers in the community. Offering IPSV training to other professionals creates an ideal opportunity for initiating conversations about the possible need for an IPSV support group. As professionals who work with domestic violence and sexual assault survivors are trained to recognize and respond appropriately to IPSV, they will become more active referral sources for support groups. Similarly, including IPSV information in community prevention and outreach programs may result in self-referrals by survivors.

Once an advocacy agency has educated its own staff and other service providers, as well as the general public, it is time to determine whether there are enough participants to form a dedicated IPSV group. The ideal size for most support groups is five to ten participants (Brown 2010). It may be worth beginning with a smaller group—no fewer than four participants—to establish the support group concept. If the agency is unable to gather a minimum number of appropriate group participants, the best course of action is to focus on broadening the scope of other support groups, as suggested above.

In a larger community, it may be possible to develop more specialized support groups, such as a group for teens, older women, or those victimized by same-sex partners. Culturally specific groups, especially those led by advocates with roots in that community, can be a strong source of support, addressing issues within the culture that may perpetuate isolation and victimization. Specialized support groups may address abuse topics more broadly, but will be enhanced by the inclusion of information about IPSV. For example, Spangler and Brandl (2011) describe the need for support groups for older women survivors of abuse, and identify some of the specific sexual abuse issues these participants may have experienced, such as abuse during caretaking, being forced to watch pornography, or being forced into certain sex acts.

## Marketing your group

Active marketing of the group produces the best recruitment results. Some suggested strategies are the following:

- Create a simple, attractive one-page flyer providing basic group information.
- Print inexpensive business cards with a contact number and a few words describing the group. Hand them out at meetings, give to clients, or set out in public areas.
- Make regular announcements in your staff meetings about the group, and be sure to distribute flyers to your colleagues.
- If you work in a multi-service agency, provide information about the group to each department.
- Ask your colleagues to bring flyers to meetings they attend.
- Call or email your contacts in other agencies.
- Place an announcement in professional newsletters.
- Don't forget to post information on your own agency's website and social media such as Facebook or Twitter.
- Offer information about IPSV and contact information for the group to partners in law enforcement, those who work in the criminal justice system, health care professionals, therapists, college student affairs personnel, disability advocates, child welfare workers, and attorneys.

The advocate's own enthusiasm and excitement about offering an innovative service are excellent marketing tools. The results of the needs assessment process will be useful in making the case for the value of an IPSV group and for obtaining any needed resources for the group.

## Deciding on group structure

Prospective facilitators will want to consider the practical aspects of forming a sustainable group. Support groups for domestic violence and sexual assault survivors often are comprised of 8 to 12 sessions, usually held on a weekly basis. Holding group sessions over a longer time period allows for the presentation of more information and can enhance participants' bonding, but group members may have difficulty committing. Most advocacy agencies have a preferred format for existing support groups, which can be used as a starting point for IPSV groups, with modifications to be made based on feedback from participants and facilitators.

Facilitators working with specific populations will want to customize the group structure. For example, homeless youth are unlikely to make a commitment to attend a 12-session closed support group. *Relationship Traffic*, a curriculum for runaway and homeless young adults, describes how the program structure works:

> In order to meet the needs of runaway and homeless youth, each session was designed to stand-alone and should make sense to a youth that had never attended the group before. In the drop-in centers, membership in the groups has been open and new participants entered freely during the series. (Hollywood Homeless Youth Partnership n.d., p.3)

## Facilitator qualifications

Because this is a psychoeducational support group model, facilitators do not need to be mental health professionals. When a mental health professional does facilitate an IPSV support group, he or she should be mindful of the boundary between psychoeducation and psychotherapy. Support groups are not the place for extensive explorations of individual histories and motives.

Regardless of the facilitator's profession, a thorough knowledge of group dynamics and the topics of IPSV, domestic violence, and sexual assault is a prerequisite for effective facilitation. Those with limited experience may wish to partner with an experienced co-facilitator and seek intensive supervision. A supervisor or colleague can offer consultation and debriefing for a solo facilitator.

Whether or not to have a co-facilitator is a personal preference that may be affected by the availability of an appropriate partner.

There are many benefits to co-facilitation, because support groups offer a complex array of dynamics that can be challenging for a single facilitator (Washington Coalition of Sexual Assault Programs 2006). On the other hand, co-facilitation requires setting aside time before and after each group session for planning and debriefing. Good communication between co-facilitators is essential for an effective group, and poorly handled conflict or misunderstanding between facilitators may be toxic.

## Screening for the group

Prior to beginning the screening process, the facilitator (in consultation with the co-facilitator and a supervisor) should establish the criteria for group admission. Some exclusionary criteria are self-evident: current psychosis or active substance abuse, inability to listen and respond to others with any sense of compassion, or being so easily triggered that the group may cause undue distress. Beyond these basics, facilitators should seek group members who seem to fit well with each other and who are able to make the commitment to regular attendance.

Because it may be difficult to assemble the desired number of survivors to begin a group, facilitators may be tempted to include a person who is not quite ready or does not seem entirely appropriate. This can create problems for that individual and for the group. Facilitators will want to be prepared with other resources (such as individual advocacy or therapy) in order to match survivors with the best possible support for their particular needs.

## Developing the curriculum

Unlike therapy or self-help groups, psychoeducational support groups generally follow an established curriculum. While the facilitator needs to be flexible enough to allow the group members to pursue topics of interest, having a structured agenda ensures that participants are provided with vital information. This is particularly important for survivors of IPSV, because so many of them do not perceive what has happened to them as sexual assault (Easteal and McOrmond-Plummer 2006). Recognition that their partners' sexual tactics were used to control and demean, and that survivors are not responsible for the violence to which they were subjected, is essential to the healing process (Bennice *et al.* 2003). For many group participants, this is a paradigm shift that is reinforced by the knowledge of the facilitator and the experiences of other group members.

While facilitators may wish to begin with a suggested curriculum such as the one developed for the Washington Coalition of Sexual Assault Programs (Levy-Peck 2009), the content of the group should be shaped by the needs of the particular participants, the community from which group members are drawn, and the facilitator's preferences. Some suggested topics include:

- an overview of IPSV, focusing on how common it is and the dynamics of the abuse

- messages from society about sexuality and the role of women, and how these contribute to sexual violence

- information about the effects of IPSV on children, if relevant to the participants

- activities designed to help participants recognize healthy and unhealthy relationships

- accurate information about sexuality, reproductive health, and reproductive coercion

- coping and self-care skills

- information and activities to support a sense of personal effectiveness and optimism

- community resources for meeting a variety of needs, such as housing, legal needs, safety, and health care

- options for activism, to enable group members to connect to the larger movement against the victimization of women and other vulnerable individuals.

For groups that focus on specific populations, the curriculum content should be tailored to the concerns of participants. For example, teens may benefit from some instruction in media literacy, so they can deal with the bombardment of messages about sexuality to which they are subjected. Lesbian, gay, bisexual, transgender, and queer/questioning individuals may wish to discuss stigma and the fear of being "outed," as well as a paucity of role models for healthy relationships.

When developing a curriculum, it is critical to match the topics to the appropriate stage of group development. During the first session, facilitators should encourage the group to establish ground rules, stressing confidentiality and commitment to the group.

Sensitive topics such as sexuality are best addressed after the group has had several sessions to establish a sense of trust and bonding. The last session should provide an opportunity for group members to review the progress they have made and to say goodbye to each other.

The group curriculum should have an overall goal, and each session should be designed to meet a clear objective. As the facilitator customizes the group curriculum for the participants, he or she should ensure that every aspect of the group is faithful to the group goal and to the objective of the particular session.

Group curricula should take into account the needs of adult learners. It is particularly important for adult learners in general, and for survivors in particular, to feel that their experiences and perceptions are valued and respected. Facilitators can convey their respect for participants by soliciting opinions and offering options to the group, and by using group input as the basis for decisions about how to proceed. For example, a choice of activities may be offered, or the facilitator may include a clip from a video that a participant has recommended. A well-designed curriculum includes activities that appeal to all of the various adult learning styles. For example, a single session may include:

- a brief opportunity for solitary reflection and writing in response to a prompt

- a discussion of a topic by pairs of participants, with or without a report back to the larger group

- a group activity that includes getting up out of their seats, such as "The Continuum of Force" (Levy-Peck 2009, p.24)

- a brief lecture, with good audiovisual aids such as video clips or poster boards

- a guided discussion.

Within each session, a predictable structure helps group participants to feel safe. The issues addressed by IPSV groups are difficult and can prompt emotional surges. In *The Courage to Heal*, Bass and Davis describe how setting a fixed time to end a writing session "creates a container that makes it safer" (2008, p.xxx). The routine of each group session creates a similar "container" for emotional safety. One curriculum format (Levy-Peck 2009) suggests starting each session with a round of brief "check-ins" comprised of responses to a prompt, such as "What is one positive thing that happened during the past week?" Each session ends with a "check-out," another round of brief responses to a prompt. It is especially important for demanding topics to be raised early in the session and for the session to end on a positive note, so that participants can more easily make the transition to their everyday lives.

Within the session structure, participants should have time to tell their stories, discuss their concerns, and keep in touch about what is happening in their lives. Facilitators will find it challenging to accomplish all of these tasks while conveying the information that is critical to a successful psychoeducational group. It may be helpful to assign time ranges to each portion of the session agenda and to keep a clock in view throughout. Sharing the agenda for each session with the group will enable participants to keep the pace appropriate to the topics to be covered. Facilitators can also identify the highest-priority topics and activities for the session, with additional material to be added if time allows.

## Group evaluation

Group evaluation is useful in many ways. It provides feedback to enable agencies to improve their support groups over time. The data generated from group evaluation may support agency funding requests and may offer a strong argument to other service providers about the value of referring individuals to support groups. Evaluation does not have to be complex or daunting, but it does need to be integrated into the group plan from the very beginning (Thomas and Pender 2008). A questionnaire tied to group objectives can be administered to participants before and after the group (e.g. during the screening process and at the last group session). In addition, participants should be offered the opportunity to provide feedback about aspects of the group experience, such as the group setting, any barriers to attendance, the usefulness of the topics, and perceptions of facilitators' effectiveness.

## Managing the group

Discussion of sexual assault can be highly triggering for survivors. Facilitators should establish a clear plan for managing distressing thoughts and feelings that are stirred up by group participation.

Each member should have access to an advocate or therapist as well as the number of a crisis line.

Because trust and betrayal are critical issues for IPSV survivors, it is particularly important that facilitators are mindful of maintaining appropriate boundaries. Group sessions should begin and end on time. In the first session, facilitators can address the possibility of the "last-minute bombshell," whereby a participant brings up an emotionally fraught topic such as suicidal feelings during the last few minutes of the session. Facilitators who have difficulty wrapping up topics and maintaining the session structure should seek supervision or consultation to improve their skills.

Some IPSV survivors may still be in a relationship with their abusers, or may re-establish contact during the course of the group. Therefore, it is critical to establish safety rules for the group similar to those for domestic violence support groups. The Stalking Resource Center of the National Center for Victims of Crime (2009) has developed a support group guide that includes an excellent discussion of group safety considerations. Group participants who are in contact with abusers will benefit from individual advocacy to address their personal safety planning issues (Davies 2009). A discussion of survivors' choices regarding contact with their abusive partners offers the opportunity to emphasize a nonjudgmental approach by all participants.

Guidelines for users of the Pandora's Aquarium website have been adapted for IPSV support groups to "help create a safe, supportive atmosphere for all group participants, no matter what their circumstances" (Levy-Peck 2009, p.57).

## Self-care for facilitators

Support groups can be both magical and maddening. There is so much beauty and power in the process of survivors supporting each other and learning about their own strengths. At the same time, participant behavior can be challenging, and the suffering of survivors is always painful for the caring professional. Some groups seem to work marvelously well; other groups, with the same curriculum and facilitators, may feel like a constant uphill climb.

Self-care begins with careful preparation. Facilitators who are not confident in their knowledge of the material to be presented or who are uninformed about group dynamics begin at a disadvantage. A good personal and professional support system is crucial for self-care.

Having a supportive supervisor or colleague to call when the group hits a snag will enable the facilitator to consider additional options and to rebound more quickly from obstacles.

Facilitators need to be careful that their group commitment does not make them feel resentful. A 12-session group may sound great initially, but facilitators may find that it limits their personal and family life for too long. Having some planned breaks, such as holding the last two sessions at two-week intervals, may alleviate some of this pressure.

Facilitators who are also survivors may find the intensity of the group even more triggering than conducting individual advocacy sessions. A frank discussion with a friend, a therapist, or a supervisor who knows the facilitator's background can help with assessing readiness to facilitate an IPSV group.

Peer supervision and periodic meetings of all support group facilitators within an agency or a community can offer excellent support. Co-facilitators need to pay careful attention to their relationship with each other and create regular meeting times. It helps to accept the fact that every facilitator will make mistakes. Facilitators who find that the group takes a great deal of emotional energy may wish to talk to their own partners or family members about giving them some time and space when they come home—or being prepared to sit down and watch a comedy together. Having a self-care plan developed in advance will lessen the possible vicarious trauma from conducting a group.

# References

Bass, E. and Davis, L. (2008) *The Courage to Heal: A Guide for Women Survivors of Child Sexual Abuse*, Fourth Edition. New York: HarperCollins Publishers.

Battered Women's Justice Project (n.d.) *Marital Rape: A Call to Advocacy*. Washington, DC: Center for Survivor Agency and Justice. Available at https://s3.amazonaws.com/s3.documentcloud.org/documents/413656/marital-rape.pdf, accessed March 15, 2013.

Bennice, J.A., Resick, P.A., Mechanic, M., and Astin, M. (2003) "The relative effects of intimate partner physical and sexual violence on post-traumatic stress disorder symptomatology." *Violence and Victims 18*, 87–94.

Bergen, R.K. (1996) *Wife Rape: Understanding the Response of Survivors and Service Providers*. Thousand Oaks, CA: Sage Publications.

Brown, N. (2010) *Psychoeducational Groups: Process and Practice*, Third Edition. New York: Taylor & Francis.

Davies, J. (2009) *Advocacy Beyond Leaving: Helping Battered Women in Contact with Current or Former Partners.* San Francisco, CA: Family Violence Prevention Center (now Futures Without Violence). Available at www.futureswithoutviolence. org/userfiles/file/Children_and_Families/Advocates%20Guide%281%29.pdf, accessed May 2, 2012.

Easteal, P. and McOrmond-Plummer, L. (2006) *Real Rape, Real Pain: Help for Women Sexually Assaulted by Male Partners.* Melbourne: Hybrid Publishers.

Finkelhor, D. and Yllo, K. (1985) *License to Rape: Sexual Abuse of Wives.* New York: The Free Press.

Hollywood Homeless Youth Partnership (n.d.) *Relationship Traffic: An Intimate Partner Abuse Prevention Curriculum for Runaway and Homeless Youth.* Los Angeles, CA: Hollywood Homeless Youth Partnership. Available at www.hhyp.org/ downloads/HHYP_RelationshipTraffic_YoungAdult.pdf, accessed May 12, 2012.

Levy-Peck, J. (2009) *IPSV Support Group Guide: A Guide to Psychoeducational Groups for Intimate Partner Sexual Violence Survivors.* Olympia, WA: Washington Coalition of Sexual Assault Programs. Available at www.wcsap.org/ipsv-support-group-guide-guide-psychoeducational-support-groups-survivors-intimate-partner-sexual, accessed February 10, 2013.

Spangler, D. and Brandl, B. (2011) *Golden Voices: Support Groups for Older Abused Women.* Madison, WI: National Clearinghouse on Abuse in Later Life. Available at www.vaw.umn.edu/documents/goldenvoices/goldenvoices.html, accessed May 8, 2012.

Stalking Resource Center of the National Center for Victims of Crime (2009) *How to Start and Facilitate a Support Group for Victims of Stalking.* Washington, DC: National Center for Victims of Crime. Available at www.victimsofcrime.org/docs/src/ support-group-guide.pdf?sfvrsn=2, accessed March 20, 2013.

Thomas, R.V. and Pender, D.A. (2008) "Association for Specialists in Group Work: Best Practice Guidelines 2007 Revisions." *The Journal for Specialists in Group Work* 33, 2, 111–17.

Washington Coalition of Sexual Assault Programs (2006) *Circle of Hope: A Guide for Conducting Psychoeducational Support Groups.* Olympia, WA: Washington Coalition of Sexual Assault Programs. Available at www.wcsap.org/circle-hope-guide-conducting-effective-psychoeducational-support-groups, accessed March 20, 2013.

CHAPTER 11

# "Invisible" Intimate Partner Sexual Violence

## PREVENTION AND INTERVENTION CHALLENGES

Debra Parkinson and Susie Reid

## Introduction

Although intimate partner sexual violence (IPSV) was legislated into the criminal codes of most of the developed world over recent decades, the concepts of wifely obligation and conjugal rights still dominate. IPSV is judged to be less injurious than stranger rape, with a less culpable perpetrator and a more blameworthy victim (Lievore 2003; Wall 2012). The low rate of reporting and the miniscule number of men serving sentences attests to this (Australian Law Reform Commission 2010; Heenan 2004; Lievore 2003; Mouzos and Makkai 2004). Yet, if we understood the true nature and cost of IPSV, it would sit with stranger rape and child sexual abuse in our perception of its assault on a civilized society (Bourke 2008).

Primary prevention of IPSV rests on a profound shift in our views of gender roles and male/female relationships. Secondary prevention (with those who are at high risk) and intervention (for those who have already been victimized) are hampered by the lack of clarity, understanding, and willingness to act by those who have the power to do so.

## Invisibility of intimate partner sexual violence: our research

In 2007, Women's Health Goulburn North East (with the support of Upper Murray Centre Against Sexual Assault) began qualitative research with 21 women, 23 health professionals, and 30 police officers in Victoria, Australia. Immediately, there were indications of the myths surrounding IPSV. Our colleagues warned us off (what they saw to be) such a nebulous research undertaking, with comments like "Hmm, it's such a gray area" and "It's just compromise, isn't it?" The accounts of the 21 women clearly revealed no such dilemma.

The women described circumstances where they had no option to say no. For some women, rape was part of their daily married life and part of a comprehensively abusive and controlled environment— vicious and impossible to circumvent. One woman had her back broken by her husband as he anally raped her. Another recounted her obstetrician stepping back from the examination table in horror, asking what happened to cause the hundreds of cuts to her vagina. Another wondered if it was really rape when she "chose" the rape over a beating, because it was quieter, and wouldn't wake the children:

> It was either do this or face the consequences. It was do this or have the crap beaten out of you. But I was thinking because I did it, I didn't complain, it was like a choice between two things. (Jacqui)

The women acquiesced to avoid other violence to themselves or others (Duncan and Western 2011). Yet, for other women in our research, the first or only rape was perpetrated by their partner after years of an ostensibly respectful and happy relationship. One highly respected man in the community raped his unconscious wife after she fell and hit her head. Another drugged his wife before assaulting her. Both marriages were decades long and previously unmarred by violence.

There was no suggestion of "compromise" or "gray areas" in the women's accounts of IPSV. These were clearly criminal acts, yet the women did not have the clarity afforded by the law to other victims of crime. DNA evidence is admissible in stranger rape cases, but in date rape and IPSV the value of such evidence is compromised by issues of consent (Braaf 2011; Du Mont and White 2007; Lievore 2005). Further complications are shared children and a shared life. The women in our research felt alone, confused, and ashamed, their confusion orchestrated by the perpetrators' claim to entitlement and society's use of euphemisms (Duncan and Western 2011; Wall 2012; Weiss 2010).

> I'd talk myself out of thinking that I'd been raped... My reaction was this can't be true. You're stupid, change your mind. (Amanda)

The women in our study could not believe the man who was meant to love them was, in fact, raping them (Heenan 2004), and their denial was reinforced by the men's implicit and explicit denial of any wrongdoing and societal apathy (Braaf 2011; Easteal and McOrmond-Plummer 2006). None of the women believed their partners would see their behavior as criminal (James, Seddon, and Brown 2002). He had a marriage certificate, he could do what he wanted with her, she was his. This notion of "male sexual proprietorship" (Braaf 2011, p.4) was upheld by professionals representing fundamental and seminal structures—the Church, the law, and the health system.

> [My church ministers] said to pray about it. It wasn't just the rape...it was a textbook abusive marriage. I said to them, "What if he kills me first?" They said, "At least you'll go to heaven"... I went to the doctor after I had my baby... I had had an emergency cesarean and he couldn't even wait for one week. It hurt so much. I told the doctor it was hurting. He said—and my husband was right there—the doctor said, "Women are built for sex. It shouldn't hurt." (Julia)

> [It's basically] domestics with a bit of sex thrown in... No, men would not call their actions rape, they would classify it as their right. If they had to be 100 percent honest they'd say, "I did take advantage of her but stuff it, she's my wife, it's Saturday night..." (Police officer)

It was not until they were out of these relationships that the women could consciously acknowledge their partner had raped them. A legal interpretation would state that rape was occurring because consent was absent, and yet the women were interpreting their rape as something their partner had a right to—until the benefit of hindsight told them otherwise (Bergen 1995). Sexual violence by a current partner has the lowest rate of reporting of all assaults (Braaf 2011; Heenan 2004; Lievore 2005; Parkinson 2008; Wall 2012). Australian Bureau of Statistics data from 2005 estimate only one in four women perceive these acts to be a crime, yet when the perpetrator was a "previous partner" or "stranger," more women perceived the sexual violence incident to be a crime. How do you prevent IPSV if it is not perceived to be a crime, and rarely treated as one?

## Difficulties with prevention: health professionals' unhelpful responses

Women's help-seeking mostly begins with their doctor (Duncan and Western 2011), as was the case for women in our research. The women were rarely able to voice their distress, instead minimizing their experience of sexual violence and using euphemisms and inferences, dropping hints and hoping that someone would help (Heenan 2004;

Wall 2012). Sexual violence is the last to be disclosed, as shame overwhelms and silences victims (Wall 2012; Weiss 2010).

Reflecting societal attitudes of conjugal rights and women's sacrifice, the doctors who could name IPSV and offer referrals rather than medication and platitudes were few. Women could not raise the issue with their doctor because *he* was male, elderly, conservative, or religious, and because they anticipated his disbelief and discomfort. Often when women tried, they were ignored by doctors who found it easier and safer to ignore the clues. Women who did ask for help often described physicians' responses as minimizing.

> *The doctors were apathetic and patronizing. "You'll be all right, dear. Go back."* (Laura)

Even when there were legal implications, responses were dismissive.

> *My doctor…said, "What caused this?" I remember saying, "I was raped by my husband"…and I wanted it documented in case I then wanted to take this bastard to court. His comment was, "Well, you'll have to be a little less physical next time."* (Fraser)

> *I went [to my GP] after I'd gone to the police… I said I'd been forced to have sex. He said, "Who with?" and I explained [who] it was. He made a note of that and to this day he's never brought it up… They just won't ask a direct question. Absolutely will shy away from it… If it hadn't been my husband, I think I would have got a different response.* (Victoria)

As Braaf (2011) notes, sexual abuse is not easy to discuss, and the sensitivities of workers must be overcome to avoid further risk to women.

> *I don't get people talking about partner rape in the general counseling setting here. But then again I must admit I don't ask. And that's something I did bring up at a staff meeting with the counselor…and they all said that it's something they don't ask clients. They are really uncomfortable with bringing it up.* (Health professional #8)

Weiss (2010) puts this down to the curious taboo on speaking of personal sexuality despite its cultural ubiquity (Wall 2012). This fear is misplaced when helping women experiencing IPSV can be as simple as asking the question and offering referrals. Even a clumsy attempt is better than avoidance.

> *A lot of GPs are so discomforted by it, they just don't ask the appropriate questions. I wish they were skilled up and didn't feel they're going to make it*

*worse. It's already very bad, there's nothing they can say that would make you feel any worse than what you're feeling.* (Louise)

Even specialist domestic violence workers indicated reluctance to speak of IPSV, seeing it as the responsibility of sexual assault workers (Braaf 2011; Duncan and Western 2011). Ironically, disservice to women can equally spring from deep empathy that blocks health professionals' ability to name partner rape. Some counselors spoke of their own discomfort, and curtailing further discussion with women as it brought up vulnerabilities for them as women, particularly if they had experienced a form of sexual assault themselves.

*I work from a feminist point of view, so for me personally, each time I hear it, I feel a sense of being a woman myself—a sense of being disempowered myself.* (Health professional #5)

*I've gone through IPSV as well when I was younger… I start feeling their pain and relive my pain.* (Health professionals focus group C)

## Secondary prevention: effective responses

The reality for workers in the health, community, and legal sectors is that they are time and resource poor, and persuading workers to attend to IPSV will depend on demonstrating that effective response can be quick and simple. Prevention involves educating professionals who may be the first point of contact for women seeking help on the prevalence and nature of IPSV, its damaging effects on women, which include the risk of repeated assaults and of homicide, and its status as a crime (Braaf 2011; Parkinson 2008). Several professionals in our research demonstrated exemplary practice. Even in the context of busy practices—and, for the doctor, ten-minute appointments—they acted on their suspicions. They were direct and open to the challenging conversations that followed their questioning.

Based on this, Women's Health Goulburn North East developed two key resources for professionals and community members: a four-step postcard and a ten-minute educational film, both accessible via the internet.

**THE FOUR STEPS**

Health professionals, religious staff, and community members can constructively respond to a woman they suspect may be suffering IPSV in just four steps:

1. ASK: "Are you safe within your relationship?" (And assure her of confidentiality.)
2. NAME IT: "What you've just described to me is rape and it's a crime."
3. RESPOND: Give contact details of the local Sexual Assault Service, Domestic Violence Service, and Police Sexual Assault and Child Abuse Unit.
4. FOLLOW UP: "Last time, you spoke about your safety. I'd like to know how you are now."

## 1. Ask

Asking this simple question has the potential to free women from ongoing sexual assault from their partner. Wall's (2012) review of the literature corroborates this, directing professionals to overcome embarrassment and speak about sexual violence in plain language, knowing women are unlikely to raise it themselves. She suggests introducing the discussion as part of universal practice to ask these questions, and emphasizing confidentiality. Such a compassionate and respectful invitation may be the first step towards preventing further sexual violence.

In our research, professionals helped women by listening, believing, and understanding the criminality of the abuse. They appreciated the gravity of the situation and did not minimize the assault or excuse the perpetrator. Crucially, they asked the questions and persisted when women alluded to what was happening to them. They questioned injuries they could see, and inquired about state of mind.

> I often find myself [having] to get over that feeling of, "That's too confronting, I shouldn't really ask that"...but if you don't ask you won't know... I have to constantly remind myself... "Is there sexual violence behind what's actually happening to this woman presenting to me?" (Health professional #12)

Those demonstrating good practice were alert to clues, such as when women requested sedatives, or used phrases like "having to do it" or had traces of bruising. They took the opportunity to help women find the truth of their partner's crime.

*They start to allude to it, they'd go, "...and sex," and shake their head. And you think, right. You start to put some frameworks around it for them. "This is what abuse is about."* (Health professionals focus group A)

One worker spoke of the importance of repeating back to women the words they have found shameful and hard to say, "so they don't feel they're the only one sitting in the room saying these things."

## 2. Name intimate partner sexual violence

Repeating the women's words is a recommended way to ease into the discussion (Duncan and Western 2011). Some theorists are hesitant to name rape for women, reminding us of different world views and cultural sensitivities (Weiss 2010). In clashes of cultural understanding, some professionals lose confidence, seeing their own reaction to IPSV or domestic violence as symptomatic of their socialization, while others restate there can be no justification for this abuse of human rights, and see an opportunity for nonjudgmental education about laws (Allimant and Ostapiej-Piatkowski 2011).

> [T]he issue of rape within a marriage is a concept that may not find recognition in minds of many women from CALD [culturally and linguistically diverse] backgrounds. It does not mean, and should never be confused with, an inability to recognise the violence occurring within such contexts. It points, however, to a world-view that does not include options for women... (Allimant and Ostapiej-Piatkowski 2011, p.7)

The women we interviewed immediately understood the assault against them, yet revised it in the light of day and in imagining how their cries for help would be interpreted by family, friends, health professionals, and police. They could not believe it and imagined that those they told would not believe it either. Feelings of "insidious and damaging" shame (Lievore 2003; Wall 2012, p.2; Weiss 2010) kept women quiet, and the refusal to name rape protected the perpetrator and shielded society.

If a woman seeks specialist help and still does not hear the words she needs to hear from professionals, nothing will change for her. When workers use euphemisms, they protect the man and disguise his criminal actions. They deny a woman the opportunity to address rape by her partner. She will go home unclear about her rights and her visceral understanding of what happened. And he will continue with his criminal actions, believing them to be his conjugal right and his privilege. Why should he identify his actions as rape when no one else does?

Naming IPSV can free women from their sense of shame and self-blame. It can be empowering.

*I couldn't call it rape for so long. Even when a psychologist was calling it rape I couldn't. I just kept saying he assaulted me. It was only a couple of weeks ago I could call it rape. A lot of searching and support helped me do that.* (Cheryl)

This practice of conscious attention to IPSV affirms women's intrinsic knowledge that their rights have been violated. Women's responses varied. Some were surprised, never expecting such compassion. Some were fearful, asking that nothing be said or done. Others were relieved.

*She said what he'd done was a crime. You need to hear that again. It sounds so silly. I considered myself to be a reasonably intelligent person but I needed to hear that.* (Victoria)

Disturbingly, some health professionals stated with conviction that it is unhelpful to name IPSV and indeed, may be emotionally and even physically dangerous for the woman. Making "a big noise" about it is to be avoided.

*I know of one [woman]…she was physically abused, her vagina was physically abused and they never reported that. I know she saw other counselors in the hospital but it was never discussed… As a worker, you have to be careful how she names it. Because…if they decide to lay criminal charges, for the physical abuse or rape, and you send her back to where she came from, the perpetrator is still there and there's a bigger payback for her. So in many ways it's better for her if she doesn't declare who did it and that it was rape, and when she goes back there may be a brief lull that he'll leave her alone. If she cries out and makes a big noise about it, there will be a payback.* (Health professionals focus group B)

This implicit suggestion—that women return quietly to continuing rapes to prevent worse violence—is flawed. This position is not defensible in relation to neglected animals, or child abuse, or theft. Why then, with women raped by their partner?

Rape is not prevented when a doctor, a counselor, a priest, or an imam shrugs his or her shoulders and speaks in euphemisms, or when police officers' first reaction is to doubt the motives of the woman, or sympathize but rarely take a case forward, or when judges allow men who plead guilty to walk away with affirmation of their character and community standing. We perpetuate men's entitlement when we refuse to name IPSV.

## 3. Respond and 4. Follow up

The postcards provide contacts for key sexual assault and domestic violence services. Practitioners can also provide details of regional specialist services and help lines. Following up is as simple as saying, "Last time, you spoke about your safety. I'd like to know how you are now."

## Social change

Despite the premise that IPSV may be the most common form of sexual assault (Bergen 1995), each woman in our research thought it was happening to her alone. It was not a publicized social issue like family violence or drug abuse (Parkinson 2008; Wall 2012).

> *Nobody else talks about this in their relationship. It's like I'm the only person that this is happening to. There's not another person saying, "My husband is doing that to me, and he's not allowed to."* (Cheryl)

If it is only happening to her, then she must be to blame. Where had she gone wrong? Was it her inability to satisfy the sexual needs of her partner? Was her body too stretched by childbirth? Was it because she had a disability? Or was she shy? Was she "cheap"? Did she attract men "like this"? What kind of signals was she sending? Was she asking for it? Was she flawed?

This individual focus is mistaken. Bergen (1995) explained that "women have historically lacked a social definition that allowed them to see the abuse as anything more than a personal problem" (p.130). IPSV is, instead, a product of gender inequality in a society which privileges masculinity and justifies male violence (Chung, O'Leary, and Hand 2006; Pease 2008). Vlais (2011) described sexual violence as "an expression of men's unearned gender-based privilege, based on a belief that they are entitled to sexual gratification and are being 'victimised' when women 'withhold' sex from them" (p.3).

Legislative change that criminalized IPSV in states and nations over recent decades was long overdue. And still, public opinion lags—snared in outdated notions of private terrain and male entitlement, and sustained by an apparent absence of legal consequences (Chung *et al.* 2006; Lievore 2003). "Who can and can't be raped" (Weiss 2010, p.287) and what is considered sexual violence are cultural precepts that remain unpersuaded by legislation.

How is social change to be effected? Two key strategies are early education on respectful relationships directed to boys and girls, and ongoing media and internet campaigns to challenge male violence and privilege. Police offered their insight on both strategies:

> *[What's needed is] education for the males—that females are not just a piece of equipment to be used whenever you want it.* (SOCAU officer)

> *I don't think [a media campaign is] going to fix the male that believes that's how he should treat his woman. The male who thinks that she's eating out of his fridge, so she's gotta come across. He can't change the essence of his personality. That's already formed. But what [the campaign] is highlighting to him is that his behavior is unacceptable.* (Uniformed officer)

## Conclusion

Euphemisms hide the criminality of IPSV. Men use them. Women use them. And more disturbingly, health and legal professionals use them. Prevention relies on our willingness to acknowledge and condemn the prevalence of IPSV.

> *To me it's one of the worst crimes. It's swept under the carpet far too much... Women need to be better informed. It needs to be presented to them with a marriage certificate.* (Amanda)

The myths that surround IPSV can be exposed through open and public discussion that is informed by feminist theory and scholarship on men and masculinities (Pease 2008). Its criminality can be upheld by prosecuting and sentencing perpetrators of IPSV. Until then, prevention will be haphazard, dependent on the fortune of individuals in finding brave professionals to help.

## References

Allimant, A. and Ostapiej-Piatkowski, B. (2011) "Supporting women from CALD backgrounds who are victim/survivors of sexual violence: challenges and opportunities for practitioners." *ACSSA Wrap No. 9.* Melbourne: Australian Institute of Family Studies.

Australian Law Reform Commission (2010) *Family Violence—National Legal Response: Final Report 114.* Sydney: Australian Law Reform Commission.

Bergen, R.K. (1995) "Surviving wife rape: How women define and cope with the violence." *Violence Against Women 1*, 2, 117–138.

Bourke, J. (2008) *Rape: A History from 1860 to the Present.* London: Virago.

Braaf, R. (2011) "Preventing domestic violence death—is sexual assault a risk factor?" *Australian Domestic and Family Violence Clearinghouse Research and Practice Brief,* (October 1).

Chung, D., O'Leary, P.J., and Hand, T. (2006) *Sexual Violence Offenders: Prevention and Intervention Approaches.* Melbourne: Australian Institute of Family Studies.

Du Mont, J. and White, D. (2007) *The Uses and Impacts of Medico-Legal Evidence in Sexual Assault Cases: A Global Review.* Geneva, Switzerland: World Health Organization.

Duncan, J. and Western, D. (2011) *Addressing "The Ultimate Insult": Responding to Women Experiencing Intimate Partner Sexual Violence.* Australian Domestic and Family Violence Clearinghouse, Stakeholder Paper 19, 1–16.

Easteal, P. and McOrmond-Plummer, L. (2006) *Real Rape, Real Pain: Help for Women Sexually Assaulted by Male Partners.* Melbourne: Hybrid Publishers.

Heenan, M. (2004) *Just "Keeping the Peace": A Reluctance to Respond to Male Partner Sexual Violence Issues.* Melbourne: Australian Centre for the Study of Sexual Assault.

James, K., Seddon, B., and Brown, J. (2002) *Using It or Losing It: Men's Constructions of Their Violence Towards Female Partners, Research Paper 1.* Sydney: University of New South Wales, Australian Domestic and Family Violence Clearinghouse.

Lievore, D. (2003) *Non-Reporting and Hidden Recording of Sexual Assault: An International Review.* Canberra: Australian Institute of Criminology.

Lievore, D. (2005) *No Longer Silent: A Study of Women's Help-Seeking Decisions and Service Responses to Sexual Assault.* Canberra: Australian Institute of Criminology.

Mouzos, J. and Makkai, T. (2004) *Women's Experiences of Male Violence: Findings from the Australian Component of the International Violence Against Women Survey Research and Public Policy, Series No. 56.* Canberra: Australian Institute of Criminology.

Parkinson, D. (2008) *Raped by a Partner: A Research Report.* Wangaratta, Victoria: Women's Health Goulburn North East.

Pease, B. (2008) *Engaging Men in Men's Violence Prevention: Exploring the Tensions, Dilemmas and Possibilities, Issues Paper 17.* Sydney: Australian Domestic and Family Violence Clearinghouse.

Vlais, R. (2011) "Engaging men on their use of sexual violence as a power and control tactic." *Australian Domestic and Family Violence Newsletter 45,* 3–4.

Wall, L. (2012) *The Many Facets of Shame in Intimate Partner Sexual Violence.* ACSSA Research Summary, January. Melbourne: Australian Centre for the Study of Sexual Assault.

Weiss, K.G. (2010) "Too ashamed to report: deconstructing the shame of sexual victimisation." *Feminist Criminology 5,* 3, 286–310.

# CHAPTER 12

# Medical Indicators and Responses to Intimate Partner Sexual Violence

Charlotte Palmer and Vanita Parekh

## Overview

Intimate partner sexual violence (IPSV) has critical immediate and long-term health consequences for women. Professional and practical responses are possible, if practitioners are caring, nonjudgmental, and attuned to the pattern of physical and mental consequences of partner sexual violence.

We will use the gendered term "woman" or "women" to respect that women numerically dominate as victims of IPSV. The relationships are principally heterosexual; however, in clinical practice we are aware of the less common but equally concerning situations of women and men in same-sex relationships being victims of partner rape (see Chapter 21). It is most exceptional but not unknown for women to be perpetrators, with men as victims.

We emphasize collaborative relationships between providers and women and their communities. But, boundary violation must be meticulously avoided through education, practice guidelines, supervision, institutional complaint mechanisms, and criminal legislation. We will retain the traditional term "patient" to refer to women seeking assistance to emphasize the special relationship of care and responsibility on the part of providers. It is most important that assessment and responses are based on the principle of autonomy, while noting that the professional must not become a passive bystander to individual experiences of terror, for fear of interfering.

## What is sexual violence by an intimate partner?

We would encourage clinicians to view a wide range of behaviors as implicated in IPSV, ranging from physically injurious forced sex to nonconsensual engagement in an intimate partner's sexual fantasies. The three behaviors researchers elicited from women in the World Health Organization (WHO) multi-country study provide a helpful and broad definition; in full they are the following:

- Was physically forced to have sexual intercourse when she did not want to.

- Had sexual intercourse when she did not want to because she was afraid of what her partner might do.

- Was forced to do something sexual that she found degrading or humiliating.

(Garcia-Moreno *et al.* 2006, p.1262)

Forced intercourse may be vaginal, anal, oral, and/or object insertion. A significant number of women are beaten before intercourse or bitten during forced intercourse (Garcia-Linares *et al.* 2005). Intercourse may also occur in front of children, or involve pornography.

## Context

The context of contact of the patient with the health professional is important to consider. It is quite variable, and will be considered briefly according to viewpoint.

### *The patient viewpoint*

The woman who presents to the clinician may have recent experiences of sexual violence by a partner. For clinical and research purposes "recent" is deemed within the last 12 months, and experiences may be multiple and current and hence she is at risk of a future reoccurrence.

In contrast, some women present with a more distant history of IPSV. The past is in the past, but exists in the present in the form of the psychological scars of traumatic memory and possible complex physical consequences.

### *The health system viewpoint*

Women who experience IPSV come into contact with the health system in a variety of ways, from primary to aged care. Of particular importance are obstetric, sexual health, drug and alcohol, and psychological services. Dental care is an area where contact has its specific challenges, as a result of acute dental injury, dental care neglect, and the difficulties encountered with accepting therapeutic instruments in the mouth.

The literature suggests increased utilization of health services by women with experiences of intimate violence (McCauley *et al.* 1995), while health status remains poor, and our experiences indicate a sad neglect of health screening and uptake of preventive health measures.

# Indicators

The clinical literature describes a number of associations (as opposed to proven causation) between experiences of violation and clinical features. There are few longitudinal studies to determine temporal relationships, which would assist in indicating causation. *We argue that, in the majority of cases, physical and psychological features are a consequence of violation.* We discuss these indicators under five points: physical indicators, psychological indicators, perpetrator and partner indicators, health risk behaviors, and disclosure and screening.

## *1. Physical indicators*

There are numerous studies supporting the association of interpersonal violence (in particular intimate partner violence) and physical symptoms (Campbell 2002; Campbell *et al.* 2002; Coker, Smith, Berea *et al.* 2000; Ellsberg *et al.* 2008; McCauley *et al.* 1995; Plichta 2004) and chronic diseases (Breiding, Black, and Ryan 2008). In some studies, an increased number of physical symptoms rather than the specific nature of individual presentations give a clue to intimate partner violence.

Chronic pain syndromes have been increasingly recognized as having causations which are complex, and now regarded as having bio-psychosocial dimensions. Embedded in the complexity are: (a) injury, and peripheral and central neural amplification of pain experiences, involving opioid, noradrenaline, and serotonin neurotransmitters; (b) psychological meaning attribution; and (c) the social dimension of adverse events such as social isolation, poverty, and lack of supportive relationships (van der Kolk *et al.* 2005). When IPSV co-exists or contributes to chronic pain syndromes, the clinical response necessarily requires an in-depth unraveling. Some of the important chronic pain syndromes are musculoskeletal pain, chronic pelvic pain, vulvodynia, interstitial cystitis, and functional gastrointestinal disorders.

149

## Physical injury

The multi-country WHO intimate partner violence study involved 24,097 women who were interviewed in ten countries. Separate questions about physical violence, sexual violence, and emotionally abusive or controlling acts were administered. Of present relevance, this study showed *it was more usual than not for sexual violence to be accompanied by physical violence.* A number of studies have supported the pattern that if there is sexual as well as physical violence, then *the physical violence is more severe.* The WHO study reported a significant need for health care for injuries (ranged from 22% to 80%). This study is supported by other studies (Coker, Smith, Berea *et al.* 2000; Garcia-Linares *et al.* 2005; McCauley *et al.* 1995) noting increased emergency department and primary care attendance in situations of intimate partner violence.

## Homicide

In the most extreme situation, physical injury leads to death. The work of Campbell, Webster, and Glass (2009) has demonstrated that sexual violence is a specific risk factor for homicide (see Chapter 4).

*The important message for clinicians is that they may see women who have survived intimate partner homicide attempts. A precedent experience may have been partner rape. And as a corollary, IPSV is a risk factor for serious injury or even death.*

## Pregnancy outcomes

Pregnancy-associated homicide by intimate partners contributes significantly to maternal mortality from all causes. In addition, intimate partner violence contributes to unwanted pregnancies, induced and spontaneous abortion, fetal loss, preterm delivery, and low birth weight (Alio, Nana, and Salihu 2009; Fanslow *et al.* 2008; Garcia-Moreno *et al.* 2006; Meuleners *et al.* 2011; Plichta 2004; Shah and Shah 2010; Taft and Watson 2007; ). Direct physical injury, inadequate antenatal care, poor diet, stress, smoking, and other substance use contribute to these adverse outcomes. McFarland (2007) reports fewer live births and more elective abortions in women who were raped at the time of conception, in contrast to women who were not raped.

## Gynecological symptoms

Chronic pelvic pain, whether dysmenorrhoea, dyspareunia, or noncyclical pain, has a demonstrable organic basis in many situations, for example when adhesions or endometriosis are present, or less commonly, when there is persistent untreated infection. A significant proportion of women though—one third to one half—with chronic pelvic pain have no organic pathology on colposcopy or laparoscopy. Latthe *et al.* (2006) extensively reviewed studies which looked at predisposing factors for chronic pelvic pain. *Sexual abuse was a significantly more likely experience in all of the above three categories of chronic pelvic pain, compared with women without chronic pelvic pain.*

The pathway by which abuse can cause pelvic pain is not well understood; however, the concept of neuropathy allows for an understanding of visceral and central sensitization and for limbic system influences. By this means, events and psychological processing can alter function and pain perception. Vulvodynia and interstitial cystitis, conditions which may often co-occur, are now receiving attention as chronic pain or neuropathic conditions in which tissue histopathology does not account for the substantial symptom burden (Micheletti, Pelissetto, and Benedetto 2009). Studies of these conditions have not shown a consistent relationship with abuse, but warrant further research.

## Gastrointestinal symptoms

Digestive and abdominal symptoms are experienced in significant excess in women who have experienced partner violence. Again, the relationship between abuse and symptoms is consistent with current understandings of pain-persistence being related to peripheral and central sensitization. There is no psychological mediator in the immediate physical pain experienced in violent anal rape.

## Pain syndromes

Increased incidences of pain of any sort have also been reported (Ellsberg *et al.* 2008; Poleshuck *et al.* 2009) in those who have experienced partner violence. Headaches and back pain, both notable for demonstrating a bio-psychosocial complexity, are particularly documented to be more prevalent in women with violent partners.

## Sexually transmitted infections

A number of studies report that women who have experienced intimate partner violence have higher reports of symptoms and diagnosis of a sexually transmitted infection (Breiding *et al.* 2008; Campbell *et al.* 2002; Coker, Smith, Berea *et al.* 2000; Smith Fawzi *et al.* 2005).When intimate partner sexual abuse is specifically examined, there is more likelihood of a report of multiple sexually transmitted infections than if physical violence alone is present in the relationship (Wingood, DiClemente, and Raj 2000). Gender power imbalance makes protective sexual measures difficult to negotiate.

The situation with HIV/AIDS is particularly concerning, and in the African situation there are reports of higher incidence of HIV diagnosis in those women who report intimate partner violence. Other concerns relate to partner violence after disclosure of positive test results; and that partner violence interferes with HIV testing and the uptake of retrovirals in the prevention of mother-to-child transmission (Kiarie *et al.* 2006).

## 2. Psychological indicators

### Distress

Edwards *et al.* (2009) explored the association of types of IPSV in a large, three-state US community study of health functioning. The presence of sexual violence resulted in a seven-fold increase in serious psychological distress, while the combination of sexual and physical violence resulted in a nine-fold increase in distress (see pp.39–40). Other studies have revealed a similar substantially high burden of psychological disorders in women who have experienced intimate partner violence (Dutton *et al.* 2005; McCauley *et al.* 1995).

Distress in women who have experienced intimate partner violence is such that prevalence of suicidality—as in death from suicide, attempted suicide (Coid *et al.* 2003; McCauley *et al.* 1995; Pico-Alfonso *et al.* 2006), and suicidal thoughts (Ellsberg *et al.* 2008)— is considerably higher than for nonabused women.

### Shame

Shame is an intense primitive and developmentally prelingual emotion. Because of the latter, it often has few words, but it is characterized by particular observable manifestations, such as averted gaze, blush, or shudder. To engender shame may be the specific intent of an IPSV perpetrator. Shame leads to self-loathing and isolation, and this may inhibit disclosure of IPSV (Wall 2012). Shame remains a powerful indicator of traumatic psychological distress, and should prompt the clinician to make further inquiry.

## Specific diagnoses

(A) POSTTRAUMATIC STRESS DISORDER

In Golding's (1999) meta-analysis of 11 studies of women subjected to intimate partner violence, 63.8 percent met the criteria for posttraumatic stress disorder (PTSD), a rate 3.7 times that of the nonabused population. Other studies support the increased rate of PTSD. According to new criteria for Posttraumatic Stress Disorder published in 2013, there are four clusters of clinical symptoms in PTSD:

1. intrusion symptoms—such as flashbacks, nightmares, and intrusive memories

2. avoidance—such as deliberately avoiding people or places that remind the person of the traumatic experience, or avoiding thinking about what happened

3. negative alterations in cognitions and mood—such as persistent negative beliefs and expectations, or persistent distorted blame of oneself

4. alterations in arousal and reactivity—such as insomnia, irritable or aggressive behavior, or being easily startled.

(American Psychiatric Association 2013)

Unlike a diagnosis of anxiety or depression, a significant traumatic event is required for the diagnosis of PTSD. The pattern of symptoms may not be seen as PTSD, if the clinician is not aware of the events of trauma. A simple screening tool asked in reference to the past month is as follows:

1. Have [you] had nightmares about it or thought about it when you did not want to?

2. [Have you] tried hard not to think about it or gone out of your way to avoid situations that remind you of it?

3. Were [you] constantly on guard, watchful, or easily startled?

4. [Have you] felt numb or detached from others, activities, or your surroundings?

(Prins *et al.* 2003, p.10)

Studies have indicated that if women are subjected to sexual violence, as well as physical and psychological intimate partner violence, the prevalence and severity of PTSD is greater (Bennice *et al.* 2003; Dutton *et al.* 2005; Golding 1999).

(b) Anxiety disorders

In the clinical setting, a woman who has experienced partner violence may present with the symptom cluster of generalized anxiety disorder, panic attacks, or a specific phobia. Coid and colleagues (2003) demonstrated a 3.31 increase in likelihood of anxiety if domestic violence is also present.

(c) Depression

Some authors particularly emphasize depression as the most important association with intimate partner violence. Hegarty *et al.* (2004) found a cohort of depressed women to be 5.8 times more likely to have experienced intimate partner violence than those who were not depressed. A Valencian study indicated that depression severity was significantly higher in those who also suffered sexual violence (Pico-Alfonso *et al.* 2006).

A strong association (comorbidity) of partner violence with anxiety, depression, PTSD, suicide attempts, illicit drug use, and alcohol misuse has been demonstrated. It may be a matter of nosological semantics that one woman's distress is referred to as depression and another's as PTSD. Identification of the specific form of distress does, however, have some relevance to therapeutic modalities. We would concur with Golding (1999), who argues that a diagnosis of PTSD incorporates and validates the traumatic event(s).

## 3. Perpetrator and partner indicators

The research of Coker, Smith, McKeown *et al.* (2000) suggests that perpetrator characteristics are very significant predictors of intimate partner violence, including IPSV. Partner risk factors appear to be stronger if there is sexual as well as physical violence. The characteristics may include:

- problem alcohol use
- problem drug use
- unemployment status
- low educational levels
- nonviolent criminal activity; this has associations with intimate partner violence (Piquero *et al.* 2006), but it is not known if this association exists with IPSV
- remaining within their current relationship (Wooldredge and Thistlethwaite 2006); however, separation may increase the risk of assault for some women (Dugan, Nagin, and Rosenfeld 2003; see also Chapter 5)
- an association between child victimization by violence and subsequent perpetration (Holmes and Sammel 2005); however, causation is very difficult to prove and the association may not hold true for IPSV.

It is not uncommon for medical practitioners, especially family physicians, to be involved in the medical care of both victim and perpetrator. This may provide many boundary and ethical issues for the doctor. Advice should be sought with regard to appropriate care for both patients; ideally, they should be managed by separate clinicians.

## 4. Health risk behaviors

A number of high-risk health behaviors have associations with the experience of intimate partner violence. The behaviors include:

- excessive alcohol use, including binge drinking
- drug use, including smoking
- a decreased level of protective behaviors such as medical checkups, having vaccinations, and healthy eating.

These health behaviors and decreased levels of protective behaviors appear to manifest as actual risk of poor health outcomes such as stroke, disability, joint disease, and heart disease (Breiding *et al.* 2008; Vos *et al.* 2006). The estimated costs of this to a community are significant (Heenan *et al.* 2004).

## 5. Disclosure and screening

There are low rates of spontaneous disclosure of intimate partner violence. Most probably there are also low rates of spontaneous disclosure of IPSV (Watts and Zimmerman 2002). In order to facilitate disclosure, screening for IPSV should be a standard practice in high-risk settings such as:

- reproductive health settings for contraception, pregnancy, antenatal, and termination consultations (Johnson *et al.* 2003)
- sexual health consultations
- psychiatry and psychological medicine consultations
- drug and alcohol consultations (Brackley, Williams, and Wei 2010), including those involving partners with a substance abuse history
- medical care for patients who disclose a past history of abuse or those who disclose intimate partner violence.

Clinicians must be prepared to offer an appropriate response to identification of partner sexual violence. Screening questions based upon the WHO definition of IPSV should be considered. Clinicians may prefer to introduce the topic; for instance:

*Has your partner ever pressured or forced you to have sex when you didn't want to? Has this ever happened with a partner in the past?*

This question is an open question and may lead to a conversation about intimate partner violence and IPSV.

Screening of potential perpetrators (i.e. asking about their infliction of violence) may also be considered in high-risk settings. Brackley *et al.* (2010) provided evidence from drug and alcohol consultations. An example is given on page 584:

*In my practice, I find some patients with similar situations to yours will on occasion yell, threaten, or hit their partners or other family members. Has this happened to you?*

Anticipation of a positive response to this question requires much thought and pre-planning, including appropriate referral networks.

# Medical responses

There is a paucity of published literature on the medical responses to disclosure of sexual violence in intimate relationships, and much of what follows is based on the authors' experiences and the more extensive literature on intimate partner violence.

## *Principles of engagement*

Medical responses need to vary according to the context of clinician and patient, as discussed above. Shame, fear, and experiences of pain need *acknowledgment and validation*. The clinician needs to *hear* that sexual violation has occurred, but there is a fine balance between intense recounting and unhelpful reliving. Descriptions of the past need to be recognized as not occurring at the moment of the patient's narration. The practitioner can initiate collaborative problem-solving in the present.

- There are a number of mandated reporting requirements. It is wise to inform the patient of mandatory provisions for reporting with regard to the safety of any persons involved and most especially children. This should occur before hearing significant content, as this respects patient autonomy and protects the clinician from what can be perceived as entrapment.

- Be nonjudgmental at all stages.

- Recognize the potential chronicity of the situation while respecting the pace of change.

- Acknowledge complexity.

- Address medical, social, and psychological needs.

- Put the patient-identified needs first.

- Follow up and review. For the sake of both patient and practitioner, it is always appropriate to offer early review, with the notion of untangling issues into manageable problem-solving projects.

## *Referral pathways*

Be prepared with knowledge of referral pathways. Compiling a compendium of local services and making time to meet the providers in these services forearms the practitioner. These services need to include advocacy (domestic violence and sexual assault), emergency housing, financial, disability, interpreter, pediatric, mental health, addiction, sexual health, forensic, and legal services. Such a compendium would seem to apply to a first world metropolis and not to a rural area in a developing country, but it is important to seek whatever resources exist. With the world becoming more electronically connected, online access to expertise is a possibility.

## Safety and well-being of all

The paramount clinical response for a clinician who has been alerted to an incident of any interpersonal violence is to determine whether violence is current, ongoing, or likely to be repeated. It should be recognized that:

- Many women who survive are not cognizant of their risk.
- Women may be immobilized by the violence; this "freeze response" can prevent women from making the necessary changes in their lives.
- Women at the point of leaving are especially vulnerable to serious injury and homicide.
- Couple counseling in a violent relationship is inappropriate and unsafe.

Clinicians need to assist women in obtaining security from a perpetrator through honing insight and practical referrals to obtain housing, financial, and legal services.

Safety from self-harm through suicide, self-injury, self-neglect, illicit drug use, or the misuse of alcohol needs to be addressed; the distress should be validated, but not the response.

The well-being and safety of a woman's children are critical, and may test the clinician's abilities to maintain a relationship with an abused woman while complying with the local jurisdiction's requirements to report that children are at risk.

## Medico-legal issues

Thankfully now, sexual violence between partners (rape in marriage) is illegal in many jurisdictions. Women need to be informed of the local law, and provided with practical directions as to how to obtain legal redress. It is of note that a legal requirement to report *any family violence* exists in some jurisdictions. In any setting, but especially when there are acute injuries, careful recording of history and physical findings is professionally essential for potential forensic purposes. Advice or referral for forensic sample collection may be indicated.

## *Attention to specific health needs*

Sensitivity to context and care of all the specific health sequelae can have life-changing consequences for abused women. It has been noted that symptoms improve when the silence is broken and a woman has been able to talk with a health professional about the abuse. Physical symptoms, whether functional or organic, require careful assessment and management. *But importantly, abuse does not preclude organic pathology.*

The specific priorities that a woman places on her needs require respect, although the physician needs to retain control over the prescribing of medication upon which dependence is possible. In this regard, we are especially cautious about prescribing benzodiazepines in the setting of trauma, as long-term adverse outcomes outweigh the immediate relief from intrusive memories.

# Education and training

We acknowledge that some practitioners may feel overwhelmed with a sense of enormity, complexity, and perhaps inadequacy when faced with a woman disclosing IPSV. Medical practitioners especially are steeped in a training weighted toward the biomedical sciences, leaving them less comfortable with social dimensions, *but they have much to offer.* They are the experts when it comes to such things as physical symptom analysis. A trial intervention in 2011 (Feder *et al.* 2011) gives some qualified cause to celebrate. In a controlled trial of general practices in the UK, four hours of training of practitioners, with quarterly follow-up clinical meetings, led to three times more women being identified as victims of partner violence and 21 times more referrals to advocacy services. This is essentially a trial of primary care case-finding and referral.

*We conclude that health care workers are in an ideal situation to assist women who are made aware of partner sexual violence, either through screening or asking about sexual violence in the presence of indicators.*

# References

Alio, A.P., Nana, P.N., and Salihu, H.M. (2009) "Spousal violence and potentially preventable single and recurrent spontaneous fetal loss in an African setting: cross-sectional study." *The Lancet 373*, 9660, 318–324.

American Psychiatric Association (2013) *Diagnostic and Statistical Manual of Mental Disorders*, 5th edition. Washington, DC: Author.

Bennice, J.A., Resick, P.A., Mechanic, M., and Astin, M. (2003) "The relative effects of intimate partner physical and sexual violence on post-traumatic stress disorder symptomatology." *Violence and Victims 18*, 1, 87–94.

Brackley, M.H., Williams, G.B., and Wei, C.C. (2010) "Substance abuse interface with intimate partner violence: what treatment programs need to know." *Nursing Clinics of North America 45*, 4, 581–589.

Breiding, M.J., Black, M.C., and Ryan, G.W. (2008) "Chronic disease and health risk behaviors associated with intimate partner violence—18 U.S. states/territories, 2005." *Annals of Epidemiology 18*, 538–544.

Campbell, J.C. (2002) "Health consequences of intimate partner violence." *The Lancet 359*, 1331–1336.

Campbell, J.C., Jones, A.S., Dienemann, J., Kub, J. *et al.* (2002) "Intimate partner violence and physical health consequences." *Archives of Internal Medicine 162*, 10, 1157–1163.

Campbell, J.C., Webster, D.W., and Glass, N. (2009) "The Danger Assessment: validation of a lethality risk assessment instrument for intimate partner femicide." *Journal of Interpersonal Violence 24*, 653–674.

Coid, J., Petruckevitch, A., Chung, W.S., Richardson, J. *et al.* (2003) "Abusive experiences and psychiatric morbidity in women primary care attenders." *British Journal of Psychiatry 183*, 332–339.

Coker, A.L., Smith, P.H., Bethea, L., King, M.R. *et al.* (2000) "Physical health consequences of physical and psychological intimate partner violence." *Archives of Family Medicine 9*, 451–457.

Coker, A.L., Smith, P.H., McKeown, R.E., and King, M.J. (2000) "Frequency and correlates of intimate partner violence by type: physical, sexual, and psychological battering." *American Journal of Public Health 90*, 4, 553–559.

Dugan, L., Nagin, D., and Rosenfeld, R. (2003) "Exposure reduction or retaliation? The effects of domestic violence resources on intimate partner homicide." *Law and Society Review 37*, 169–198.

Dutton, M.A., Kaltman, S., Goodman, L.A., Weinfurt, K. *et al.* (2005) "Patterns of intimate partner violence: correlates and outcomes." *Violence and Victims 20*, 5, 483–497.

Edwards, V.J., Black, M.C., Dhingra, S., McKnight-Eily, L. *et al.* (2009) "Physical and sexual intimate partner violence and reported serious psychological distress in the 2007 BRFSS." *International Journal of Public Health 54*, 37–42.

Ellsberg, M., Jansen, H.A., Heise, L., Watts, C.H. *et al.* (2008) "Intimate partner violence in the WHO multi-country study on women's health and domestic violence: an observational study." *The Lancet 371*, 9619, 1165–1172.

Fanslow, J., Silva, M., Whitehead, A., and Robinson, E. (2008) "Pregnancy outcomes and intimate partner violence in New Zealand." *Australian and New Zealand Journal of Obstetrics and Gynaecology 48*, 4, 391–397.

Feder, G., Davies, R.A., Baird, K., Dunne, D. *et al.* (2011) "Identification and Referral to Improve Safety (IRIS) of women experiencing domestic violence with a primary care training and support programme: a cluster randomised controlled trial." *The Lancet 378*, 9805, 1788–1795.

Garcia-Linares, M.I., Pico-Alfonso, M.A., Sanchez-Lorente, S., Savall-Rodriguez, F. *et al.* (2005) "Assessing physical, sexual, and psychological violence perpetrated by intimate male partners toward women: a Spanish cross-sectional study." *Violence and Victims 20*, 1, 99–123.

Garcia-Moreno, C., Jansen, H.A., Ellsberg, M., Heise, L. *et al.* (2006) "Prevalence of intimate partner violence: findings from the WHO multi-country study on women's health and domestic violence." *The Lancet 368*, 1260–1269.

Golding, J.M. (1999) "Intimate partner violence as a risk factor for mental disorders: a meta-analysis." *Journal of Family Violence 14*, 2, 99–132.

Heenan, M., Astbury, J., Vos, T., Magnus, A. *et al.* (2004) "The health costs of violence, measuring the burden of disease caused by intimate partner violence. A summary of findings." *VicHealth 2004* (reprint 2010).

Hegarty, K., Gunn, J., Chondros, P., and Small, R. (2004) "Association between depression and abuse by partners of women attending general practice: descriptive, cross sectional survey." *British Medical Journal 328*, 7440, 621–624.

Holmes, W.C. and Sammel, M.D. (2005) "Brief communication: physical abuse of boys and possible associations with poor adult outcomes." *Annals of Internal Medicine 143*, 8, 581–586.

Johnson, J.K., Haider, F., Ellis, K., Hay, D.M. *et al.* (2003) "The prevalence of domestic violence in pregnant women." *BJOG: An International Journal of Obstetrics & Gynaecology 110*, 3, 272–275.

Kiarie, J.N., Farquhar, C., Richardson, B.A., Kabura, M.N. *et al.* (2006) "Domestic violence and prevention of mother-to-child transmission of HIV-1." *AIDS 20*, 13, 1736–1739.

Latthe, P., Mignini, L., Gray, R., Hills, R. *et al.* (2006) "Factors predisposing women to chronic pelvic pain: systematic review." *British Medical Journal 332*, 749–755.

McCauley, J., Kern, D.E., Kolodner, K., Dill, L. *et al.* (1995) "The 'battering syndrome': prevalence and clinical characteristics of domestic violence in primary care internal medicine practices." *Annals of Internal Medicine 123*, 10, 737–746.

McFarland, J. (2007) "Pregnancy following partner rape: what we know and what we need to know." *Trauma, Violence, & Abuse 8*, 2, 127–134.

Meuleners, L.B., Lee, A.H., Janssen, P.A., and Fraser, M.L. (2011) "Maternal and foetal outcomes among pregnant women hospitalized due to interpersonal violence: a population based study in Western Australia, 2002–2008." *BMC Pregnancy and Childbirth 11*, 70. doi:10.1186/1471-2393-11-70

Micheletti, L., Pelissetto, S., and Benedetto, C. (2009) "Is vulvodynia a somatoform disorder?" *Expert Review of Obstetrics and Gynecology 4*, 2, 119–123.

Pico-Alfonso, M.A., Garcia-Linares, M.I., Celda-Navarro, N., Blasco-Ros, C. et al. (2006) "The impact of physical, psychological, and sexual intimate male partner violence on women's mental health: depressive symptoms, posttraumatic stress disorder, state anxiety, and suicide." Journal of Women's Health 15, 5, 599–611.

Piquero, A.R., Brame, R., Fagan, J., and Moffitt, T.E. (2006) "Assessing the offending activity of criminal domestic violence suspects: offense specialization, escalation, and de-escalation evidence from the Spouse Assault Replication Program." Public Health Reports 121, 4, 409–418.

Plichta, J.B. (2004) "Intimate partner violence and physical health consequences: policy and practice implications." Journal of Interpersonal Violence 19, 11, 1296–1323.

Prins, A., Ouimette, P., Kimerling, R., Cameron, R.P. et al. (2003) "The primary care PTSD screen (PC-PTSD): development and operating characteristics." Primary Care Psychiatry 9, 9–14.

Poleshuck, E.L., Bair, M.J., Kroenke, K., Watts, A. et al. (2009) "Pain and depression in gynecology patients." Psychosomatics 50, 3, 270–276.

Shah, P.S. and Shah, J. (2010) "Maternal exposure to domestic violence and pregnancy and birth outcomes: a systematic review and meta-analyses." Journal of Women's Health 19, 11, 2017–2031. doi:10.1089/jwh.2010.2051

Smith Fawzi, M.C., Lambert, W., Singler, J.M., Tanagho, Y. et al. (2005) "Factors associated with forced sex among women accessing health services in rural Haiti: implications for the prevention of HIV infection and other sexually transmitted diseases." Social Science and Medicine 60, 4, 679–689.

Taft, A.J. and Watson, L.F. (2007) "Termination of pregnancy: associations with partner violence and other factors in a cohort of young Australian women." Australian and New Zealand Journal of Public Health 31, 2, 135–142.

van der Kolk, B.A., Roth, S., Pelcovitz, D., Sunday, S. et al. (2005) "Disorders of extreme stress: the empirical foundation of a complex adaptation to trauma. Journal of Traumatic Stress 18, 5, 389–399.

Vos, T., Astbury, J., Piers, L.S., Magnus, A. et al. (2006) "Measuring the impact of intimate partner violence on the health of women in Victoria, Australia." Bulletin of the World Health Organization 84, 739–744.

Wall, L. (2012) The Many Facets of Shame in Intimate Partner Sexual Violence (Research Summary). Melbourne: Australian Institute of Family Studies, Australian Centre for the Study of Sexual Assault. Available at http://www.aifs.gov.au/acssa/pubs/researchsummary/ressum1/, accessed March 15, 2012.

Watts, C. and Zimmerman, C. (2002) "Violence against women: global scope and magnitude." The Lancet 359, 9313, 1232–1237.

Wingood, G.M., DiClemente, R.J., and Raj, A. (2000) "Adverse consequences of intimate partner abuse among women in non-urban domestic violence shelters." American Journal of Preventive Medicine 19, 4, 270–275.

Wooldredge, J. and Thistlethwaite, A. (2006) "Changing marital status and desistance from intimate assault." Public Health Reports 121, 4, 428–434.

CHAPTER 13

# Counseling Specific to the Survivor of Intimate Partner Sexual Violence

Elizabeth Layton

## Understanding intimate partner sexual violence in counseling

If you are a counselor, you may come into contact with a client who has experienced, or is experiencing, intimate partner sexual violence (IPSV). Because of the relationship between rapist and victim, it is common for many people, including counselors, to discount IPSV and its effects, even though the effects can be longer-lasting than for other types of rape and sexual assault (Bergen 1996; Finkelhor and Yllo 1985). Throughout this chapter, I hope to shed light on some of the difficulties such a survivor may face and how to help her through disclosure. In order to exemplify the main issues, I have used a fictitious client, who for convenience will be known as Mary. However, everything Mary presents is grounded in real-life counseling situations I have experienced over the years in working with survivors of IPSV. The examples I use are by no means exhaustive and I would urge any counselor to undertake further research to deepen knowledge, understanding, and empathy towards a client experiencing IPSV.

Another important point to consider (if you are a not a counselor working for a victim advocacy agency) is your role in referring an IPSV survivor client to advocacy services for legal, medical, and safety issues. This necessary step may be crucial in ensuring the client's continued well-being and safety. Please see Chapter 8 in this book for clarification of the role of an advocate.

# Is it my fault?

*When I explained to my doctor about what was happening to me he said I should go back to my husband and try to sort out our differences. Sexual problems are not uncommon in a relationship, and the fact that I was suffering with depression may be a factor in my sexual dysfunction. I remember feeling shocked and unable to reply. But then I began to think, perhaps it is me; maybe I'm just being a prude or something by not enjoying what he did to me, you know, frigid. I walked away wondering, is it my fault?*

Allaying any fears this survivor may have of receiving similar treatment and avoiding more traumatization is crucial in laying the groundwork for a successful outcome. It is vitally important for such a client to feel she is believed. Counselors must avoid minimizing clients' feelings, as this may wound them further. Conveying openness, reassurance, trust, and empathy, and ensuring a nonjudgmental, nonthreatening atmosphere, helps to get the counseling relationship off to a good start. This will ensure that your client feels safe, and will enable her to talk about the experiences she has endured.

*My last counselor cried when I told her what happened to me; I felt bad for upsetting her and a bit confused. I felt embarrassed and I didn't know what to do.*

The above is an example of what a counselor should not do. The counselor's inability to deal with this client's grief compounded the client's sense of shame and helplessness. While all survivor stories are distressing, some of what you hear may be particularly harrowing, even to an experienced counselor. It is vital that you are prepared and able to help support a survivor who has disclosed IPSV to you. Self-care and supervision are also important for your own well-being as well as the client's.

# Understanding and challenging stereotypes

As other chapters in this book will show, IPSV can happen in any type of relationship—heterosexual or lesbian, gay, bisexual, or transgender (LGBT). Victims may be any age from teenagers to elders, and from any class, culture, or background (Winters 2008; see also Chapter 19). Different age groups need consideration and have specific issues relevant to their group (see Chapter 23). For example, a young teenager may only recognize IPSV as "bad sex." She may suffer from self-esteem issues and believe that her boyfriend may leave her if she doesn't give in to his demands. Increasingly, young teens are *enduring* their first experiences of sex and sexual exploration, rather than it being a natural and enjoyable occasion, and sadly many young teenagers are reporting that their first experience of intercourse and sexual intimacy was forced (Ryan, Manlove, and Franzetta 2003).

Although IPSV is more likely to be associated with domestic violence (Russell 1990), one challenge is to understand that rape and sexual assault can happen in relationships where no other violence or abuse has occurred previously (Easteal and McOrmond-Plummer 2006). Another point to understand is that rape isn't always physically violent; it can occur through coercion and other forms of intimidation (Finkelhor and Yllo 1985). Furthermore, because of the dynamics of this type of relationship, the client may have experienced consensual sex as well as rape and sexual assault; this is even more confusing for the client and may make her doubt herself even further. Because of this, your client may still have feelings for her abuser (Easteal and McOrmond-Plummer 2006).

IPSV may involve forms of sexual humiliation that the abuser knows disturb his partner, such as getting her to dress a certain way, sadomasochistic sex including verbal abuse, taking sexually graphic photographs, or orchestrating other men and women to have sex with her. A key point is that this betrayal of trust by someone who is supposed to love and cherish her is particularly hurtful and confusing for a survivor. There may be added complications or anxieties about health risks and sexually transmitted disease (Finkelhor and Yllo 1985).

The survivor of IPSV is also in the unfortunate position of seeing her rapist day after day. If the couple have children together and are separated, in most cases the survivor is still subject to having contact with her rapist. This may have a tremendous ongoing emotional and psychological impact (Easteal and McOrmond-Plummer 2006). Explaining how cultural and social norms encourage negative stereotyping and victim-blaming may help a survivor to understand what has happened to her and lessen her induced feelings of shame and guilt.

# Establishing the counseling relationship

Whenever your client discloses this trauma—whether in the very first session or when it emerges in later sessions—one of the most beneficial things you can do as her counselor is to say these three important words: *I believe you.*

This is important because it validates your client's feelings, all those thoughts that have been circulating in her mind, and the hurt she has locked away because she thought she was wrong to feel this way. Your accepting, empathic, and nonjudgmental attitude is key to building that all-important rapport. Your client will need to feel emotionally and physically safe with you, before you can begin exploring this issue deeper with her. She may say she feels embarrassed, confused, or not sure whether it was really rape at all. The next crucial idea you can convey to her is: *It's O.K. to feel hurt/angry/sad/confused. What you have to say is important and I am listening.*

Person-centered counseling (PCT) has had a very positive outcome for many of my clients. I believe this is because of the client's need to receive unconditional positive regard and empathic understanding first and foremost. It is best to consider each person on an individual basis and tailor a plan or strategy that addresses her needs. Some clients benefited in particular from applying certain Cognitive Behavioral Therapy (CBT) techniques, particularly where the client was exhibiting acute stress and anxiety, symptoms of posttraumatic stress disorder (PTSD), or depression.

Another group that needs to be considered is older women. Even if they are not experiencing IPSV now, they may have endured it for much of their lives. It is also very possible that they could have suffered with PTSD that was not recognized in the way we understand it today. This age group may face social constrictions that have not allowed them to speak out and find their voice to be able to seek help and support. They may not have received any recourse to justice due to the social stigma they faced and the skepticism and possible derision received from police, the justice system, and other authorities (Office for Victims of Crime 2012). Counseling can play a vital role in allowing a client the validation and legitimization of her experience and help with finding a way to healing.

## Placing the blame where it belongs and naming rape

Because of the way much of society is constructed and the values that affect our core beliefs about ourselves and our relationship to the world around us, we often live with the idea of shame. Shame is a social construct to make people adhere to a perceived way of life.

Social hierarchy and power imbalance result in victim-blaming. The abuser will blame his victim because he has no ability or desire to take responsibility for his own actions. Family, friends, and the wider community may victim-blame for similar reasons but also because they wish to distance themselves from unpleasant occurrences, using faulty thinking which goes along the lines of, "If I don't do what she does, and I don't behave like her, then it will never happen to me." While naming IPSV is an important step in recovery, timing is critical. Remembering that some women have no name to give IPSV, see Chapter 11 about simple but sensitive ways to ask about and name it with clients.

Unfortunately, this only reinforces the abuser's behavior and makes it harder for a survivor of IPSV to come forward. So not only does such a client have to deal with the trauma, but she also has to carry around with her all these unhelpful attitudes and values which she may internalize. Here you can help her deconstruct these ideas, and help her understand where any possible shame and guilt may be stemming from and why people victim-blame. This leads to another very important and vital part of her journey to recovery: understanding that *it's not her fault.*

> Counselor: *So on the one hand he was telling you how bad you were in bed and he might find another lover, then almost immediately after, telling you he loved you and wanted a family with you. That sounds very unsettling and confusing for you. How did it make you feel at the time?*
>
> Mary: *Confused. Hurt. He treated me really well normally; it was just sex that was a problem for us. He would often say that I just lay there, like a piece of meat. But I didn't know what sex was supposed to be like. So when he said I was rubbish in bed, I blamed myself because I didn't know anything.*
>
> Counselor: *So you were a young woman, it was your first sexual as well as romantic relationship. Yet he was 25 and had previous relationships, with two children by his ex. Yet he blamed you for an unsatisfying relationship, Mary?*
>
> Mary: *Yes, that's right. But that's wrong, isn't it? He should have known better.*
>
> Counselor: *How do you feel about that now?*
>
> Mary: *I guess looking at it that way, perhaps it wasn't my fault. Just at the time I thought it was. But it isn't, is it?*
>
> Counselor: *No, it wasn't your fault, Mary.*

It may take a number of sessions to reach this point, and it is important to go at the client's pace. Some clients may come to you and say they have been raped and want to talk about it from the start. Others may be describing rape but not seeing it as such because of their beliefs. Rushing them to come to terms with what has happened may leave them feeling emotionally unsafe. This may result in them leaving the session distraught with overwhelming feelings and memories, which may lead to them harming themselves or not coming back to counseling because they feel unable to deal with it.

> Counselor: *Could I just bring you back to something you said earlier? You said that according to him you were like a piece of meat. That sounds verbally and emotionally abusive. How did you feel about him saying that?*
>
> Mary: *Horrible. A bit worthless actually, and he never cuddled me afterward. I see now, he was already chipping away at me. So when he kept on and on at me to start a family I finally gave in and I got pregnant when I was 18.*

Helping the client to come to terms with how her abuser made her feel and helping her to understand that she was not to blame for the physical and psychological abuse is also important to her recovery. She may feel that somehow she deserved the abuse. Perhaps when confiding in a family member those ideas about her behavior and that of the abuser were reinforced. You can help this client to discover a different point of view and lay the responsibility of blame where it firmly belongs, with the abuser. If your client is uncertain about this at first, you can use methods to explain the cycle of abuse—that is, explaining how it works, showing her a diagram such as a power and control wheel, and asking her to see if she notices any similarities. A power and control wheel that is adapted to include rape and coercive sexual behavior is presented in Chapter 9.

> Mary: *I had my doubts about marrying because he got a bit jealous. He'd call me a slut. The sex wasn't any better; in fact after the birth of my second child it got worse.*
>
> Counselor: *In what way did it get worse, Mary?*
>
> Mary: *I was useless in bed. I couldn't please him and he'd find someone else. When I said we shouldn't get married then, he would change and say it didn't matter, but being a proper family did matter to him, more than anything. And that was really important to me too.*
>
> Counselor: *Was he aware of how much this meant to you?*

Mary: *Yes he was. (Mary sighs and shakes her head.) Even then he was manipulating me. Now I don't know if he ever loved me at all.*

This can be a tricky point in the counseling process. Moving from self-blame and disbelief to understanding the reality of the relationship should be handled with great sensitivity. Letting go of long-held beliefs that may have been her only way of surviving the trauma can leave the client feeling lost or empty, and if not handled carefully may impress upon her a sense of worthlessness. Here, you need to consider positive reinforcement and help her to see herself in a new light. You can begin the process of rebuilding her self-esteem and confidence. Here is one way to do that:

Counselor: *If it were one of your closest friends or one of your children who had been through what you have, and had just said the exact same thing to you, would you still value her and see her as deserving to be loved and cherished?*

Mary: *Yes, I would. And I would tell her that I love her very much.*

Counselor: *That she deserves to be loved and find a relationship where she is cherished? (Mary nods.) Then if you have so much love and compassion for them in your situation, can you find the same love and compassion for yourself?*

Mary: *Oh, I hadn't thought about it like that before.*

Counselor: *How would having this compassion change the way you feel about yourself?*

Mary: *I'm not sure. Um, loved, valued, like actually, I'm O.K. Bad stuff happens but that doesn't make me a bad person.*

## Symptoms of posttraumatic stress disorder

In order to be able to deal with the often repeated assault and trauma, a survivor develops one or more defense mechanisms. For example, she decides that much of the sex that is forced on her is actually O.K. and just a normal part of their relationship (Bergen 2006). She may experience dissociation from her surroundings, creating a fantasy world where this is happening to someone else or is not happening at all. This survival skill is to protect the psyche during and after experiencing the trauma and allows survivors of IPSV to go on functioning as best they can day after day. Some clients may describe severely traumatic dissociative states such as derealization, depersonalization, and memory loss (Herman 1992). Co-morbid conditions aimed to attain avoidance of painful feelings, such as self-harm, eating disorders, or substance abuse, may require other forms of professional support as well as counseling (Matsakis 1992). The client may benefit from visits to a supportive doctor, local support groups, and specialist therapists in drug and alcohol abuse. As a counselor, you can play a vital role in supporting any ongoing treatment and help the client to identify and cope with the triggers in her daily life to assist her in regaining control.

There may also be the added burden of guilt and shame exacerbating these symptoms due to social stigma, a feeling of not being able to cope and perhaps not being able to function well on a daily basis. If children are involved she may feel she failed to protect them, or that her suffering rendered her unable to meet all the child's needs.

While these symptoms and feelings can happen during or just after a trauma such as rape, the effects can also occur many years later. A survivor may feel she has moved on and pushed these traumatic events out of mind, yet years later the memories come flooding back either through nightmares, flashbacks, or persistent and disturbing thoughts. This can happen either in a new relationship which is a happy and fulfilling one, or because of a simple trigger such as a word, sound, sight, taste, touch, or smell. The client may go into a spiral of depression, feel intense anger, and go on to experience a range of PTSD symptoms (Easteal and McOrmond-Plummer 2006).

Here, Mary has experienced a flashback resulting in a state of dissociation. The counselor seeks to ground Mary and reconnect her with the present. The counselor keeps her voice calm and reassuring, but avoids whispering. The reason for this is that Mary's partner may have whispered to her while carrying out the abuse.

Counselor: *Mary, are you O.K.? (No response.)*

Counselor: *Mary, can you hear me? This is what I'd like you to do right now. Feel the material of the chair beneath your fingers. What does it feel like? Press your feet into the floor. Feel how solid it is. Listen to my voice. It's just you and me in the room, we were just talking. You are safe here, Mary. Come back to me, Mary.*

Counselor: *Mary, are you feeling O.K. right now?*

Mary: *Uh? Oh, yes, yes I'm O.K. Feel a bit tired all of a sudden.*

Counselor: *We've been sitting here awhile. Would you like to stand up and stretch your legs, stamp your feet? We'll do it together.*

The counselor remains focused on the client and seeks to ensure the client feels as safe and as grounded as possible.

Sometimes flashbacks may result in overwhelming emotion for Mary which she is unable to stem, ending in a panic attack. She experiences this a great deal in her life. Mary's stressors are certain smells and loud bangs or knocks at the door. Teaching Mary these grounding exercises, methods to help her to calm her breathing, and some focusing meditation, may help her to overcome her immediate panic. As the counselor explains how stress works and the nature of the "fight or flight" response, she begins to understand what is going on in her body and this diminishes her fear. Over time she reports that the panic attacks are gradually lessening.

Mary also reports feeling very uncomfortable in the presence of men and feels overwhelmed and panicked if they come too close, but is unable to voice how she feels. Teaching Mary how to voice her feelings and thoughts through role-play will help develop her confidence. This will enable Mary to cope with situations where she feels uncomfortable and allow her to express her feelings clearly in a positive way (Clark and Beck 2010). Other interventions which Mary agrees to practice include keeping a diary to record her thoughts and feelings, which she finds useful at night when she is having difficulty sleeping, and practicing distraction techniques for when the emotional stress or disturbing thoughts are beginning to build. These measures can help to head off symptoms of PTSD such as panic, repetitive negative thoughts, and overwhelming emotions (Rosenbloom and Williams 2010).

Other useful strategies to help challenge negative thought patterns may include Rational Emotive Behavior Therapy (REBT) and CBT worksheets such as depression, stress, and anxiety recording. You may also want to include a suicide safety plan worksheet. Mindfulness meditation techniques are also useful for helping a client to lower the fear response, relax, and stay in the present.

# Helping loved ones understand

The mental health consequences of rape and sexual violence in any form can have a devastating impact on the client, her life, and her family and friends. Not only will she have to cope with her own trauma, but also the feelings of others around her. She may be anxious about how others perceive her. They may fail to understand how she is feeling, and the resulting sense of isolation may compound her distress, resulting in a much higher risk of developing depression,

PTSD, self-harming behavior, suicide, and substance abuse. The long-term consequences of IPSV can impact work, family life, and new partnerships.

Helping family members or new partners to understand what is happening can greatly improve relationships and enable them to support a survivor more fully. This can be done by extending counseling to them, setting up a support group, and offering information about IPSV and PTSD. It is important for those who care about survivors to also look after their own well-being, because listening to what their loved one has gone through can lead to them experiencing emotional trauma too. Like counselors, if friends and family members don't look after their own well-being, they can experience "burnout." A counselor can help them to understand how to handle this situation sensitively so the survivor doesn't feel rejected.

## Safety of the client

If your client is still in a relationship with her abuser, it is worth devising a safety plan. This can cover safety during the relationship, and if the client may leave, the plan can enhance safety during the entire period of time from contemplating leaving until after the separation (Davies 2008). This can include a suicide safety plan and what to do if in physical danger. If you are inexperienced in working with IPSV survivors it will be essential that you refer your client to a domestic violence or sexual assault advocate who is specifically trained in working with safety issues.

Supporting a client through recovery and healing is some of the most rewarding work a counselor can undertake. When your client is safe, feeling empowered, has the necessary coping skills, and is coping well, reassure her that when this counseling relationship comes to an end, it is the start of a whole new beginning for her.

## References

Bergen, R. (1996) *Wife Rape: Understanding the Response of Survivors and Service Providers.* Thousand Oaks, CA: Sage.

Bergen, R.K. (2006) *Marital Rape: New Research and Directions.* VAWnet Applied Research Forum, The National Online Resource Center on Violence Against Women. Available at http://www.aifs.gov.au/acssa/pubs/researchsummary/ressum1/, accessed July 7, 2012.

Clark, D. and Beck, A. (2010) *Cognitive Therapy of Anxiety Disorders: Science and Practice.* New York: Guilford Press.

Davies, J. (2008) *When Battered Women Stay: Advocacy Beyond Leaving.* Harrisburg, PA: The National Resource Center on Domestic Violence. Available at http://new. vawnet.org/Assoc_Files_VAWnet/BCS20_Staying.pdf, accessed July 7, 2012.

Easteal, P. and McOrmond-Plummer, L. (2006) *Real Rape, Real Pain: Help for Women Sexually Assaulted by Male Partners.* Melbourne: Hybrid Publishers.

Finkelhor, D. and Yllo, K. (1985) *License to Rape: Sexual Abuse of Wives.* New York: The Free Press.

Herman, J. (1992) *Trauma and Recovery: From Domestic Abuse to Political Terror.* New York: Basic Books.

Matsakis, A. (1992) *I Can't Get Over It: A Handbook for Trauma Survivors.* Oakland, CA: New Harbinger Publications Inc.

Office for Victims of Crime (2012) *Assisting Older Victims of Intimate Partner Sexual Violence.* Washington, DC: Office for Victims of Crime. Available at http://ovc. ncjrs.gov/ovcproviderforum/asp/Sub.asp, accessed March 3, 2012.

Rosenbloom, D. and Williams, M. (2010) *Life After Trauma: A Workbook for Healing.* New York: Guilford Press.

Russell, D. (1990) *Rape in Marriage.* Bloomington, IN: Indiana University Press.

Ryan, S., Manlove, J., and Franzetta, K. (2003) *The First Time: Characteristics of Teens' First Sexual Relationships.* Washington, DC: ChildTrends. Available at www. childtrends.org/files/firsttimerb.pdf, accessed July 7, 2012.

Winters, M. (2008) "Making the connections: advocating for survivors of intimate partner sexual violence." *Connections 10,* 1, 10–14.

# CHAPTER 14

# Responding to Christian Survivors of Intimate Partner Sexual Violence

Barbara Roberts

Sexual relations, according to the Bible, are to be confined to marriage, so I will be referring to husbands and wives rather than "intimate partners." Christianity doesn't endorse premarital sexual involvement, but as it sometimes happens, much of what I say can apply to premarital relationships as well as marriage.

Counselors need to be "as wise as serpents" (Matthew 10:16) because abusers are manipulative and will try to enlist them as allies, excusing their behavior by suggesting, for example, that their wives have unfairly withheld sex. Even domestic violence experts can be taken in by abusers who are showing their Dr. Jekyll face, because abusers are masters at camouflage. But it is possible to identify the characteristic language of abusers when they drop the Jekyll facade and start showing their abusive Mr. Hyde persona (Bancroft 2002). To sharpen your antennae in this regard, do a category search for "the language of abusers" at the blog A Cry For Justice (Roberts 2012a). As for male victims of sexual abuse by wives, while this does occasionally occur, spousal abuse is overwhelmingly a gendered crime committed by men (Bancroft 2009).

If a male plans to counsel a Christian woman who is disclosing sexual abuse, he must monitor his own motives. Too many ministers have taken advantage of women who sought guidance from them. If you believe this may be an issue for you, refer the woman to someone who can safely handle the situation. As an adjunct to counseling with you, please consider referring your client to rape crisis or domestic violence services, where advocates are trained to work with the trauma she has sustained.

In preparing for this chapter, I asked survivors "Do you tell others about the sexual abuse?" at the blog A Cry For Justice. Many Christian women responded to my post, chronicling the sexual abuse they'd received from their so-called Christian husbands, and the usually appalling response they got when they disclosed. If you are counseling victims, I advise you to read their stories and to review the topic "sexual abuse" on that blog. In addition, clergy should read the *Pastors and Abuse* series by Pastor Jeff Crippen (2012b), and do further reading (see References below). Adequate study of the reality of marital rape is also a must; other chapters in this book will be advantageous here.

A Christian woman told me that she was raped by her husband and fled the house, then reported the rape to her pastor, who accompanied her back to her house to collect some clothes. While they were there, the husband arrived. The wife was in the bedroom. Taking a chair, her husband placed it just inside the bedroom door and planted himself on it, directly facing her, while she was going through the chest of drawers. The pastor was outside the bedroom and didn't intervene. When the woman and her pastor were back in his car, she told him how scared she'd felt when her husband sat there blocking the bedroom door. The pastor said he didn't see that there was any intimidation. This story illustrates that sometimes pastors are told the facts about rape, and *they just don't get it.* They don't understand that the victim is scared of her husband. This insensitivity is based on male privilege: some men may not understand how much privilege they have in this world, and how easy it is for men to intimidate women. However, it is true that some men do understand their privilege, and are not willing to relinquish this for the sake of justice to women. So, such treatment of a disclosure may come down less to ignorance than to enshrined values that devalue women and make ongoing danger to them possible. It's essential that the safety of an abused woman is your priority and not, for example, the idea that marriages should be saved at all costs.

## Men who rape their wives shouldn't be treated as Christians

Unbiased reading of the Bible leads one to conclude that men who abuse their wives should not be treated as if they are believers. Christians are told in 1 Corinthians 5:11 not to associate with anyone who claims to be a believer who is sexually immoral or greedy, an

INTIMATE PARTNER SEXUAL VIOLENCE

idolater or verbally abusive, a drunkard or a swindler. Do not even eat with such a person. So-called "Christians" who do these heinous things are to be stripped of their church membership. Jesus gave instructions for disciplining members of the church in Matthew 18:15–17 and said that if the offender fails to truly repent, he must be treated as an unbeliever. But the church has chronically and sinfully ignored these injunctions and failed to excommunicate perpetrators of abuse who profess to be believers. Abusers are skilled at enlisting allies in the church, and many Christians cannot detect phony repentance, so they fall into the abuser's manipulative web. This causes immense anguish for victims.

When a woman has been sexually abused by her "Christian" husband, what ought to take place if the church adheres to biblical principles? Biblically obedient church leaders should:

- Firmly and openly take the side of the victim—as Lundy Bancroft points out, neutrality is *not* neutral in domestic violence; neutrality serves the interests of the perpetrator (2002, p.287).

- Obey 1 Corinthians 5:11–13—purge the evil person from among you. Treat the offender as an unbeliever.

- Evaluate any show of repentance from the abuser most stringently, using a tool like my "Checklist for Repentance" (Roberts 2009); God does not grant forgiveness to apologetic but unrepentant people.

- Insist the husband confess all his crimes to the police and serve any sentence imposed, if this is appropriate for the woman, after having consulted with her.

- If appropriate, insist he attend a men's behavior change group and do everything reasonable (at arm's length) to make restoration to the victim, without in any way using that as an excuse to harass or intimidate her.

- Protect the victim by barring the offender from attending her church.

Of course, most churches don't do any of this, but we can help survivors by telling them what a biblical response *ought* to look like. When survivors feel let down by the inadequate response of their churches, they can be comforted and empowered by knowing what the Bible really teaches for their situation, and how far short their church may have fallen in carrying out these principles. This helps them understand why they might be feeling angry at the church.

Anger at the woeful responses of the church is not ungodly bitterness that a victim needs to repent of; it is justified and righteous anger, the same kind of anger that God has for those who ignore the cries of the oppressed (Crippen 2012a). Feeling supported and vindicated by the Word of God may galvanize a victim to take the necessary steps to protect herself from future abuse, whether it be from her husband, or from the church.

## Making church a safe place to disclose

If family violence is never mentioned from the pulpit, victims feel excluded. When a minister indicates interest in addressing family violence, this can be lifesaving for victims. Preach about abuse from the pulpit. For exemplary sermons to help encourage disclosure, see the Sermon Series on *Domestic Violence and Abuse* (Crippen 2010).

Many churches have strong interdictions against gossip and "being judgmental," so victims feel they mustn't speak ill of their husbands. Christians need to be taught that it is good to appropriately denounce evil (Roberts 2008).

If a woman even *hints* at being mistreated by her husband, you should say, "Would you like to tell me more about that?" This invitational approach is not overly probing, but it conveys to her that you are interested and it might be safe to disclose to you. Women who disclose domestic abuse are unlikely to disclose the *sexual* aspects of the abuse, and professionals don't tend to ask—but they should. Research indicates that women who are asked about sexual abuse are likely to disclose (Bergen 1996).

## If a woman discloses to you, watch your choice of words

Use reflective and empathetic listening. Pay careful attention to the victim's story and then repeat the most important points back to her to show her you have heard and take her report seriously. State the obvious: she is describing crimes and mistreatment. You don't have to repeat the graphic detail, but you should summarize the conduct of the abuser.

Use active verbs that hold the perpetrator accountable, and make it crystal clear that the victim is not to blame. When using the word "you" to refer to the victim, try to make it the object of a transitive verb in which the perpetrator is the agent. Talking about "what he did to you" is better than saying "you endured this mistreatment," because the victim may hear "you endured this mistreatment" as implying that she was silly for putting up with it.

Words like "guilt," "evil," "unrighteous," "sinful," and "wicked" are part of Christian vocabulary and will resonate meaningfully for Christian victims, so it's fine to use them when describing the actions of the abuser. A victim needs moral reassurance to counteract the blame-shifting techniques used by her abuser, and when the reassurance is given in Christian vocabulary it is immensely helpful.

Try to acknowledge and honor the ways she has responded to the abuse. Victims respond to abuse in many creative, intelligent ways to strive to maintain their dignity and integrity (Renoux and Wade 2008; Wade 1997). For example, a woman's decision to "permit" unwanted sex may spring from her knowledge (based on bitter experience) that if she resists, the perpetrator will abuse the children the next day. Reflect this back to her: "Whenever you tried to resist, he punished both you and the kids. You chose to let him rape you that night because you wanted to protect your children."

## The right outlook is outrage

While she is telling her story, express outrage at the way her husband has mistreated her. Don't pity her but share sadness alongside of her ("weep with those who weep," Romans 12:15). She will feel she has a companion, not an aloof or neutral judge. If you don't show indignation at her husband's sins, she may feel that you don't really support her, or that you've only partly believed her. She will conclude that you believe what her husband did is "not that bad." Her doubt about whether she has enough reason to complain has probably been plaguing her already; you need to decisively explain to her that, "What your husband has done to you is very bad: it's criminal, it's wicked! And your emotions are completely normal and reasonable under the circumstances."

It's not wise to feign empathy, and it's not wise to intensively counsel victims unless you actually *feel* empathy to some extent. Apathy towards the needy is a serious sin (Ezekiel 16:49). Counselors *must* see abuse as a moral issue where the blame lies with the perpetrator, or they will not be able to convey "you are not to blame" to the victim. And when victims suspect they are being judged as partly or wholly to blame, it is like having caustic soda poured in their wounds.

## What to say to the victim

- What he did to you was awful.
- It is not your fault.
- He broke your trust.
- He manipulated you by distorting scripture.
- He coerced you.
- He ignored your pleas.
- He insulted, slandered, degraded, violated, and raped you. Rape is any kind of penetration to which you did not freely give consent at the time. Marital rape *is rape*, even if people tell you it isn't.
- It's okay to feel devastated. In your inmost self you have *been* devastated. So your feelings are normal and healthy. Crying is one of the best ways to heal from trauma (Bancroft 2012).
- It is perfectly natural that you don't want to have intimacy with your husband. You are refusing to be content with being abused—and that is a sign of your health and dignity (Renoux and Wade 2008; Wade 1997).
- When a man abuses his wife, it may sap any sexual desire she might have had for him. It is senseless to expect a woman to have sexual desire for a man who is repeatedly nasty to her.
- You don't have to heed the advice of people who tell you to put it behind you or use other clichés that imply it's not that bad.
- Rape, coercive sex, and any sexual touching that is unwanted are all crimes. Do you want to go to the police? Would you like me to help you to do that?
- You are in a high-risk situation, because victims of spousal sexual abuse are at more risk of being killed by their spouse than those who are simply verbally abused or battered

(Campbell 2002; see also Chapter 4). I can give you referrals to counseling and support services, and I can help you access those services. Under no account will I ask you to engage in couples counseling, and I will not talk about what you've told me with your husband, unless you give me your explicit permission.

## Explore religious beliefs that constrain women from getting free

Christian women usually want to deal virtuously with abuse. They are afraid of displeasing God and disobeying the Bible, and they are perplexed by misunderstandings of Scripture. The Bible does not in any way permit sexual abuse, but many Christians misunderstand the way scriptural principles all fit together without contradiction. Often this happens because certain verses are overemphasized at the expense of other verses. Sometimes it happens because the meaning of a scripture is twisted by abusers. Many pseudo-Christian husbands use spiritual abuse to enforce compliance with their sexual abuse. The most common scriptural misunderstandings and their antidotes are listed below.

### *Submission*

> Wives submit to your own husbands as to the Lord. For the husband is the head of the wife even as Christ is head of the church, his body, and is himself its Savior. Now, as the church submits to Christ, so also should wives submit in everything to their husbands. (Ephesians 5:22–24)

"Submit in everything" cannot mean submit to sin, since God never calls us to comply with sin. Christ as head of the church does not abuse his flock, he nourishes, protects, and cherishes it; and this is how a husband should treat his wife. Husbands should not treat their wives harshly (Colossians 3:19). A wife is never required to submit to sexual abuse from her husband, and the Bible recognizes that sexual abuse contaminates the body and soul at a deep level (Roberts 2012b). The Bible's teaching on wifely submission cannot require a wife to submit to the sin of abuse (Bryant 2002; Tracy 2008).

## *Authority in the marriage bed*

For the wife does not have authority over her own body, but the husband does. Likewise the husband does not have authority over his own body, but the wife does. (1 Corinthians 7:4)

Many Christians, and especially abusive husbands, think this means the wife has no right to withhold her body from her husband. But in reality, this verse permits a wife to say no to sex. Look at the second half of the verse: "the husband does not have authority over his own body, but the wife does." Therefore, she can tell his body to not do things to her body. She has authority to tell his body what it can and cannot do to her body!

So if a husband says, "You must let me do this to your body because I have authority over your body," the wife can say back to him, "No; I have just as much authority over your body as you have over mine, so if I tell you not to do that to me, you mustn't do it. Our authority over each other's bodies is equal and reciprocal, so neither of us can force the other to do anything they don't want to do!" (Davis 2009).

Biblical sex is to be engaged in by mutual agreement and for mutual enjoyment. If one spouse does not feel comfortable with something, that thing shouldn't be done. There is no other way of understanding 1 Corinthians 7:4. Women have been trained to think that they have no authority in the marital bed and that men have all the rights. But women have just as many rights and just as much authority as men in the marital bed. In fact, one could argue that the marital bed is *the* area of marriage where gender equality is most explicitly commanded, since of all the scriptural passages which could be said to endorse gender equality in marriage, 1 Corinthians 7:4 most explicitly endorses the equal authority of wives and husbands.

Another scripture that is often twisted to enforce compliance with abuse is Hebrews 13:4. I know of a case where a husband continually told his wife that he thought God would approve of all the acts he wanted her to perform in the bedroom, and that God meant it to be that way. She felt her husband was saying that if she didn't do those things she would be displeasing God, because God was "for" it and she was against it, so she was against God. The husband quoted Hebrews 13:4 that "marriage is honorable in all and the bed undefiled" (King James translation) to say that nothing you do in the marriage bed is wrong. The woman felt that their relationship wasn't really about God, and it certainly wasn't about her, it was just about him.

The husband also used the Song of Solomon to support his claims, although he had never read it! He just read something about the Song of Solomon in a book that he purchased to defend his position on "freedom" in the bedroom.

Hebrews 13:4 says, "Let marriage be held in honor among all, and let the marriage bed be undefiled, for God will judge the sexually immoral and adulterous" (English Standard Version). Here, the word "let" is directive rather than permissive, just as when Paul directs husbands to love their wives by saying, "Let each one of you love his wife as himself" (Ephesians 5:33). Marriage is not a license for perverse, unnatural, painful, or nonconsensual sex. It is not an instruction that "anything goes" simply because the couple is legally married.

## The frequency of sex

The Bible counsels couples not to unduly deprive one another of sexual relations lest they be tempted outside the marriage (1 Corinthians 7:5). The vast majority of Christian wives give their husbands sex with reasonable frequency, despite what abusive husbands might claim. Sexual abuse in marriage more often comes from the husband's insistence, to which he will brook no opposition, that his wife have sex excessively often. Many women who have lived with sex-addicted husbands have no idea what "normal" is, either in frequency or types of activity. (For a compelling account of such a marriage, see Ida Mae 2012.)

## Premarital dilemmas

If a woman has sex before marriage, that doesn't mean she is married. When a Christian girl has had sex with her boyfriend, she is often told she must marry him in order to stop the sin, which is terribly harmful advice if the man is showing red flags of being an abuser. In *The Bible's View on Pre-marital Sex—Is the Remedy Always "Get Married"?* (Roberts 2012c), I explain that when a man has sex with an unbetrothed young woman he does not always have to marry her.

## Forgiveness

Many Christians are confused about the concept of forgiveness and therefore plagued by false guilt. Three very different things are labeled "forgiveness" and the way to bring clarity is to distinguish among them (Kerry 2008; Tracy 2005, pp.180–193).

1. *Judicial forgiveness* is what God does when He forgives those who repent of their sins and trust in Jesus as their Lord and Savior. Only God can forgive the guilt of sin; judicial forgiveness is His province alone.

2. *Psychological forgiveness* is the mental processing and emotional release that accompanies the recognition and remembrance of abuse, and the renouncing of *personal* vengeance—but it doesn't have to entail renouncing any pursuit of justice through the courts or church officials. There is no correct timetable for psychological forgiveness. We do not accuse someone who suffers with broken bones of being unforgiving if their fractures don't heal immediately, but when someone has been ravaged emotionally and sexually, Christians often judge them by how quickly or slowly the healing comes. When Christians push such judgments, they are re-fracturing the victims.

3. *Relational forgiveness* is the harmonious reconciliation of the relationship with the abuser. A person can forgive psychologically without ever having to extend relational forgiveness. This is where Christians most grievously conflate the three kinds of forgiveness. There is no requirement in Christianity to reconcile relationally with someone who has abused you, especially if the abuser still remains dangerous. The Bible endorses divorce for spousal abuse.

(Roberts 2008)

Forgiveness is not forgetting (as in amnesia). Forgiveness is not just a feeling; it is an act of will. And forgiveness is not tolerance: you may forgive people, but you don't have to tolerate what they have done.

# References

Bancroft, L. (2002) *Why Does He Do That? Inside the Minds of Angry and Controlling Men.* New York: Berkley.

Bancroft, L. (2009) *Domestic Violence in Popular Culture Part 2.* Video available at www.youtube.com/watch?v=xuY_mUopIc0, accessed June 21, 2012; transcript available at www.notunderbondage.blogspot.com.au/2012/04/lundy-bancroft-says-right-outlook-is.html, accessed June 21, 2012.

Bancroft, L. (2012) *A Powerful Key to Healing from Trauma.* Available at http://lundybancroft.blogspot.com.au/2012/01/powerful-key-to-healing-from-trauma.html, accessed June 21, 2012.

Bergen, R. (1996) *Wife Rape: Understanding the Response of Survivors and Service Providers.* Thousand Oaks, CA: Sage.

Bryant, C.J. (2002) *Sabotaged Submission.* Available at http://graceinabundance.com/userfiles//SabSub%20rev%202009.pdf, accessed June 21, 2012.

Campbell, J. (2002) "Health consequences of intimate partner violence." *The Lancet* 359, 1331–1336.

Crippen, J. (2010) *Sermon Series on Domestic Violence and Abuse.* Available at www.sermonaudio.com/search.asp?seriesOnly=true&currSection=sermonstopic&SourceID=crc&keyworddesc=Domestic+Violence+and+Abuse&keyword=Domestic+Violence+and+Abuse, accessed June 21, 2012.

Crippen, J. (2012a) *How Can I Know If I Am Bitter or Righteously Angry?* Available at http://cryingoutforjustice.wordpress.com/2012/05/27/how-can-i-know-if-i-am-bitter-or-righteously-angry-by-jeff-crippen, accessed June 21, 2012.

Crippen, J. (2012b) *Pastors and Abuse Series.* Available at http://cryingoutforjustice.wordpress.com/2012/06/19/pastors-and-abuse-confronting-and-dealing-with-abusers-by-jeff-crippen/2012/06/19/pastors-and-abuse-confronting-and-dealing-with-abusers-by-jeff-crippen/, accessed June 21, 2012.

Davis, C. (2009) *Sermon on 1 Corinthians 7:1–7.* Available at www.mendingthesoul.org/files/2006/11/wabc053109_sermon.mp3, accessed June 21, 2012.

Kerry, B. (2008) *Sermon: Breaking Barriers to Intimacy with God.* Available at www.notunderbondage.com/pdfs/BobKerreysforgivenesssermon.pdf, accessed June 21, 2012.

Mae, I. (2012) *Sex in an Abusive Marriage.* Available at http://thoroughlychristiandivorce.wordpress.com/2012/01/28/sex-in-an-abusive-marriage-part-1, accessed June 21, 2012.

Renoux, M. and Wade, A. (2008) "Resistance to violence: a key symptom of chronic mental wellness." *Context* 98, 2–4. Available at www.notunderbondage.blogspot.com.au/2011/11/resistance-to-violence-chronic-mental.html, accessed June 21, 2012.

Roberts, B. (2008) *Not Under Bondage: Biblical Divorce for Abuse, Adultery and Desertion.* Ballarat: Maschil Press.

Roberts, B. (2009) *Checklist for Repentance—When Being Sorry is Genuine.* Available at www.notunderbondage.com/resources/ChecklistForRepentance.html, accessed June 21, 2012.

Roberts, B. (2012a) *Do You Tell Others About the Sexual Abuse?* Available at http://cryingoutforjustice.wordpress.com/2012/05/08/do-you-tell-others-about-the-sexual-abuse, accessed June 21, 2012.

Roberts, B. (2012b) *Sexual Abuse in Marriage—What Should a Christian Wife Do?* Available at http://cryingoutforjustice.wordpress.com/2012/06/11/sexual-abuse-in-marriage-what-should-a-christian-wife-do, accessed June 21, 2012.

Roberts, B. (2012c) *The Bible's View on Pre-Marital Sex—Is the Remedy always "Get Married"?* Available at http://cryingoutforjustice.wordpress.com/2012/06/15/the-bibles-view-on-premarital-sex-is-the-remedy-always-get-married, accessed June 21, 2012.

Tracy, S.R. (2005) *Mending the Soul: Understanding and Healing Abuse.* Grand Rapids, MI: Zondervan.

Tracy, S.R. (2008) *What Does "Submit in Everything" Really Mean?* Available at www. cbe.org.au/media/docs/SubmitinEverythingTJ.pdf, accessed June 21, 2012; originally published in *Trinity Journal 29,* 285–312.

Wade, A. (1997) "Small acts of everyday living: everyday resistance to violence and other forms of oppression." *Contemporary Family Therapy 19,* 1, 23–39.

CHAPTER 15

# Law Enforcement Response to Intimate Partner Sexual Violence

Mike Davis

## The importance of informed response to intimate partner sexual violence

As law enforcement we can and do have tremendous impact on people's lives. Often, police are a victim's first contact with someone who has the power and authority to deliver help and justice. Therefore, law enforcement must have a trained response to domestic violence (DV) and its related crimes, just as we do to a bank robbery in progress, a school shooter, or a bomb threat. Our training must allow us to become more sophisticated than abusers, so that we can counter these crimes and effectively deal with them. When crimes like intimate partner violence (IPV) are not properly dealt with, we see a continuance of violence and an escalation of violence, which can result in fatalities. As public servants charged with maintaining safety, police officers must take any form of IPV very seriously.

## Identifying intimate partner sexual violence

### Intimate partner sexual violence: a hidden crime

Victims of intimate partner sexual violence (IPSV) often do not match the stereotyped image of a rape victim. There is a common misperception, shared by law enforcement, that in order to have a "real rape" the suspect should be a stranger to the victim and have used extreme force such as a weapon; seriously assaulted the victim, resulting in visible injuries; or kidnapped her (Long 2009; see also Chapter 2). But the overwhelming majority of sexual assaults do not occur in circumstances like that. Law enforcement knows what to do in the stranger scenario but may not have the right response to sexual assault when it occurs in an intimate partner scenario (Archambault 2002).

IPSV is an underreported crime:

The closer the relationship between the female victim and the offender, the greater the likelihood that the police would not be told about the rape or sexual assault. When the offender was a current or former husband or boyfriend, about three-fourths of all victimizations were not reported to police. (Rennison 2002, p.3)

In my experience, it is very rare for a DV victim to call police and report a sexual assault. Some victims do not know that IPSV is a crime, because the offender has told them it is not (National Center for Women and Policing 2009). It has always surprised me how many victims say, "He never hit me, he only raised his fist to me."

A woman may call to report burglary, stalking, telephone harassment, restraining order violation, death threat, or another DV crime because those crimes are less difficult to report. Cases of IPSV are so humiliating and degrading that victims do not want to discuss them with a stranger, much less face potentially embarrassing questions and relive the event. Coercive and degrading sexual tactics are common in DV cases whether there is overt IPSV or not (Logan, Cole, and Shannon 2007). Victims call the police or someone calls for them to report the other DV crimes, usually because something has happened that scared them.

## Using a specialized domestic violence report and victim statement to uncover intimate partner sexual violence

Asking the right questions is the first step in an effective strategy to deal with the crime of IPSV. Many times when police arrive at a DV scene it is a chaotic, emotional situation in which things can easily be overlooked and a traumatized victim may not be able to disclose all of the crimes occurring. As law enforcement, we must have a trained response in which we recognize this. One way to do so is for law enforcement to have a specialized DV report which includes a victim statement that fully asks about the incident being reported, including the context and history of the DV. Such a statement can help to uncover other related crimes such as harassment, death threats, assaults, stalking, child abuse, weapons offenses, animal cruelty, and sexual violence.

We have found the routine use of the victim statement to be effective for many reasons. In addition to uncovering crimes that may be easily overlooked, the information the statement provides about the context of the violence gives us a starting point for investigation and a furtherance of any probable cause. It can assist in determining the primary aggressor. It allows the victim another avenue for communication of events that may not otherwise be documented. The statement can also be used as substantive evidence if the victim recants or the suspect opens the door to a contradiction of the statement. The use of the statement is not a substitute for a complete investigation and gathering of evidence or witness statements, but it is a helpful investigative tool to fully address the range of possible DV incidents (see *City of Vancouver Police Department Domestic Violence Victim Statement*, Washington Association of Sheriffs and Police Chiefs; Office of Crime Victims Advocacy 2009, p.84.)

## Thorough investigation of intimate partner sexual violence

A full and complete investigation is helpful in establishing the severity of the crime and the history of DV, which is relevant for the issuance of protection orders, obtaining victim compensation, medical treatment, sentencing, probation and parole supervision, and batterer treatment. In my experience, many DV and IPSV offenders have multiple victims and are serial abusers. If a suspect moves on to a new victim, the prior DV investigations will be relevant. If the history includes different protection orders with multiple protected persons, this is an indicator of a serial abuser.

Law enforcement should be prepared and trained for a disclosure of an extensive history of DV and be able to respond to the victim that IPSV is not uncommon in DV situations. The right officer is the one who "gets it" and does a thorough evidence-based case, while treating all the parties involved with dignity and respect. If a male officer is competent he can do the interview and investigation just fine.

This is an excerpt from the protocol developed by the Clark County Police Department in Washington State:

Potential questions and responses:

- Did your partner force you to have sex against your will?

- Has your partner ever threatened to hurt you, a family member, your pet, or destroy your property to force you to have sex in the past?

If yes:

Investigator: *I am sorry to say that is not unusual in DV situations. A definition of what you are asking may be needed—threaten to hurt you, other family member, pet, or destroy property. Follow up investigative questions as needed. You should receive medical care to ensure any injury is attended to. I would also suggest a rape exam to gather evidence and to check for internal injuries. You may want to call the sexual assault program for assistance. Here is their contact information.* (Washington Association of Sheriffs and Police Chiefs; Office of Crime Victims Advocacy 2009, p.38)

## Allowing time for more information to emerge

Law enforcement should read the victim statement at the scene and be prepared for disclosures of crimes and IPSV that may not have been discussed on first contact with the victim.

Law enforcement can establish rapport with the victim by expressing concern for the victim's safety and letting her know that the officer wants to know more about what is going on. Often, victims have never had anyone express concern and interest in what is happening and the severity of the DV or sexual assault.

Once the victim is calmed and feels safer, and the officer has established a connection, the victim will often recall and disclose events that did not come out initially. If IPSV is disclosed, let the victim discuss it in terms with which she is comfortable. It is particularly important to maintain privacy during the communication with the victim in order to maintain her dignity (United Nations Task Force on Drugs and Crime 2010) and to respect her desire to shield her children from hearing about her sexual victimization. Once a sexual assault is disclosed, employ sexual assault policy and protocols.

## Using the opportunity to provide help

Police may be the only ones either required by statute or in a position to give DV victims a notification for advocacy and victims' rights. That is one of the reasons it is important to uncover what is going on, in order to provide resources to help victims and get them to enhanced safety planning. This is also an opportunity to include information about IPSV in the DV information packet. Some US jurisdictions are including the safety cards available in English and Spanish developed by Futures Without Violence (Futures Without Violence 2012). Specific information about the services offered by local sexual assault and domestic violence advocacy agencies should also be included in the DV packet.

## Overcoming the challenges of intimate partner sexual violence investigation

### Understanding victim recantation

I always anticipate the victim will recant, and as I am going through the case I anticipate why. The most common reasons for minimization or recantation are fear, dependence of the victim on the suspect, worries about losing custody of children, pressure from friends or family, concern about not being believed, hesitancy about the criminal justice system, intimidation by the suspect, and loss of privacy (Police Executive Research Forum 2012). Police officers should keep in mind that sexual assault by a partner is not something many people would want to discuss with police or deal with in a court setting, due to the stigma attached to it.

The victim may recant as soon as the emergency call is over or well into a trial. "A victim's reluctance to participate is neither indicative of a false report nor reason to forego a strong, evidence-based investigation" (International Association of Chiefs of Police n.d., p.2).

### Overcoming lack of apparent injury

Officers can overcome the challenge of lack of injury with a detailed victim statement identifying the history of DV, fear induced in the victim, and the context of the violence. We need to focus on the force used and the fear placed in a victim and why a victim would feel coerced. We need to corroborate the victim's report with the circumstances to build a case. Oftentimes we are quick to assume there is a lack of evidence when there is a lack of physical injury; we need to look beyond injury alone. Many times we stop the investigation short when there may be evidence by witnesses, electronic messages, or other sources that do support a case for IPSV, or an assault with sexual motivation.

## *Extending the investigation to identify IPSV*

A common dynamic and defense for IPSV is the "she likes kinky sex" defense. I recall a violent felon who locked his live-in girlfriend in a house, terrorized her, punched holes in a wall, and started fires in the house. The victim fled to a neighbor's for help while she was half-clothed, with her breasts exposed. Upon contact with the police, the suspect stated, "She likes rough anal sex with sex toys and strangulation." He then produced a collection of anal sex porn videos. In fact, the victim did engage in consensual rough sex in the past, but in this case the evidence was overwhelming that the victim was held in her home and terrorized. This act was not consensual; it was an act of DV and IPSV. In order to put all this together we needed to know the history of DV, the fear, the force used, and the context of the violence. Many of these victims are dismissed before a thorough evidence-based case is investigated.

Here is an example of a case that benefited from extended investigation:

> A woman called police more than once to report harassing phone calls. The follow-up interview with the victim led me to enhance the way we work DV and IPSV cases. The woman was very accustomed to having threatening calls from her ex-husband, the father of her child, who lived in another state. This initially appeared to be a stalking case. During an interview while we obtained the history, frequency, and severity of abuse, she disclosed very humiliating sexual violence. It included her being "inspected for cheating" and drug-facilitated sexual assaults. The violence even extended to other family members and arrests had been made. The case had gone on for years and prior restraining orders had expired. The victim was being stalked by the suspect, who contacted the neighborhood places where she would do her errands and asked store clerks to report to him when she was there and what she was wearing. The suspect would use this information to scare and intimidate the victim. The suspect played on cultural barriers in the victim's diverse community to gain information from well-intentioned community members. The victim had tried to report the abuse to her family members but due to cultural expectations she was disregarded. I contacted a detective in another state and stalking charges were placed on the suspect with the use of our DV reports.

## Changing the approach to intimate partner sexual violence cases

As a result of cases like this, all DV calls in which there is a crime are now screened for all potential crimes, including IPSV. When interviewing the victim and forced sex or IPSV is disclosed, we caution officers to be prepared for what they might hear. Law enforcement should be prepared to hear about humiliating IPSV as well as related crimes, and may also hear of drug trafficking, parole violations, weapons offenses, and the like. It is critical to have a trained police response to get the victim to safety and to get detectives or specialty units involved. In rural or small departments, responding officers should be prepared to work the case themselves and further interview the victim.

The case of the woman who initially called to report harassing phone calls changed how we interview victims. When a sexual assault is disclosed in my jurisdiction, we are required to offer the victim a sexual assault advocate or a personal representative who may accompany her during an in-depth interview. Along with others, I recommend this practice (Women's Justice Center 2010). Often what the police officer may miss, the advocate will pick up on and vice versa. As police, we need to use all of our resources to capacity, and two heads are better than one (although of course the roles and responsibilities of law enforcement and advocates are different). Communicate with the advocate for the safety of the victim.

Also, I have found that when the police show empathy and an understanding of victimization, the victim feels comfortable to disclose. When this happens, victims may feel a bonding with the officer and there needs to be a professional boundary the officer does not cross. Victims may see an empathetic officer as their rescuer in time of need. When an interview is done with two professionals—two officers, or an officer and an advocate—there is less of a possibility of the victim "falling in love" with the officer. We now interview victims with two people.

## Developing an effective response to victims with disabilities

There may be particular challenges in responding to cases involving victims from the deaf community. Often when police have contact with deaf individuals, an exchange of notes is their form of communication.

That may be fine for very basic safety and factual information, but it is no substitute for a trained sign language interpreter. An interpreter can provide a more accurate representation of the victim's concerns and information. For an in-depth interview, I recommend using video recording of the victim and the interpreter. In the US, the National Sheriffs' Association (2008) has detailed recommendations for responding to victims with a variety of disabilities.

## Dealing with language barriers

In a case I handled that brought home the importance of addressing language barriers, a non-English-speaking woman was arrested for assaulting her husband by stabbing him with a pencil. Further investigation revealed prior hang-up calls from the residence to the emergency dispatcher, and in fact the arrested female was being abused by her husband. The incident with the pencil was self-defense, although the husband called the police. The use of interpreters revealed the suspect husband was having sex with his wife in front of her small children. He was likely grooming the children for abuse, and the victim was submitting to sex only after he unlawfully imprisoned her in the home, taking the phone away from her and isolating her. The case was effectively concluded, but it highlighted the need to consider the use of an interpreter, even on what appears to be a simple case. If there is a language barrier it can result in an even bigger obstacle to justice for a victim. At my agency every police officer is issued a cell phone and we have a language line for 24-hour access to interpreters. Unless emergency and immediate safety concerns exist, it is best not to use friends or family as interpreters in DV situations (Law Society of England and Wales 2012).

## Strategies to deal with intimate partner sexual violence offenders

### Interview the offender promptly

Often, attention is focused on blaming the victim for DV or IPSV. I focus attention on what the suspect does. In my experience, the interview with the suspect and the suspect examination are often delayed and problematic. For example, police have arrived at the scene of DV and uncovered IPSV, and the offender has fled. The offender may already have warrants or may be violating and/or absconding from parole or probation—or he may simply have fled the scene to avoid police. A common scenario in the US is that a DV detective is looking for the offender and the offender is arrested by patrol officers of another jurisdiction.

If the suspect is available, he should be interviewed as soon as possible, preferably before he gets an attorney or gets on the phone at jail and starts calling the victim or potential witnesses. When I believe the window of opportunity for interviewing is tight, I expedite the process. I carry a digital recorder, as all police officers should, and I have conducted interviews in the back of a police car or before we got to jail. It is not uncommon in my unit for us to do many interviews of DV suspects on scene or immediately after being located.

Police can eliminate possible defenses simply by getting a statement as soon as possible. Questioning should be done prior to arraignment but after the suspect is read his rights. Procedures may need to be modified for agencies outside the US, which have different requirements. Once the investigation has yielded enough facts and evidence to obtain a suspect statement, do it as soon as practical to lock that suspect into a story, which may change over time. Many of these statements are easily disproven by a good evidence-based case that anticipates possible defense strategies (Archambault 2002).

## Go the extra mile to get a suspect statement

A common defense will be "she attacked me" or "the sex was consensual." The totality of the circumstances can show the acts were not consensual and there was force used. The bottom line is we need the statement and what evidence the suspect may present along with it. When we do not get the suspect interviewed, the case is more challenging. Every interview we ever do, no matter how short, is worth it; for example, the suspect may talk about new witnesses and present alibis that do not hold up. The most common scenario is the suspect realizing after the interview and "seeing our hand" that he should plead guilty—and many have done so. Plea bargains save victims (and their children) from the further traumatization of a trial.

## Locate the offender

Law enforcement personnel should be aware of the system their agency uses for notification that a sought-after person is arrested elsewhere. Be prepared to receive notice 24 hours a day so you can get to the interview as soon as practical. Many agencies will attach a warrant notification slip to their warrants to notify you, or flag a name so that other officers know you are looking for that suspect and will notify you when they have contact with him.

## Prepare for the interview

I ask the arresting officer about the circumstances of the arrest and the suspect's demeanor. I have the case file with me, including DV history, criminal history, and photos of the victim and evidence. I usually interview the suspect with another officer. The second officer may be the suspect's parole or probation officer. It could also be the officer who took the initial report or the case detective. A parole officer may have rapport with the suspect and have additional knowledge of the suspect's work, probation conditions, vehicles the suspect drives, or other victims he has assaulted.

## Nuts and bolts of interviewing intimate partner sexual violence suspects

I start the contact with the suspect by introducing myself and the other officer. I let the suspect know I am concerned about the case and I want to get his side of the story. I build rapport with him and tell him I will read him his rights. I get the suspect settled in a comfortable interview room with privacy, usually at the jail. I make sure he has water and a comfortable seat, and that we do not have distractions. I make an audio or video recording of the interview with his consent and his rights on the record.

I start with what I call my comparison questions. These questions are nonadversarial and meant to be easy for the suspect to answer—things like his name, date of birth, what city he was born in, and his address and phone number. I am looking at his mannerisms in reaction to these questions to establish a baseline of nondeceptive communication skills and demeanor.

I try to get basic facts about his relationship with the victim, thereby establishing the basis for an intimate partner DV case.

This usually involves asking about where they met, how long they have dated, where they have lived, who works and how much is the rent, and who pays the rent. I am establishing them as household members or intimate partners and I may ask if they have a sexual relationship and if they have children in common. I am also trying to establish who wields the power and control as the suspect describes the dynamics of the relationship. For example, I may learn that he met her at rehab, he pays the rent, it is his place, they have lived together for a year, she is scared he will kick her out, and she has nowhere to go.

I let the suspect give his side of the story. Then I confront him with the facts of the case and get his explanations for the crime— or as many offenders call it, "the accident" or unintentional act, or consensual act. I then re-confront with the evidence and photos of any injuries, and let him minimize or confess. I give him an opportunity to "sugar coat" incriminating statements and admissions; interviewers call this letting him have an "out" or explanation.

I ask if he thinks the victim is or has ever been scared of him. If so, then why? I get amazing responses and confessions in this manner. I ask about his criminal history. I recall one DV offender who had numerous prior sexual assault arrests and no convictions. Ask about the history so that door can be opened later in court if possible. Confront him with any deceptive statements and ask why.

## Coordination with system partners
### An innovative team model
In my jurisdiction, a specialized unit called the Domestic Violence Prosecution Center (DVPC) is an innovative arrangement for prosecution, police, victim advocates, probation/parole officers, and community partners to address all DV crimes, including IPSV. In conjunction with the victim statement, the DVPC has had a major impact on prosecution and overall DV response.

Members of the DVPC such as prosecutors, victim advocates, police, probation, and parole have a trained response to the issue of victim recantation so that the case does not just go away; rather, the reason for recantation is addressed and dealt with. Professionals are co-located and have easy access to each other and work as a team on cases.

Another innovation that promotes positive results in IPSV cases is the cross-deputization of prosecutors at the DVPC. If the case moves from misdemeanor to felony, it stays with the same prosecutor and advocate, often resulting in a higher conviction rate and less frustration for both victims and law enforcement. Having a co-located, dedicated, and well-trained team results in easier and more effective interviews of victims and witnesses.

### Community partners and police training

One way for a community to address IPSV is to train police and community partners together. These partners may be emergency dispatchers, prosecutors, probation officers, child protection investigators, and advocates. You may consider participating in cross-training sexual assault advocates and DV victim advocates (see Chapter 9). To address teen relationship abuse, work closely and train with police officers assigned to schools and gang units. In Washington State, a grant project supported the creation of training resources on IPSV for police officers (Washington Association of Sheriffs and Police Chiefs; Office of Crime Victims Advocacy 2009).

## Self-care and the stress of working intimate partner sexual violence cases

Working in DV/IPSV can be emotionally and physically draining. I spent years on call and had most days off interrupted by a phone call and then going into work at a crime scene or to interview a suspect. Then there were the trials and "crisis of the day" that came every day, such as a surveillance looking for a stalker or assisting another agency. Every person working in this field must determine how long he or she can do it before a break is needed. All of us have a different timeline.

The words that best describe what many go through is "compassion fatigue." Know that when fatigue sets in it is healthy and acceptable to take a break. Also, have other interests that make you feel good.

When I am training police officers who seem burned out or lacking in compassion, I remind them, "Always remember that the victim is someone's daughter, sister, or mother. If your daughter, sister, or mother went to the police, are you the person you would want to respond and investigate?"

# References

Archambault, J. (2002) *Dangerous Liaisons: Effectively Recognizing and Responding to Sexual Assault.* Available at www.iowacasa.org/UserDocs/E1_Archambault_DANGEROUS_LIAISONS_PPT_Notes.pdf, accessed January 20, 2013.

Futures Without Violence (2012) *Safety Cards: Did You Know Your Relationship Affects Your Health?* San Francisco, CA: Futures Without Violence. Available at https://secure3.convio.net/fvpf/site/Ecommerce/42226815?VIEW_PRODUCT=true&product_id=1722&store_id=1241, accessed March 1, 2013.

International Association of Chiefs of Police (n.d.) *Sexual Assault Incident Reports: Investigative Strategies.* Available at www.theiacp.org/LinkClick.aspx?fileticket=PxEJMvQbU7c=&tabid=392, accessed December 1, 2012.

Law Society of England and Wales (2012) *Use of Interpreters in Criminal Cases.* London: The Law Society. Available at www.lawsociety.org.uk/advice/practice-notes/interpreters-in-criminal-cases, accessed March 4, 2013.

Logan, T.K., Cole, J., and Shannon, L. (2007) "A mixed-methods examination of sexual coercion and degradation among women in violent relationships who do and do not report forced sex." *Violence and Victims 22*, 1, 71–94.

Long, J.G. (2009) "Intimate Partner Sexual Assault." In *Sexual Assault in the Context of Domestic Violence.* Olympia, WA: Washington Coalition of Sexual Assault Programs. Available at www.wcsap.org/sexual-assault-context-domestic-violence, accessed February 3, 2013.

National Center for Women and Policing (2009) "Successfully Investigating IPSV: Considerations for Law Enforcement." In *Sexual Assault in the Context of Domestic Violence.* Olympia, WA: Washington Coalition of Sexual Assault Programs.

National Sheriffs' Association (2008) *First Response to Victims of Crime.* Available at www.ojp.usdoj.gov/ovc/publications/infores/pdftxt/FirstResponseGuidebook.pdf, accessed January 17, 2013.

Police Executive Research Forum (2012) *Improving the Police Response to Sexual Assault.* Available at http://policeforum.org/library/critical-issues-in-policing-series/SexualAssaulttext_web.pdf, accessed January 21, 2013.

Rennison, C.M. (2002) *Rape and Sexual Assault: Reporting to Police and Medical Attention, 1992–2000.* Washington, DC: Bureau or Justice Statistics, US Department of Justice. Available at http://bjs.gov/content/pub/pdf/rsarp00.pdf, accessed April 12, 2013.

United Nations Task Force on Drugs and Crime (2010) *Handbook on Effective Police Responses to Violence Against Women.* New York: United Nations. Available at www.unodc.org/documents/justice-and-prison-reform/Violence_Against_Women_handbook.EN.pdf, accessed January 18, 2013.

Washington Association of Sheriffs and Police Chiefs; Office of Crime Victims Advocacy (2009) *Manual for Law Enforcement Agencies: Stalking and Sexual Assault within the Context of Domestic Violence.* Available at www.waspc.org/files.php?bfid=3305, accessed August 16, 2013.

Women's Justice Center (2010) *Advocating for Victims of Sex Crimes During the Police Investigation.* Available at www.justicewomen.com/handbook/advocatingsexcrimes.html, accessed January 17, 2013.

CHAPTER 16

# Forensic Medical Assessment in Intimate Partner Sexual Violence

Vanita Parekh and Angela Williams

## Overview

Health care workers have a crucial role in supporting people who experience intimate partner violence (IPV). The accurate recording of history and findings from patients by their health care worker may benefit patients' cases greatly should they choose to enter the legal system (Easteal and Feerick 2005). Health care workers may be anxious regarding both documentation of the history and findings, as well as the delivery of medico-legal information (reports and courts) to the criminal justice system. Whilst their evidence may be considered at best corroborative in this forum, patients may experience significant benefits, including early identification of health-related issues and injuries, improvement in health outcomes, validation of the patient's report, and assistance with future reporting.

Forensic medicine is the discipline of medicine that pertains to the law. Despite a significant component of the consultation revolving around accurate documentation, collection of forensic specimens, and the recording of evidence (the forensic component), the medical component is always the priority. IPV and intimate partner sexual violence (IPSV) are known to be significant risk factors in the morbidity and mortality of a person and carry the potential of serious and persistent health sequelae (Campbell 2002; see also Chapter 4). Data specifically addressing IPSV are scarce; however, the rate of disclosure of IPV appears to be higher in pregnant women and in the postnatal period (Keeling and Mason 2011). The early involvement of a health care worker who provides medical care and is informed of the forensic elements of the examination is therefore essential to the ongoing health and wellbeing of a patient and the progression of a case through the legal system.

# Identifying intimate partner violence and intimate partner sexual violence

Whilst there are studies, surveys, and reported crime data to suggest that IPV affects between 10 percent and 50 percent of women in their lifetime (Heise, Ellseberg, and Gottemoeller 1999), as well as men and young people, the actual disclosure by victims of their experiences of violence is considered low (Mouzos and Makkai 2004). Many victims never tell anyone about IPV, let alone report to an authority on the matter. Patients may seek medical care for the long-term physical and emotional effects of IPV without disclosing a history of violence. This is also true of patients with acute injuries (such as fractures) following violence who present to emergency departments with alternative explanations of their injury causation. It is therefore important that the practitioner consider the possibility of IPV when assessing patients in their care and be prepared to offer medical and forensic contributions to their management.

In most cases of sexual assault, the offender is known to the victim. There is an overwhelming predominance of partner and ex-partner offenders who are often involved in multiple acts (sexual, physical, emotional, and financial) of violence, on multiple occasions (Australian Bureau of Statistics 2005). Health care workers should give careful consideration to asking victims of IPV whether there have been incidences of sexual assault. Victims of IPV and sexual assault are often forensically and medically managed in a similar way.

# Barriers to reporting

There may be reluctance from the victim to report IPSV in the first instance, and she may recant at a later date. A number of barriers to reporting to police and health care workers exist for those who experience IPSV, including the relationship with the offender, shared children, lack of finances and support systems, and past history of abuse. Previous experiences with health, legal, and police systems and professionals may adversely influence decisions to report. Health care workers providing care should bear in mind the reluctance to report, barriers to reporting, and the possibility of subsequent engagement in the legal process. Health care workers should communicate to the victim that their primary focus is the health and welfare of the patient. In particular, patients should be told that they have the right to withdraw from services offered by health, police, or legal systems.

## Connection to advocacy services

Many jurisdictions have advocacy, support, and other agencies to assist victims of interpersonal violence including IPSV. Full details regarding referral and process may be found in Chapter 12 in the "Medical responses" section.

## The investigation of intimate partner sexual violence

IPSV investigation is primarily the role of law enforcement agencies. Assistance from health care workers in this investigation (with the patient's consent) can greatly assist law enforcement agents in their decision-making about allegations and processes. Health care professionals may also work with child protection, housing, and other support agencies. Forensic evidence collection principles that apply to sexual violence will apply similarly to IPV.

## Preparation prior to the forensic medical examination

Contemporaneous recording from the medical consultation enables the evidence to be presented before the legal system in the most robust manner. Preparing the case and the documentation at the time of the examination will prove highly valuable should the health care worker be required to provide evidence in legal proceedings, as the courtroom requires accurate descriptions of events (particularization) at the time at which they occurred. Where further information or assessment comes to light, the health care worker should note additional information, including the date and time it was added to the medical record.

### Recording of the details of initial contact involving the case

Written details about the involvement of the health care worker provide the context for the consultation setting for future reference and legal purposes. Identification of the referral source begins the recording of a series of events (with accurate times/dates) and a clear identification of the involvement of each person. The details recorded initially should be regarded as early information, but may need to be further explored in order to direct the consultation.

## Early agency briefing

Information given by police and other agencies should be detailed and documented, as well as the identity, role, and position of the referral source. Information from the referral source should be kept informative and concise as it may be the source of legal argument in the future.

## Setting up the consultation

A quiet, safe consultation space that provides for privacy, confidentiality, and discretion is preferable. This environment promotes the exchange of difficult information, especially as the patient will provide details of a reported assault. Certain aspects of the history may need to be clarified and documented; a safe and secure consultation space can benefit the patient's ability to speak freely. Where the primary purpose of the examination is to conduct both the forensic and medical components to contribute to the justice system, the health care worker should ensure the patient knows that, with her consent, the information obtained will be shared with a third party. Rapport building is fundamental to providing forensic and medical care; further details are found in Chapter 12.

## Precise and contemporaneous record-keeping

Precise and contemporaneous record-keeping cannot be over-emphasized; it may be many years before any records may be used for evidentiary purposes. Where possible, documentation of the patient's words will limit misinterpretation or misunderstanding of the content of the history. The health care worker can clarify the patient's meaning through direct questions.

## Process of obtaining consent

Obtaining valid consent must precede the forensic medical assessment. Not only does it provide the permission to examine the patient, but it also demonstrates to the patient that her concerns are being taken seriously. Consent should be obtained for:

- history
- examination
- collection of specimens for medical investigations to diagnose any medical problems
- collection of specimens for forensic purposes
- photography for the specific purposes of record, to provide future opinion, for peer review, and for teaching of other specified groups, such as police, doctors, or nurses
- treatment of any identified medical conditions and injuries
- permission to access medical records related to current or past reports
- permission to notify counselors or other persons (as relevant) of attendance
- permission to notify law enforcement agencies.

A consent form with the above information should be included in the patient's record. If consent is provided by another person or agency, or there are any limitations to consent, this information should be recorded specifically. Where practicable, the consent form should be signed by the person providing consent and witnessed by the health care worker.

## The presence of third parties during the consultation

A support person may be present during the consultation upon the patient's request. During a forensic medical examination, it is important that the support person is not the person to whom the first complaint was made, as this may compromise the validity of their evidence should it ever be required. The authors' experience is that the most appropriate person is an independent advocate or medical chaperone—that is, a nurse with appropriate training—and this preference should be clearly explained to the patient so that she is fully informed of the reasoning. The role of the support person should be clarified with the patient. The role may vary depending upon whether the support person is chosen primarily to support the victim or to assist in the clinical aspects of the examination or both of these roles. This will limit the likelihood of miscommunication, reduce the potential for DNA contamination, provide support for the victim, and ensure the rapport between the health care worker and the patient remains intact.

## Aspects of the history provided by the patient

A history of the offense should be obtained using the patient's words where possible. It is important to record:

1. time and date of the assault

2. time since the assault

3. the location of the assault

4. assailant details, limited to the relationship between the offender and the patient

5. details of the reported violence including:

    a. drug and alcohol use by the offender and patient

    b. areas of the body that have been involved in any altercation

    c. the nature of any object(s) used to inflict any trauma

    d. specific questions about attempted strangulation and head injury

6. whether any sexual assault acts have occurred, with particular reference to oral, vaginal, and anal penetration; all forms of penetration (or attempted penetration) are considered by patients to amount to sexual assault and therefore it is important to ask about these

7. current symptoms, including difficulty breathing, vocalizing, or swallowing; pain, bleeding, or injury; and genital symptoms (pain or bleeding)

8. medical treatment already received including details of who provided the care, when, where, and the type of any care provided

9. any relevant medical, surgical, or psychiatric history, including details of any allergies and medications

10. the family tree including relevant parties and children; this should include the biological relationships of each child and the location of each child

11. housing (consideration should be given to the ability to access safe housing)

12. safety issues, including the presence of a safety plan, support persons, and agencies

13. any previous episodes of violence by the same and other partners.

## Clinical examination of the patient

### General considerations

Much has been written about forensic medical examinations in the key forensic medicine textbooks. This section will identify the key issues; further reference may be required from forensic medicine textbooks. Useful readings are given at the end of this chapter.

It is important to recognize the amount of courage that it takes for a person to disclose IPV of any form and to subject themselves to an intimate medical examination. At all stages of the consultation this should be acknowledged, and permission should be sought for each part of the consultation—for example, the history, the examination, disrobing, and photography. Attention should also be given to ensuring safety, dignity, privacy, and confidentiality.

### Documentation of findings

The identity of any person present for the examination apart from the examiner and patient should be recorded. The patient's general appearance should be noted objectively—for example, "tearful" rather than "upset." Any other initial observations should be noted, including mental state, cognitive or physical impairments, or signs of intoxication.

The examination will be guided by the history of the reported assault, although a complete external examination is best practice. Negative findings (such as the absence of injuries, signs, and symptoms) must also be reported alongside signs of recent injury, illness, and any other notable feature. If a complete examination is not undertaken, this should be recorded.

Medical findings should, where practicable, be documented on body charts in order to detail each injury. Where appropriate photography equipment is available, injuries should be photographed and a record kept of the date, time, and photographer.

## Nongenital injury

Any wounds identified on the body should be classified into the following categories: abrasions, bruises, lacerations, incised wounds, and burns. In order to accurately describe a wound, detail regarding the wound site, size, shape, surrounds, color, margins, foreign debris, age, and depth is required. Particular attention should be given to injury patterns that may assist in identifying the mechanism of injury. For example, careful photo-documentation or drawings should be included to detail patterns of bite marks, implement marks (e.g. sole of shoe, edge of knife), patterns of burns (splash, scald, radiation), or injuries that mimic each other (e.g. multiple blows with similar objects) or are in close proximity (e.g. fingertip marks).

The examiner should be sure to examine all body parts (with consent), as it is common to have injuries obscured by clothing or in places where the victim was not aware of the presence of injuries. Injuries to the head and neck, chest and back, and arms and legs are common, including on the scalp, behind the ears, on the backs of arms, and on breasts. Consideration should be given to the seriousness of the injury and need for referral to the emergency department or other specialists for ongoing investigation and medical management.

## Genital-anal injury

It is important to note that frequently there may be no signs of injury, genital or otherwise, in those who experience IPSV. There is conflicting published research with regard to the prevalence of genital injury from a sexual assault committed by an intimate partner (Moller et al. 2012; Palmer et al. 2004). There may indeed be little difference in prevalence between injury in these assaults versus sexual assault by an unknown assailant (Jones et al. 2004). A speculum may be used in the process of the examination. Injuries should be recorded, and any foreign material should be collected for forensic analysis. With consent, the examination should include careful inspection of the external genitalia and anus with consideration of an internal examination where appropriate.

## Collection of DNA

Collection of DNA should be considered; however, it should be noted that, in cases of IPSV, the presence of DNA may exist from recent sexual activity, routine household contact, contamination, and transference from shared objects and people. However, the collection of such samples may be necessary to corroborate case details and exclude persons of interest.

## Collection of forensic specimens

Forensic specimens may be collected at the time of the examination. Examples include cases where the clothing and the underlying wound may together tell a story or blood and/or urine are required for the purpose of toxicological analysis. Care must be taken to ensure the integrity and continuity of any forensic specimens collected. Advice should be sought regarding packaging and labeling, storage and handling, and maintaining the continuity of the chain of evidence.

## Documentation of other aspects of the consultation

Details of any medication or treatment provided should be recorded, and if possible, contact with the patient's regular medical provider should be made with the patient's consent.

# The impact on children of witnessing intimate partner violence and intimate partner sexual violence

Much work has been done (Richards 2011) on assessing the impact that IPV has on children and young people exposed to violence in their family or household. Results of studies have shown that children and young people exposed to IPV have an increased risk of problems with mental health, behavioral, and learning difficulties. The emotional effects of witnessing IPV in the family can be severe and lifelong. Whilst direct injury (such as when a child is assaulted by a parent) and indirect injury (resulting from getting in the way of an assault on a parent) may be identified and managed, they can be significant and require a concurrent forensic medical assessment. Short-term health effects and the long-term health issues of IPV (direct or witnessed) contribute to the child's risk of morbidity and mortality and are indeed considered cumulative with each subsequent event. As described in the section on "Custody and visitation" in Chapter 18, the effect of

IPSV on children has been largely overlooked, but growing up in a household where IPSV takes place may pose unique risks to children.

Where IPV is occurring in a family in which children are raised, health care workers must consider their role in mandatory reporting. Each health care worker should be familiar with the reporting requirements within his or her jurisdiction. Mandatory reporting should be documented within the medical notes as well as any concerns and discussion with the patient.

## Follow up of a patient presenting after an episode (or many episodes) of intimate partner sexual violence

As discussed earlier, serious and persistent health sequelae have been identified as a result of IPV and can significantly contribute to the risk of morbidity and mortality in individuals. The most common health sequelae are covered in Chapter 12 and (as identified by Breiding, Black, and Ryan 2008) include:

- mental health issues—depression, anxiety, suicide, and eating disorders
- substance use and abuse—illicit drugs, medications, alcohol, and smoking
- obstetric and gynecological illness/disorder—pregnancy and postnatal complications, sexually transmitted illnesses, and cervical cancer
- gastrointestinal complaints—nausea, abdominal or pelvic pain, vomiting, or difficulty eating
- pain disorders.

A follow-up consultation should be conducted two weeks after the initial consultation (not withstanding the need to seek medical care in the meantime) to ensure obstetric care and sexual health needs are identified and managed. It is ideal to encourage an ongoing relationship with a trusted health care provider to minimize the risk of long-term problems related to the assault.

# References

Australian Bureau of Statistics (2005) *Personal Safety Survey*. Canberra: Australian Bureau of Statistics. Available at www.abs.gov.au/ausstats/abs@.nsf/mf/4906.0, accessed March 23, 2013.

Breiding, M.J., Black, M.C., and Ryan G.W. (2008) "Chronic disease and health risk behaviors associated with intimate partner violence—18 U.S. states/territories, 2005." *Annals of Epidemiology 18*, 538–544.

Campbell, J. (2002) "Health consequences of intimate partner violence." *The Lancet 359* (April 13), 1331–1336.

Easteal, P. and Feerick, C. (2005) "Sexual assault by male partners: is the license still valid?" *Flinders Journal of Law Reform 8*, 2, 185–207.

Heise, L., Ellsberg, M., and Gottemoeller, M. (1999) "Ending violence against women." *Population Report, Series L, No. 11*. Baltimore, MD: Johns Hopkins University School of Public Health.

Jones, J.S., Wynn, B.N., Kroeze, B., Dunnuck, C. *et al.* (2004) "Comparison of sexual assaults by strangers versus known assailants in a community-based population." *American Journal of Emergency Medicine 22*, 6, 454–459.

Keeling, J. and Mason, T. (2011) "Postnatal disclosure of domestic violence: comparison with disclosure in the first trimester of pregnancy." *Journal of Clinical Nursing 20*, 1–2, 103–110.

Moller, A.S., Backstrom, T., Sondergaard, H.P., and Helstrom, L. (2012) "Patterns of injury and reported violence depending on relationship to assailant in female Swedish sexual assault victims." *Journal of Interpersonal Violence*, doi:10.1177/0886260512441261.

Mouzos, J. and Makkai, T. (2004) *Women's Experience of Male Violence: Findings for the Australian Component of the International Violence against Women Survey*. Canberra: Australian Institute of Criminology Research and Public Policy. Available at www.aic.gov.au/publications/current%20series/rpp/41-60/rpp56.aspx, accessed July 22, 2012.

Palmer, C.M., McNulty, A.M., D'Este, C., and Donovan, B. (2004) "Genital injuries in women reporting sexual assault." *Sexual Health 1*, 55–59.

Richards, K. (2011) "Children's exposure to domestic violence in Australia." *Trends and Issues, No. 419*. Canberra: Australian Institute of Criminology.

# Useful reading

Payne-James, J., Busuttil, A., and Smock, W. (2003) *Forensic Medicine: Clinical and Pathological Aspects*. Cambridge: Greenwich Medical Media.

Stark, M.M. (2011) *Clinical Forensic Medicine: A Physician's Guide*, Third Edition. New York: Humana Press.

White, C. (2010) *Sexual Assault: A Forensic Clinician's Practice Guide*. Manchester, UK: St. Mary's Sexual Assault Referral Centre.

World Health Organization (2003) *The Guidelines for Medico-Legal Care for Victims of Sexual Violence*. Available at http://whqlibdoc.who.int/publications/2004/924154628X.pdf.

CHAPTER 17

# Advice for Criminal Justice Staff and/or Advocates to Aid Intimate Partner Sexual Violence Survivors

Patricia Easteal AM

## Introduction

In this chapter, I give advice to professionals and support people who have a client facing court, to ensure that they prepare her for the numerous obstacles that may appear in her path to seeking justice. Previous chapters have described how rape culture myths permeate the community and the criminal justice system. There seems to be a cognitive continuum, with "authentic rape" or "real rape" (e.g. where the rapist is a stranger who uses physical force; the victim sustains injuries, and reports the incident immediately) at one end and "not quite legitimate assault" (which might involve nonphysical coercion, delay in reporting, and/or victim "provocation") at the other end (Edwards *et al.* 2011; Estrich 1987; Stubbs 2003). These beliefs about "real" rape are ingrained within our communities. For instance, Clark (2007) found that 98 percent of Australian respondents believed that these types of myths were relevant in determining the "seriousness" of a sexual assault. Judges, jurors, and legal practitioners are not immune to these beliefs (Easteal and Gani 2005; Neame and Heenan 2003; S.C. Taylor and Mouzos 2006; N. Taylor and Gassner 2009). For example, although the immunity of husbands from prosecution and a "license to rape" have been abolished for decades in Western industrial countries around the world, partner rape has particularly low reporting, prosecution, and conviction rates (Easteal and Feerick 2005; Easteal and Gani 2005; Heenan and Murray 2006; Kelly, Lovett, and Regan 2005; Lievore 2003, 2005). Judicial use of phrases like "little short of rape" and "special relationship" to describe violent marriages and sexual assault are indicative of how some judges perceive intimate partner sexual violence (IPSV) to be at the less "real" rape end of the continuum (Easteal 1998; Easteal and Gani 2005). These sexual assaults may be seen as less severe or even acceptable (Kennedy *et al.* 2009). For instance, Justice Hulme stated in his decision in a case of sexual assault against a woman who was once in a consensual sexual relationship with the defendant:

> Although fearful of the Appellant the Complainant at least knew him and no doubt was capable of making some assessment of the situation... The case was not one where a victim walking through a lonely street or park at night is seized by a complete stranger about whom she knows nothing and who, for all the victim knows, may well kill her when the intercourse is over... (*Boney* v. *R* 2008, 106)

Sentencing language like this illustrates some judges' perception of the greater harm of rape by a stranger:

> ...the facts in this case are most serious. They are disturbing in that they occurred...in circumstances where you did not know the victim prior to this assault. It is also disturbing that this offending occurred in her bedroom at the university premises, and that she was entitled to feel safe. Your behaviour was totally unacceptable. (*R* v. *Ipia* 2008, 3)

> ...an extremely serious example of the offence of rape... Such conduct was craven and despicable... She was unknown to you, taken from the street where she had the right to feel safe. She was attacked without explanation and suffered extremely serious injuries. (*R* v. *Gill* 2008, 46–47)

*Tip: Prepare your client or the person whom you are supporting for attitudes like these held by some players in the criminal justice system. Give her a copy of this book to read with bookmarks for the sections like this chapter that will help provide an understanding of rape myths and the courts. Knowledge is power.*

## Attrition

Be aware that the women who are pushing through into the courts represent the very tip of the iceberg of IPSV victims. In the context of the mythology about "real rape" it is not surprising that the high rate of discontinuances or dropping of charges that we see in all sexual assault cases is even higher in partner rape (Heenan 2004; Lea, Lanvers, and Shaw 2003). Prosecutors are looking for the most *solid* cases to run with, since they know that the chances of conviction in sexual assault matters are low. Therefore, if there are any differences between what a victim said to police in different interviews and/or in her preliminary hearing testimony, the prosecutor may label the victim as "not reliable" and drop the case, thus preempting the defense from raising these discrepancies at trial. Prosecutors are also more likely to pursue a case if there is forensic evidence.

*Tip: If you are supporting a victim, encourage her to have an examination, and it may be a good idea to make her aware that what she says seemingly in an unofficial way to a police officer at the hospital may be compared with a later statement.*

A victim sometimes requests that charges be dropped. She may be influenced (perhaps subtly and sometimes very directly) by the police and/or the prosecutors who advise that there is little hope of a guilty verdict (Easteal and Feerick 2005). Or, her cross-examination at the committal hearing (indictment) may have been an ordeal and therefore she may simply lack the energy to continue.

*Tip: Police, prosecutors, and support workers could be more sensitive to the power that they may wield in influencing the victim and more aware of their words and tone.*

A paper-based committal is therefore ideal since it reduces the number of times (in theory) that a victim witness will be cross-examined. In some areas (e.g. in Australia all states and territories except New South Wales and Tasmania) there are laws allowing for the recording of witnesses' evidence at a special hearing held before the actual trial. This also theoretically restricts the "cross" to once.

*Tip: Find out if your jurisdiction provides for applications for paper committals and/or pre-recording.*

Be aware that even if there are provisions for "paper-based" committal proceedings for adult victims of sexual assault, the court may still require the woman to attend to give evidence and be cross-examined in some of these jurisdictions. The legislative statutes are usually written to allow for discretion (Kennedy and Easteal 2011). It is not uncommon for the defense to apply to cross-examine the complainant.

Also, the special pre-recorded evidence may only apply to a certain subgrouping of victims such as "vulnerable" or "special." How "vulnerable" and "special" are interpreted and applied may preclude some victims from consideration. There may be provisions allowing for the re-use of victim witness evidence at subsequent hearings. The witnesses and trials that the provisions cover differ from country to country and state to state.

*Tip: Be aware these provisions may only be available to specific categories of witnesses and often have preconditions that need to be fulfilled before they are ordered. Expert evidence showing the vulnerability of the victim witness might be necessary (Kennedy and Easteal 2011).*

# Trial

If the case makes it through the prosecutors' filtering, aside from the fact that it may take years before it goes to court, the complainant needs to be prepared by a support person for certain realities of the courtroom. She may experience frustration since she has no lawyer or advocate in the trial. The defendant may not be cross-examined about matters that she feels are relevant. Further, the judge may not allow certain evidence like history of domestic violence even though such evidence may be vital, and its inadmissibility may contribute to an acquittal. The complainant might feel invalidated and isolated:

> I was on the stand for a day and a bit, really a day and a half. It was a terribly traumatic experience. I kept on trying to talk to my QC [Queen's Counsel, or prosecutor] and he kept on saying you're just another witness. If you tell me anything that's not in your statement I'll have to tell the other side so I don't want you to tell me anything… He kept on saying I'm not your QC, you're just another witness… I just found the whole thing very distressing. (Easteal and McOrmond-Plummer 2006, p.199)

*Tip: One answer to these issues is to make victim support/advocacy a higher priority (Victorian Law Reform Commission 2004). Work in your community to ensure that there is a process whereby someone guides and mentors the victim from the initial complaint to the final court hearing. This would ideally be someone who has some authority and the spirit to insist that justice is done. In addition, prepare the person you are assisting through the criminal justice process by forewarning them about these potential sources of frustration for rape victims.*

Rape victims' evidence in general is seen as intrinsically unreliable and that sexual assault allegations are "very easy to fabricate but extremely difficult to refute" (Victorian Law Reform Commission 2001, p.155). There is however a gradation of credibility based on attributes of the victim, with some victims seen as more unreliable than others. Those that are seen as *extra* unreliable do include partner rape victims (Easteal and Feerick 2005; Heenan and Murray 2006; Lievore 2005). These victims may be seen as especially unreliable since delayed reporting can lead to the disappearance of evidence and can then be used against the woman in court to further discredit her as a witness. The rape myth operating here is that the "good" victim reports immediately. With IPSV, as discussed in earlier chapters, prompt disclosure and reporting are not the norm.

As is so often the case in all sexual assault trials, it is the IPSV complainant's words that end up being on trial. Heenan (2004, p.7) describes it this way:

> ...securing convictions in male partner rape cases remains difficult for prosecutors. Like most rape trials, the defence is likely to devote considerable attention to attacking the victim's character and credibility. Where there has been a relationship history, the defence has a greater pool of information about the complainant to draw on in reconstructing a version of events set on undermining what she alleges happened. At best, the approach is designed to raise a reasonable doubt about her veracity in the minds of the jury. At worst, she will be exposed to a gruelling process of cross-examination that will remain transfixed on the detail of previous consensual sexual activity she once engaged in with her partner—the man she now accuses of rape.

Indeed, the woman may be made to recount every painful detail of the rape, and may be publicly attacked and blamed by the defense in a courtroom dominated by males (Parkinson and Cowan 2008).

> To be honest, if I was ever in a position where any of these things had happened to me, I don't think I would go to the police. It's not the police, it's the justice system. You can't find justice in an unjust system and that's what it is. (Sexual Offences Child Abuse Unit officer) (Parkinson and Cowan 2008, p.96)

## Cross-examination: consent

The interpretation of the meaning of consent or its negation (the lack thereof) continues to be problematic. As sexual assault is a criminal offense, the burden of proving each element of the offense beyond reasonable doubt lies with the prosecution. Thus, the prosecution must prove (generally, across jurisdictions) that the defendant had sexual intercourse with the complainant without her consent (physical element) and that the defendant knew, or was reckless to the possibility, that the complainant was not consenting (fault element). The centrality of consent to both the physical and fault elements of the offense of sexual assault is problematic, and these problems seem to be magnified in the context of partner rape. Unsurprisingly though in a partner context, proving a lack of consent (the physical element) or an absence of consent that the defendant knew of, but chose to ignore (the fault element), is difficult because of the history of consensual intercourse. The underlying premise seems to be that if the victim has had consensual sex with her ex-partner the day before or even months before, any future act loses potential interpretation as rape (Easteal and Feerick 2005). Even if evidence of the complainant's sexual reputation is not admissible and evidence of the complainant's sexual activities is not admissible in a sexual offense proceeding without leave of the court, this does not usually apply to evidence of specific sexual activities between the victim and the accused in sexual offense proceedings. For Australian examples see the Criminal Procedure Act 1986 (NSW), s293; Evidence (Miscellaneous Provisions) Act 1991 (ACT), s51(2); and *Taylor* v. *R* [2009]. As Heenan (2004, p.8) observed in her sample of Victorian trials:

> The aim of defence barristers in these cases was unashamedly directed at suggesting that consensual sex was more likely to have occurred on the occasion in question, just as it had in the past. Across the five trials, women were asked how often they had sex, when they started having sex, and whether they could speak to the general health of their sexual relationships. They were challenged about their versions of the regularity of sex, their alleged refusals to engage in sex, and their claims to often appease their male partners through submitting to sex.

*Tip: Check your jurisdiction's laws regarding evidence of previous consensual sex. Make sure that the complainant knows the type of questions that she is likely to be asked.*

# Importance of domestic violence history in arguing lack of consent

From the perspective of the partner rape victim, *fear* of physical force may be the source of coercion. If evidence of prior violence is not admitted and the incident is looked at in isolation from prior abuse, then the threat of force that vitiates or negates the victim's consent may not be comprehended. Evidence of prior violence is necessary to bring context to the victim's fear of the defendant, her feelings, and the reasons for her reaction at the time. As discussed in earlier chapters, other manifestations of domestic violence are not an uncommon backdrop to partner rape. Therefore, evidence of prior abuse can be vital to securing a conviction and to discharging the onus of proving that the defendant knew that the complainant was not consenting. This is demonstrated in *R* v. *C* [2003], where the court upheld the decision of the trial judge to admit the complainant's account of the circumstances leading to the rape:

> The appellant said he wanted to "make up" for hitting her, and asked to "make love," and the complainant said "no" but as she explained in her evidence, "I had to say it very gently because from past experience... I thought he would have done it again" (that is, hit her).

Some judges, who are perhaps more wary of "relationship evidence," are less likely to allow such evidence to be admitted. Judicial reasons include risk of unfair prejudice and the accused's right to a fair trial.

*Tip: Recognize the importance of antecedent violence and possibly use expert witness testimony or expert reports.*

# Cross-examination: consistency

The complainant may be cross-examined about a variety of issues that are designed to make her lose credibility. And, credibility as a witness unfortunately is equated with consistency. Rationality and logic work positively towards a witness's credit, whereas signs of emotion and trauma are likely to have an adverse effect (Heydon 2000). The victim witness is expected to remember every detail and be able to particularize. Defense lawyers' cross-examinations are often exhaustive and aimed at confusing the complainant about a number of details so that she appears unreliable. A witness may be asked questions that she can only answer "Yes" or "No" to, but which are impossible to answer in that way. The questions may be asked in a nonchronological sequence to confuse her further. Any evidence of inconsistency within a victim's testimony tends to be construed as evidence that the complaint was false, as opposed to appreciating how the trauma of sexual assault and how the discourse of "real rape" and a "culture of skepticism" may influence her memory and narrative of events (Kelly *et al.* 2005, pp.49–50).

*Tip: Advise the person you are supporting or your client to expect a focus on minor details, such as the precise sequence of events. In the context of partner rape in particular, these tactics work against the complainant, and consequently overshadow the actual rape. Have enough "rehearsals" with the victim-witness that she either has the level of detail at hand or you develop strategies of response. Develop a plan to assist her in dealing with confusion. Inform her that she can ask the judge for time out for a glass of water. Encourage her to make eye contact as much as possible with you or with another support person. Help establish a "reality check" by developing some signals. For example, advise her that you will touch your forehead as if to say, "This lawyer is trying to play with your head." If you clasp your hands it can be a message of strength and union.*

## Special measures

Laws have been enacted around the world in an attempt to provide the victim witness in rape cases with respect and dignity during the prosecution process. For example, following a famous English case (*R* v. *Ralston Edwards* 1996) where the accused personally cross-examined the victim for six days wearing the same clothes that he wore when he committed the offense, resulting in the victim having to leave the witness stand to be physically sick, a number of legal systems now prohibit examination by a self-represented accused.

There are now usually provisions in place for victims to have a support person present whilst they give their evidence. For instance, questions that barristers or attorneys can ask are regulated to some extent by law. Note though that regulations tend to be phrased with discretionary language. Prosecutors' and judges' discretion is exercised within a broader legal and social context, one that is susceptible to influence by the common societal beliefs about "real" rape and what constitutes a "vulnerable" witness, just to name a couple (Kennedy, Bartels, and Easteal 2012). For example, in the Australian Capital Territory, in deciding whether to order that the court be closed to

INTIMATE PARTNER SEXUAL VIOLENCE

the public, the court must consider whether the witness wants to give evidence in open court; and [whether] it is in the *interests of justice* that the witness give evidence in open court" (Evidence (Miscellaneous Provisions) Act 1991 (ACT), s81D(3)). What is seen as constituting the interests of justice depends upon the interpretation of the individual judicial officer.

Another example of a gray-colored (open to interpretation) measure to protect victim safe speaking: all Australian jurisdictions now have provisions in place that allow for the use of audiovisual links or closed circuit television and screening arrangements, although in some jurisdictions they are only available for children and "special witnesses."

*Tip: Check to see if courts can be closed in your area. Find out if your jurisdiction allows the adult rape victim witness to give her testimony in another room or with a partition. She will feel more comfortable and safer if she's not in the same room as her perpetrator. And check for indeterminate or "gray" language such as "vulnerable" and "special," ensuring that the person you are supporting will be considered as eligible for protective measures.*

## Final comments

There has been substantial reform to sexual assault laws, including the laws governing procedure and evidentiary principles in recent years. Unfortunately, in the context of partner rape, defendants continue to escape prosecution and victims continue to feel unheard and dissatisfied with the process. Further reform of the relevant laws would be helpful. However, education of police, the judiciary, and law enforcement officials is more likely to have a lasting positive effect. Existing laws are not perfect, but any reform will be ineffective unless accompanied by widespread education and efforts to increase community and criminal justice system perceptions that partner sexual assault is of equal (if not more) seriousness to sexual assault by a stranger, and should be treated by the legal system in the same way.

*Tip: Learn about the reforms of sexual assault laws in your area. It is vital that legal reform and educational campaigns are underpinned with the victim's reality and not with silencing her voice or with misperception about certain issues, which only perpetuate rape mythology. If you work in the criminal justice system, continue to battle the permeation of the myths by challenging the practices discussed in this chapter.*

# References

Clark, H. (2007) "Judging rape: public attitudes and sentencing." *ACSSA Newsletter.* Melbourne: Australian Centre for the Study of Sexual Assault. Available at www. aifs.gov.au/acssa/pubs/newsletter/n14pdf/n14_5.pdf, accessed November 3, 2012.

Easteal, P. (1998) "Rape in Marriage: Has the License Lapsed?" In P. Easteal (ed.) *Balancing the Scales: Rape, Law Reform and Australian Culture.* Sydney: Federation Press.

Easteal, P. and Feerick, C. (2005) "Sexual assault by male partners: is the license still valid?" *Flinders Journal of Law Reform 8,* 2, 185–207.

Easteal, P. and Gani, M. (2005) "Sexual assault by male partners: a study of sentencing factors." *Southern Cross University Law Review 9,* 39–72.

Easteal, P. and McOrmond-Plummer, L. (2006) *Real Rape, Real Pain: Help for Women Sexually Assaulted by Male Partners.* Melbourne: Hybrid Publishers.

Edwards, K., Turchik, J., Dardis, C., Reynolds, N. *et al.* (2011) "Rape myths: history, individual and institutional-level presence, and implications for change." *Sex Roles 65,* 761–773.

Estrich, S. (1987) *Real Rape: How the Legal System Victimises Women Who Say No.* Cambridge, MA: Harvard University Press.

Heenan, M. (2004) *Just "Keeping the Peace": A Reluctance to Respond to Male Partner Sexual Violence.* Melbourne: Australian Centre for the Study of Sexual Assault. Available at www.aifs.gov.au/acssa/pubs/issue/i1.html, accessed September 3, 2012.

Heenan, M. and Murray, S. (2006) *A Study of Reported Rapes in Victoria 2000–2003.* Melbourne: Office of Women's Policy. Available at http://mams.rmit.edu.au/igzd08ddxtpwz.pdf, accessed March 23, 2013.

Heydon, J.D. (2000) *Cross on Evidence.* Sydney: LexisNexis.

Kelly, L., Lovett, J., and Regan, L. (2005) *A Gap or a Chasm? Attrition in Reported Rape Cases.* Home Office Research Study 293. London: Home Office Research, Development and Statistics Directorate.

Kennedy, J., Easteal, P., and Bartels, L. (2012) "How protected is she? 'Fairness' and the rape victim witness in Australia." *Women's Studies International Forum 35,* 334-342.

Kennedy, J. and Easteal, P. (2011) "Shades of grey: indeterminacy and sexual assault law reform." *Flinders Law Journal 13,* 49–77.

Kennedy, J., Easteal, P., and Taylor, S.C. (2009) "Rape mythology and the criminal justice system: a pilot study of sexual assault sentencing in Victoria." *ACSSA Aware 23,* 13–22.

Lea, S., Lanvers, U., and Shaw, S. (2003) "Attrition in rape cases: developing a profile and identifying relevant factors." *British Journal of Criminology 43,* 3, 583–599.

Lievore, D. (2003) *Intimate Partner Sexual Assault: The Impact of Competing Demands on Victims' Decisions to Seek Criminal Justice Solutions.* Available at www.aifs.gov.au/conferences/aifs8/lievore.pdf, accessed November 3, 2012.

Lievore, D. (2005) "Prosecutorial decisions in adult sexual assault cases." *Trends and Issues in Crime & Criminal Justice 291.* Available at www.aic.gov.au/documents/8/C/1/%7B8C1609DA-6C67-4BAB-BF86-5D92564410E1%7Dtandi291.pdf, accessed February 3, 2012.

Neame, A. and Heenan, M. (2003) "What lies behind the hidden figure of sexual assault?" *ACSSA Briefing 1*. Melbourne: Australian Centre for the Study of Sexual Assault. Available at www.aifs.gov.au/acssa/pubs/briefing/acssa_briefing1.pdf, accessed November 3, 2012.

Parkinson, D. and Cowan, S. (2008) *Raped by a Partner: Nowhere to Go, No-One to Tell.* Victoria: Women's Health Goulburn North East.

Stubbs, J. (2003) "Sexual assault, criminal justice and law and order." *Women Against Violence 14*, 14–26.

Taylor, N. and Mouzos, J. (2006) *Community Attitudes to Violence against Women Survey: A Full Technical Report.* Canberra: Australian Institute of Criminology. Available at www.aic.gov.au/documents/3/8/C/%7B38CD1194-9CE2-4208-8627-7C32B4B238F2%7D2006-11-violenceAgainstWomen.pdf, accessed November 3, 2012.

Taylor, S.C. and Gassner, L. (2009) "Stemming the flow: challenges for policing adult sexual assault with regard to attrition rates and underreporting of sexual offences." *Police Practice and Research 11*, 3, 240–256.

Victorian Law Reform Commission (2001) *Sexual Offences: Law and Procedure. Discussion Paper.* Melbourne: Victorian Law Reform Commission. Available at www.lawreform.vic.gov.au/projects/sexual-offences/sexual-offences-discussion-paper, accessed October 3, 2012.

Victorian Law Reform Commission (2004) *Sexual Offences: Final Report Summary.* Melbourne: Victorian Law Reform Commission. Available at www.lawreform.vic.gov.au/projects/sexual-offences/sexual-offences-final-report-summary, accessed February 3, 2012.

# Cases

*Boney* v. *R* (2008) NSWCCA 165, 106.
*R* v. *C* (2003) QCA 561.
*R* v. *Gill* (2008) VCC 0027.
*R* v. *Ipia* (2008), VCC 0355.
*R* v. *Ralston Edwards* [1996] EWCA Crim 1679.
*Taylor* v. *R* [2009] NSWCCA 180.

# Legislation

Criminal Procedure Act (1986) New South Wales.
Evidence (Miscellaneous Provisions) Act (1991) Australian Capital Territory.

CHAPTER 18

# Intimate Partner Sexual Violence and the Courts

Lynn Hecht Schafran

At a National Judicial Education Program presentation on intimate partner sexual abuse, Wisconsin Judge Jeffrey Kremers posed this question to his colleagues: "If a partner is controlling, abusive, and violent in the kitchen, the living room, and in public, why would he stop the abuse at the bedroom door?" This is a question everyone in the court system needs to ask.

US courts have only recently begun to focus on intimate partner sexual violence (IPSV) because marital rape has only recently become a crime. Although the first state to eliminate its marital rape exemption did so in 1976, it took decades before the complete exemption was eliminated under all state, federal, and military law. Today, several states and jurisdictions retain special qualifications for marital rape, such as a requirement that the couple be living apart. With the advent of gay marriage, the question arises as to how the marital rape laws will be interpreted and applied in the five states and one jurisdiction with statues requiring that the persons involved in a sexual assault be of the opposite sex, or that the victim be female, for there to be a chargeable offense.

This is in contrast to Australia and the UK, where the marital rape exemption was abolished with none of these qualifications. Australia repealed the exemption in common law in 1991. The UK did so in 1991 after agitation by groups such as Women Against Rape (WAR). As in the US, however, the law as written and the law as applied are two different things.

Moreover, because the US justice system began to take domestic violence seriously at a time when marital rape was not a crime, IPSV was all but invisible to the courts as that reform movement evolved. And because that movement initially focused on married victims, when it embraced unmarried victims the invisibility of IPSV was extended to them as well. It was as if sexual abuse and battering were two types of violence against women that ran on parallel tracks but never intersected.

Today we know better, and it is critical that judges and court personnel know, too. To assist the courts in dealing with IPSV, the National Judicial Education Program (NJEP), a project of Legal Momentum in cooperation with the National Association of Women Judges, created an interactive web course, *Intimate Partner Sexual Abuse: Adjudicating This Hidden Dimension of Domestic Violence Cases.* Funded by the State Justice Institute and the Department of Justice Office on Violence Against Women, it is free at www.njep-ipsacourse.org. This web course is based on US law, but it includes extensive law-related and interdisciplinary information about all aspects of IPSV that will be useful in any jurisdiction. Similarly, although the web course is focused on judges, it is used by justice system professionals of all kinds: judges, lawyers, law enforcement, victim advocates, sexual assault nurse examiners (SANEs), and others.

A prime example of what happens when judges do not understand IPSV is the case of Dr. Amy Castillo, a pediatrician in Baltimore, Maryland. In 2008, Amy was divorcing her increasingly violent, erratic, and suicidal husband, Mark, who told her the worst thing he could do to her would be to kill their three children and leave her alive. Amy obtained a Temporary Protective Order against Mark. At the hearing for the Final Protective Order the defense attorney brought out that Amy had sexual relations with Mark shortly before seeking the order. The judge was unable to grasp that this was not a romantic reconciliation but rather a terrified woman acquiescing to a violent man's sexual demand to protect her children and herself from further harm. The judge denied the Final Protective Order and awarded Mark unsupervised visitation. Shortly after, Mark drowned the three children in a hotel room bathtub (NJEP 2009, Module II). Acquiescence out of fear is *not* consensual sex. But when a domestic violence victim engages in sexual relations with the abuser, judges often misconstrue it as inconsistent with a claim of dangerousness and fear. Courts must recognize the nuances of what constitutes IPSV; the fact that teens, the elderly, and same-sex partners can be victims; the critical implications for risk assessment; and the difficulties of trying an IPSV case to a jury. Judges need to understand that if they do not treat IPSV offenders seriously, more people may be victimized. A man who sexually abuses one partner is likely to sexually abuse others (DeKeseredy and Rogness 2004).

# Risk assessment

In domestic violence cases, courts consider risk when granting or denying protection orders, setting bail, considering probation rather than incarceration, awarding custody and visitation, and determining the conditions to be imposed on the offender in all these situations. IPSV is an important factor in risk assessment because it presages increasing physical and sexual violence, potential lethality for the victim and others, and risks to children. Professor Jacquelyn Campbell, a leading US researcher on domestic violence fatalities, found that, taking all other risk factors into account, a batterer who subjects his partner to forced sex as well as physical violence is twice as likely to kill her as a batterer who subjects his partner to physical violence only (Campbell *et al.* 2003). These findings correlate with those of psychologist David Adams, who interviewed incarcerated wife murderers and women who survived their partners' attempted femicides or near-fatal beatings. The men said they were never even sexually coercive, much less assaultive. Three quarters of the women said their partners raped them (Adams 2007). Moreover, the batterer may also kill children, other family members, bystanders, or himself, and the victim may kill herself or the abuser (NJEP 2009, Module III; Schafran 2010). For more information on IPSV and potential lethality see Chapter 4.

Fully informed risk assessment requires a full picture of the violence in domestic violence cases, but a major difficulty facing the courts is IPSV victims' reluctance to disclose (NJEP 2009, Module V). In a study of 148 women seeking orders of protection, 68 percent said "yes" to one or more of five behaviorally based questions about sexual abuse. Yet none of these women included sexual abuse as grounds for the orders they sought (McFarlane *et al.* 2005). Women do not disclose IPSV for several reasons. It is too personal and humiliating. They do not know it is against the law. They have been cautioned by victim advocates and prosecutors not to talk about it because when a domestic violence victim accuses her partner of any type of sexual misconduct her credibility becomes even more suspect. The sad facts are that women are considered the less credible sex in all aspects of life, domestic violence victims are often dismissed as hysterical or manipulating the system for an advantage in a divorce or custody case, and the history of rape law reveals a deep distrust of women and fear of false allegations (Schafran 1985, 1995).

Some judges do not recognize the red flags for IPSV when they see them. As in Dr. Amy Castillo's case described above, many judges perceive a woman's having sex with her partner as a proxy for "everything's fine." In an international child abduction case, an American woman married to a Hungarian man and living in Hungary fled to the US with her two children. When her husband sought the children's return she claimed that his abuse was terrorizing her and their children, and that under the international treaty provision that bars return when there is grave risk to children's physical and psychological well-being, return should be denied. A US federal court ordered her return in a decision which included descriptions of coercive control, such as forcing the wife to sit silently and watch the husband eat, and then this description of the husband's behavior when he left the home after an "incident": "Jennifer testified…that when he returned, he ordered Jennifer to 'take her place' in their bed" (*Dobos* v. *Dobos* 2009, p.11). This is a man who considers his wife property, sexually available to him under any circumstances, but the judge did not recognize the husband's "order" as a red flag for IPSV. Mr. Dobos was like many batterers, who believe that having sex after a frightening or violent incident constitutes an apology, when it is actually a continuation of the batterer's coercive control (Bergen 1996; NJEP 2009).

Judges need to be alert to the warning signals for IPSV and know how to use behaviorally based questions to elicit the information needed for risk assessment. If a woman says her partner dragged her into the bedroom and beat her, if there is no jury present the judge might ask: "What happened next? Did he make you do anything sexual that you did not want to do?" Her partner could have beaten her anywhere in the house. Why did he drag her into the bedroom (NJEP 2009, Module XII)?

Judges should ensure that the intake forms and risk assessment instruments that court clerks, victim witness advocates, and probation officers use with domestic violence victims include IPSV. Women may not immediately check that box, but it cues them that sexual violence, even within marriage, is against the law, and may encourage disclosure in the future. Campbell's Danger Assessment, for example, asks victims, "Has he ever forced you to have sex when you did not want to?" (Campbell 2004).

Judges should also require that the batterer intervention programs to which their probation departments send offenders deal with IPSV.

Some programs address IPSV as a matter of course; others address it only if it is raised by an offender or someone in the partner's program; and some do not address it at all (NJEP 2009, Module XII).

## Custody and visitation

There is a vast literature on the negative impact of domestic violence on children and why batterers should not be awarded sole or joint custody or unsupervised visitation (Bancroft and Silverman 2002; Jaffe, Crooks, and Poisson 2003; Schafran 2003). When the mother has been sexually as well as physically abused, the harm to the children is particularly grave, but the impact of IPSV has not received the attention it warrants. In "Children's exposure to intimate partner sexual assault," Kathryn Ford observes:

> The sexual abuse of a parent has been seriously neglected—despite its potentially severe traumatic impact on children and association with greater risk to the safety and well-being of children and adult victims... [I]ntimate partner sexual assault is associated with more severe depression, anxiety, and behavior problems in the children of adult victims, as compared to those whose mothers have been physically, but not sexually, abused.
>
> As a result of their exposure to sexual assault, children might also internalize distorted and unhealthy messages about gender and sexual consent. (Ford 2008, pp.143–145)

There is also a greater risk of direct physical and sexual assaults on the children. According to domestic violence expert Lundy Bancroft, "A history of sexual assaults against the mother...[is] linked to increased risk of sexual abuse of the children and increased physical danger" (Bancroft 1998, p.7).

The standard for determining custody and visitation in US law is the best interests of the child. Every state requires that domestic violence be considered as a factor in awarding custody and visitation. This is also true in Australia where protection from violence is one of the primary considerations in the best interests of the child principle used to determine parenting orders under the Commonwealth Family Law Act. Given the harm to children posed by domestic violence and IPSV, one would expect that judges, custody evaluators, and lawyers appointed to represent children in these cases would be knowledgeable and concerned about these issues. Unfortunately, many are not (Saunders, Faller, and Tolman 2011; Schafran 2003).

Certainly there are decisions sensitive to the risks in these cases. In one such case, the court ruled that because the father raped the mother during the marriage and engaged in sexually inappropriate conduct with their daughter, the mother should be awarded sole custody and the father ordered to participate in closely supervised therapeutic visitation (*C.B.* v. *J.U.* 2004). In another case, the defendant committed marital rape and other violence and continued to harass his family from prison. The court held that the rape and the continuing risk of physical and psychological harm to the children and their mother required that he be denied visitation either in person or by phone, and limited him to writing to his children four times a year, with the letters to be read by the children's law guardian and their mother, with no response required (*Matter of B.G.* v. *A.M.O.* 2008).

But many more decisions reflect ignorance or indifference to domestic violence and IPSV. For example, a Massachusetts lawyer appointed to represent two children wrote that although the mother's claims of abuse—including marital rape—appeared valid, there was no credible evidence that the children had been victimized by or had witnessed the violence between their father and mother. This lawyer argued that the children were not harmed by their father's violence but rather by their mother's taking them out of school and fleeing to a shelter in another county, so custody should be awarded to the abuser (Schafran 2003). One of the greatest problems facing women in US courts today is the award of joint or sole custody or unsupervised visitation to violent men (Saunders *et al.* 2011).

## Jury selection

Seating a fair jury in any sexual violence trial is challenging (Schafran 1992), but in IPSV cases at present it is even more so. Compounding the fact that many in the jury pool are likely to adhere to general rape myths, such as "real rape" is committed by weapon-wielding strangers and "real victims" immediately report, when the defendant is an intimate partner there are unique myths to be uncovered. Since the 1980s, studies of attitudes toward wife rape have found that some people do not believe that husbands ever use force to compel their wives to have sex; some believe it is rare; some believe wives have no right to say no; and many do not think IPSV harms the victim because she is used to having consensual sex with her abuser (Basile 2002; Ferro, Cermele, and Saltzman 2008; Gordon and Riger 1989). In one study, respondents asked to rank the severity of 140 crimes ranked "forcible rape of a former spouse" below "stealing $25" (Finkelhor and Yllo 1985).

Identifying fair jurors in IPSV cases requires that judges conduct or permit a thorough jury selection process in which jurors are questioned not only about their belief in rape myths, but whether they believe in the possibility of marital rape and whether they consider IPSV so harmful that a perpetrator should be subjected to criminal punishment. Questions must be specific to the case. Child sexual abuse juries have hung because a juror was certain no adult could be sexually attracted to a child. An IPSV case involving an elderly husband who rapes his elderly wife in her nursing home bed could go similarly awry without focused questioning on beliefs about sex and the elderly. Voir dire, as the jury selection process is known, is not foolproof, but it is the only mechanism we have for identifying biased jurors. Unfortunately judges often place strict time limits on voir dire or deny permission to ask critical questions, preventing attorneys from eliciting the information needed to challenge for cause those jurors who cannot deliberate fairly (NJEP 2009, Module VIII).

## Cultural defenses

Cultural defenses excuse or mitigate a criminal act on the ground that, because it is accepted behavior in the defendant's culture, he or she lacked criminal intent. A marital rape defendant from a country where this is not a crime might claim that he should not be charged with rape because he had no intent to break a law. US courts have sometimes misused cultural defenses to excuse physical and sexual violence against women and children (NJEP 2009, Module XI).

An example of a court's wrongly admitting a cultural defense is a 2010 IPSV case in the US: A young Muslim woman who had entered into an arranged marriage was subjected to sexual abuse and repeated rapes by her husband as punishment for her shortcomings as a homemaker. She obtained a Temporary Order of Protection and sought a Final Order. After her husband and his imam testified that Islamic law required a wife to comply with her husband's sexual demands, her petition was dismissed by the Family Court judge who viewed the husband's actions as culturally acceptable and consistent with his religious beliefs. The judge ruled that because the defendant believed he was acting within his religious rights he lacked specific intent to commit a sexual assault. The New Jersey Appellate Division reversed the decision. It found that the family offenses at issue required only general intent, so that the lower court's reliance on lack of specific intent was an error. The defendant's state of mind—did he *think* he was committing a criminal act—did not matter. It was his *doing* the criminal act that mattered. The appellate court also discussed the limitations of the cultural defense, determining that free exercise of religion did not exempt an individual from generally applicable laws of criminal liability (*S.D.* v. *M.J.R.* 2010).

Some scholars advocate a limited approach to allowing cultural evidence in order to maintain gains in areas such as violence against women while minimizing cultural stereotyping. Proponents recognize that while cultural evidence has been used to practically legitimize gender-based violence, it may also aid in defending women whose actions were shaped by a culture in which women are devalued and marginalized (Maguigan 1995).

Mother/child-murder/suicide cases are an example. In mainstream US culture, this is seen as the worst kind of crime. But in some Hispanic and Asian cultures it is culturally acceptable in certain situations. The crime would be for the mother to kill herself and leave her children behind, uncared for, or in the hands of an abusive parent. A case of this kind involving IPSV, domestic violence, and child sexual abuse is that of Juana Leija, a Mexican woman living in Houston, Texas. She and her seven children were physically and sexually abused every day of their lives by their husband/father. She sought help but did not find it. She tried to drown her children and herself. Two of the children died. The mother and five children survived. She explained that she wanted to end her own and her children's lives because she knew her husband would one day kill her and she did not want her children to stay with him or someone else who would mistreat them. When the circumstances of her life became known, her attorney was able to present her case in the context of the legend of La Llorona—the "weeping woman" of Mexican and Mexican-American culture—who drowned her child and herself when that seemed the only way out of an intolerable situation. Juana Leija was given a sentence of ten years' probation and, with help from several agencies, was able to rebuild her life (Heinzelman 1998; Mason 1989).

## Intimate partner sexual violence and self-defense

In 2011 a New York jury acquitted Barbara Sheehan of manslaughter in the shooting death of her husband on the grounds of self-defense. Raymond Sheehan was extremely violent and controlling and subjected his wife to what *The New York Times* called "bizarre sexual rituals," forcing her to enact his sexual fantasies. The prosecutor trivialized this as "kinky sex," claiming Barbara shot Raymond merely because this disgusted her (Bilefsky 2011). Under US law self-defense is a subjective test. The individual raising it must genuinely and reasonably believe herself to be in immediate danger of severe injury or death. Professor Jacquelyn Campbell testified as an expert witness in this trial, explaining that when there is sexual abuse, coercion, or assault in a domestic violence case it must not be dismissed as "kinky sex," but understood as a red flag for escalating violence and possible lethality. The victim who believes herself to be in life-threatening danger in a situation like Barbara Sheehan's has reason to hold that belief.

## Conclusion

Because domestic violence victims also being subjected to IPSV may be unable to fully disclose when they first turn to the courts, ensuring victim safety, crafting effective protective orders, and making appropriate dispositions in IPSV cases is challenging. Despite emerging awareness that forced sex in a relationship is a red flag for risk assessment, the issue is often overlooked in order of protection and pretrial release determinations and in treatment programs for batterers and sex offenders in both prisons and the community. The harm to past victims and possible future victims from the invisibility of IPSV is compounded when the system becomes aware of the offense but minimizes its impact out of a mistaken belief that forced sex by an intimate partner is less harmful than forced sex by a stranger.

By taking a leadership role in their courtrooms and court systems, judges can maximize the potential for developing information about IPSV in the domestic violence intake process, in court hearings, and in pre-sentence reports, and can require that the treatment programs their courts use for batterers and sex offenders address IPSV with specificity. Through the dispositions they make and the sentences they impose in these cases, judges can send a message to victims, offenders, and the community that they understand the immense harm of IPSV, that it is a crime, and that it will be treated with the utmost severity. In Fall 2012, New York County (Manhattan) inaugurated a specialized court to hear criminal misdemeanor and felony IPSV cases, which is the first of its kind in the country. Located within Manhattan's existing Integrated Domestic Violence (IDV) Court, the Intimate Partner Sexual Assault (IPSA) Court provides in-person training about IPSV for existing IDV court staff and stakeholders, enhanced services for victims of IPSV, enhanced screening by the District Attorney's Office for instances of sexual assault within existing domestic violence cases, and frequent and tailored judicial monitoring and offender program response (pre- and post-disposition). Prior to opening the IPSA Court, court administrators and the NY County District Attorney's office worked together to identify those cases that should be heard by the IPSA Court. The existence of this specialized court response to IPSV continues to raise awareness among NYC-based criminal justice system stakeholders, advocates, and community members about the prevalence of and trauma caused by IPSV. One year following its inception, the IPSA Court project has sparked a dialogue among existing domestic violence and sexual assault criminal justice system players and advocacy organizations about the importance of collaboration in order to ensure a more holistic response to victims of IPSV. The experience of this dedicated IPSV court will have lessons for us all.

# References

Adams, D. (2007) *Why Do They Kill? Men Who Murder Their Intimate Partners.* Nashville, TN: Vanderbilt University Press.

Bancroft, L. (1998) *Understanding the Batterer in Custody and Visitation Disputes.* Available at www.lundybancroft.com?page_id=279, accessed August 13, 2012.

Bancroft, L. and Silverman, J.G. (2002) *The Batterer as Parent: Addressing the Impact of Domestic Violence on Family Dynamics.* Thousand Oaks, CA: Sage.

Basile, K. (2002) "Attitudes toward wife rape: effects of social background and victim status." *Violence and Victims* 17, 3, 341–354.

Bergen, R.K. (1996) *Wife Rape: Understanding the Response of Survivors and Service Providers.* Thousand Oaks, CA: Sage.

Bilefsky, D. (2011) "An abused wife? Or an executioner?" *The New York Times,* September 25. Available at www.nytimes.com/2011/09/26/nyregion/an-abused-wife-or-an-executioner.html?pagewanted=all, accessed August 17, 2012.

Campbell, J. (2004) *Danger Assessment.* Available at www.dangerassessment.org/DA.aspx, accessed August 20, 2012.

Campbell, J., Webster, D., Koziol-McLain, J., Block, C. *et al.* (2003) "Risk factors for femicide in abusive relationships: results from a multisite case control study." *American Journal of Public Health 93*, 7, 1089–1097.

DeKeserdey, W. and Rogness, M. (2004) "Separation/divorce sexual assault: the current state of social scientific knowledge." *Aggression and Violent Behavior 9*, 6, 675–691.

Ferro, C., Cermele, J., and Saltzman, A. (2008) "Current perceptions of marital rape: some good and some not-so-good news." *Journal of Interpersonal Violence 23*, 6, 764–779.

Finkelhor, D. and Yllo, K. (1985) *License to Rape: Sexual Abuse of Wives.* New York: Holt, Rinehart, and Winston.

Ford, K. (2008) "Children's exposure to intimate partner sexual abuse." *Family & Intimate Partner Violence Quarterly 1*, 2, 141–149.

Gordon, M. and Riger, S. (1989) *The Female Fear: The Social Cost of Rape.* Urbana, IL: University of Illinois Press.

Heinzelman, S. (1998) "'Going Somewhere': Maternal Infanticide and the Ethic of Judgment." In P. Heald (ed.) *Literature and Legal Program Solving: Law and Literature as Ethical Discourse.* Durham, NC: Carolina Academic Press.

Jaffe, P.G., Crooks, C.V., and Poisson, S.E. (2003) "Common misconceptions in addressing domestic violence in child custody disputes." *Juvenile and Family Court Journal 54*, 4, 57–68.

Maguigan, H. (1995) "Cultural evidence and male violence: are feminist and multicultural reformers on a collision course in criminal courts?" *New York University Law Review 70*, 1, 36–99.

Mason, D. (1989) "An act of love?" *St. Petersburg Times* March 12, p.1F.

McFarlane, J., Malecha, A., Watson K., Gist, J. *et al.* (2005) "Intimate partner sexual assault against women: frequency, health consequences, and treatment outcomes." *Obstetrics & Gynecology 105*, 1, 99–108.

National Judicial Education Program (NJEP) (2009) *Intimate Partner Sexual Abuse: Adjudicating This Hidden Dimension of Domestic Violence Cases,* free web course at www.njep-ipsacourse.org.
>    Module I. Defining Intimate Partner Sexual Abuse and Its Prevalence
>    Module II. Victims and Offenders
>    Module III. Risk Assessment
>    Module IV. Why Victims Don't Report
>    Module V. Institutional Responses
>    Module VI. Custody and Visitation When Intimate Partner Sexual Abuse is a Factor
>    Module VII. Jury Selection
>    Module VIII. Evidentiary Issues
>    Module IX. Marital Privilege and Confidentiality of Victim Records
>    Module X. Cultural Defenses and Cultural Evidence
>    Module XI. Orders of Protection, Pre-Trial Release and Dispositions
>    Module XII. Recommendations for Improving Court Response to Intimate Partner Sexual Abuse

Saunders, D., Faller, C., and Tolman, R. (2011) *Child Custody Evaluators' Beliefs About Domestic Abuse Allegations: Their Relationship to Evaluator Demographics, Background, Domestic Violence Knowledge, and Custody Visitation Recommendations.* Washington, DC: National Institute of Justice, US Department of Justice. Available at http:// ssw.umich.edu/about/profiles/saunddan/Custody-Evaluators-Beliefs-About-Domestic-Abuse-Allegations-Final-Tech-Report-to-NIJ-10-31-11.pdf, accessed March 23, 2013.

Schafran, L.H. (1985) "Eve, Mary, Superwoman: how stereotypes about women influence judges." *The Judges' Journal 24*, 1, 12–17 and 48–53.

Schafran, L.H. (1992) "Importance of voir dire in rape trials." *Trial 28*, 8, 26–27.

Schafran, L.H. (1995) "Credibility in the courts: why is there a gender gap?" *The Judges' Journal 34*, 1, 5–9 and 40–42.

Schafran, L.H. (2003) "Evaluating the evaluators: problems with outside 'neutrals.'" *The Judges' Journal 42*, 1, 10–15 and 38.

Schafran, L.H. (2010) "Risk assessment and intimate partner sexual abuse: the hidden dimension of domestic violence." *Judicature 93*, 4, 161–163.

# Cases

C. B. v J. U. 2004 NY Slip Op 51181U, 798 N.Y.S.2nd 707 (2004)

*Dobos* v. *Dobos* (2009) 2009 U.S. Dist. LEXIS 127474 (S.D. Ohio, July 9).

Matter of B.G. v. A.M.O. 2008 NY Slip Op 09483, 57AD3d 246 (2009)

*S.D.* v. *M.J.R.* (2010) N.J. Super.Lexis 143.

# PART 4

# Reaching and Assisting Different Populations

# CHAPTER 19

# Cross-cultural Perspectives on Intimate Partner Sexual Violence

Marianne Winters and Isabel Morgan

## Introduction

Milagros is a 29-year-old mother of three children. She is a student, raising her family on public assistance while she finishes her degree. While pregnant with her middle child, she emigrated from Guatemala to the US with her husband and their oldest child. Her husband has a permit that allows him to work and he is on the path to citizenship. Milagros left him after his beatings and sexual abuse became unbearable following the birth of their third child. When the Department of Revenue sought child support from her ex-husband—because of the welfare benefits her family receives—he retaliated by requesting shared legal custody and unsupervised visits with his daughter, their youngest child, who is now seven.

As a toddler, this child witnessed her father beating and verbally abusing her mother and older siblings. Milagros knew that her daughter could be at risk because her husband used to threaten to sexually abuse the girl to secure Milagros' silence about being raped by her husband. Because Milagros was not properly served with her ex-husband's motion to the court, she was absent at the hearing and therefore the abusive father was temporarily granted his request. Since the court order was written in English and Milagros did not fully understand the contents, she did not respond and did not obey the order. Soon thereafter, she was served with a complaint for contempt for not obeying the new visitation order. She then called a local domestic violence program.

What happens next will depend, in part, on the counselor's understanding of the myriad of issues presented by Milagros and her children. As an immigrant to the US, Milagros needs an informed advocate—someone who knows the law and the ways that a survivor of domestic violence could get protection. The counselor also needs to understand how the sexual abuse (including the assaults inflicted on Milagros and the threat of abuse toward her daughter) affected Milagros: her reactions, decisions, emotions, and responses to the situation. Further, the counselor needs to understand the cultural implications of the physical and sexual abuse. Milagros was raised in a culture that emphasizes family and staying in a marriage through thick and thin. She has strong religious roots and relies on her faith for guidance and strength.

Therefore, in order for the counselor/advocate to form a productive and positive relationship with Milagros, she must understand the issues of intimate partner sexual violence (IPSV) and also must be able to bridge the cultural and linguistic gap by understanding the culturally based reactions to the abuse as well as societal barriers to safety and justice.

Effective response to IPSV is the place where the movements to end and address domestic violence and sexualized violence come together. IPSV is often closely associated with many other forms of abuse including physical, financial, emotional, spiritual, and cultural. Women from racial and ethnic minority groups are disproportionately affected by intimate partner violence (IPV), reporting higher incidences of each kind of violence: rape, physical assault, and stalking (Tjaden and Thoennes 2000). From the perspective of a survivor of color, an immigrant survivor, or an economically marginalized survivor, IPSV may be culturally condoned and isolating (Easteal 1996), while the response of service providers may be incomplete or culturally incompetent (Bent-Goodley 2007; Lipsky *et al.* 2006).

While other authors have convincingly made the point that IPSV must be addressed through an integrated approach, this chapter argues for the necessity to incorporate a deeper understanding of culture and the intersectionality of oppressions in order to adequately and appropriately address the impact of IPSV on survivors from marginalized communities. We emphasize a cross-cultural perspective because awareness of the culturally based perspectives and interactions between service providers and survivors are key to building a supportive and relevant relationship that can help to promote safety, healing, and justice. It is our belief that full integration of these issues at every level is essential, as a framework for social and political movements against IPSV and for providing culturally competent support and advocacy for survivors of IPSV. This requires utilizing a perspective that addresses the intersections of oppressions as they operate in the lives of survivors and in the families, neighborhoods, and communities that are connected to each survivor.

It is important to recognize that the content in this chapter is written within the context of the US, terminologies (i.e. race or minority group) may not have the same meaning in another cultural setting. Furthermore, all relevant cultural differences are not accounted for in this reading. Nevertheless, this does not take away from the points regarding the importance of using a holistic approach—one that incorporates an intersectionality model to address IPSV.

## Applications of the reproductive justice framework in the intimate partner sexual violence movement

The dialogue of the movement against domestic violence and sexualized violence was originally fueled by a feminist framework from the perspective of white middle-class women. While a primarily gender-based analysis was important in understanding many of the dynamics and experiences of survivors of IPSV, the rhetoric was perceived as exclusionary of many communities, in particular women of color (Pro-Choice Public Education Project 2004; Smith 2005). Since many organizations and efforts to address violence against women grew out of these predominantly white and middle-class efforts, the responses often fell short of meeting the needs or experiences of women of color, non-English-speaking women, or poor women. It became clear to many involved in this work that a broader and more complex understanding and analysis was needed in order to address the range of survivors from across all cultures, races, and economic experiences.

The reproductive justice framework, introduced in the 1990s, offers a model for an effective approach to IPSV. The reproductive justice framework moves the work to secure reproductive rights into a social justice framework. While the key concepts recognized by the reproductive justice framework are the "right to have children, not have children, and to parent the children [one] has in a safe and healthy environment" (SisterSong 2013), the social justice lens opens the dialogue to include freedom from violence and oppression as key conditions necessary in order to secure reproductive justice. This provides an important common language and framework, and places the work to end racism and other oppressions squarely in the middle of the work to end interpersonal violence. The language used in the reproductive justice movement demonstrates an understanding of the importance of using a multi-oppression model to analyze reproductive health issues while also establishing parallels between reproductive rights and other social justice issues (Kimala 2010). A similar model can be utilized when viewing IPSV through a social justice lens, while maintaining an understanding how multiple identities can shape individual experiences. In addition to the emphasis on building safety and healing for individual survivors, the reproductive justice framework emphasizes support for entire communities in building justice. The right to live free from violence is a cornerstone in this work and by definition moves the discussion from an individual perspective to a societal one.

The principles of the reproductive justice movement make sense in terms of the issues surrounding IPSV. Survivors of IPSV from marginalized groups must have the opportunity to raise awareness about how their experience is uniquely situated at the intersections of their multiple identities. Organizers in movements against IPSV can and must make active strides to avoid ethnocentric, racist, and elitist views and instead create culturally competent and survivor-centered programs and relief services for all survivors of IPSV. Furthermore, it is important to recognize that many studies on IPSV may have neglected to include a diverse participant sample. The extent to which the data can be generalized to the greater population is limited and therefore inappropriate to use for framing counseling and advocacy services for survivors from marginalized communities. How then do we analyze IPSV through a multi-oppression lens to provide the appropriate resources to survivors?

## Introduction to intersectionality

Working effectively with survivors of IPSV requires an approach that is based on an understanding of the intersectionality of oppressions. To understand this concept, two definitions by Canadian political theory professor Anna Carastathis (2008) are helpful:

- Oppression—the constellation of structural economic, political, and psycho-social relations that systematically confine or reduce the life choices of a social group.

- Privilege—unearned advantages which are conferred systematically to members of a social group, in virtue of their group membership.

Intersectionality, a term coined by Kimberlé Williams Crenshaw (1989), refers to an understanding that people's lives and situations are shaped by more than one factor at a time. These factors operate in an interrelated manner to determine social inequality and therefore affect barriers to services and safety. An understanding of intersectionality serves to explain how multiple forms of oppression and privilege may impact a survivor's ability to access resources, advocate for herself, and seek help (Easteal 1997; Sokoloff and DuPoint 2005; West 2004).

As service providers begin to understand the multifaceted experiences of survivors, they are reminded that many survivors are targeted due to their race, religion, immigration status, and educational and economic backgrounds. Someone may also hold privilege in some areas, and be the target of oppression in other areas. For example, a woman may be privileged economically, but be targeted because of her race or sexual orientation. Intersectionality is a paradigm shift—in actuality a paradigm expansion—from a focus on a single social root cause of violence (i.e. sexism) to a multi-layered and multi-dimensional view that incorporates racism, classism, homophobia, ethnocentrism, and sexism to understand the lived experiences of women of color and marginalized groups.

Think about the example of Milagros. Many factors impact the ways in which she is targeted by oppression. She is an immigrant in the US, is a single parent, and is living in poverty. However, she also has some supportive factors. She is no longer living in the day-to-day fear of violence; she is a student and therefore has access to education and to the hope for financial self-sufficiency. She also speaks English as well as Spanish. Her faith and connection to a faith-based community provide her with a support system and promote her strengths and values. A counselor who looks at her situation holistically, with an understanding of intersectionality, will see this multidimensional picture and will be more likely to promote her strengths while supporting her in the areas where she is targeted.

## Institutional barriers for intimate partner sexual violence survivors

Intersectionality is a lens through which we can understand an individual's vulnerability and reactions to IPSV. At the same time, it can be a helpful perspective that informs us of the ways in which institutions and systems can either be helpful in responding, or may act as additional barriers to safety and justice. It is helpful to consider an intersectional approach to the institutions, political structures, and economic systems that impact survivors.

## Economic disadvantages

It is no secret that survivors of IPSV have historically faced difficulties in the judicial system, at social service agencies, and in educational, medical, and faith-based institutions. Intersectionality helps us understand how some survivors are more likely to successfully navigate gender barriers due to certain privileges that allow them access to resources, such as education and fluency in the dominant spoken and written language.

Economic resources establish a means for transportation, parking, information gathering, paying for legal help, and having the flexibility of time off from work and child-rearing responsibilities to seek assistance. When the economic lives of survivors and their families are viewed through an intersectionality lens, we understand the difficulties that women encounter in establishing financial self-sufficiency and we understand the ways that financial abuse is used to maintain control over a victim. Many people assume that leaving and perhaps going to shelter will eliminate the abuse entirely. For most survivors, however, leaving means financial uncertainty and disruption of many of the sources of stability for their families. For survivors of IPSV, it can mean the need to access job training; find a new job; secure housing, new schools, and daycare for the children; and overcome the financial aspects of the relationship—all while dealing emotionally with the impact of the abuse. Intersectionality also helps us remember the emotional impact of classism and how building a financial structure for a family is made difficult due to oppression.

Consider how institutional oppression may affect the experience of survivors as you provide services.

## Limitations of judicial system remedies

Policies and procedures, created by law or through regulation, often include hidden biases against women of color and other marginalized groups. This can take the form of required documents of identification, eligibility requirements, and possible legal remedies available.

The judicial system delivers a set of responses and consequences based on a certain set of goals and values. Typically, the focus is on reprimanding perpetrators for their crimes and not necessarily on alleviating victims' pain and addressing their needs. Penalties usually center on incarceration, control of behavior as a threat of incarceration, monetary fines, and system fees. A study evaluating the satisfaction of court outcomes among a population of black women from the US with histories of abuse found that women preferred counseling and substance abuse treatment services for the abuser as an alternative to incarceration to address the "root cause" of the perpetrators' abuse (Bell et al. 2011).

The face of justice is relative to each survivor, based on his or her individual experience. For communities of color, the remedies most often sought by the judicial system may not, in fact, represent justice to a victim, due to the history of maltreatment and overrepresentation of men of color in correctional systems. Consider Milagros, for example, who has three children fathered by the abuser. Incarceration would disrupt his ability to make an income and provide child support, which in turn would result in reduced resources for the family, putting them at risk for deepening poverty and homelessness. Poverty and homelessness put Milagros at risk of being accused of neglect and losing her children.

An understanding of intersectionality helps us to see why this survivor may not report to the police and follow through with prosecution. It also helps organizations learn to provide advocacy as viewed through the lens of the survivor's understanding of justice and safety and not through our own individual or organizational values. Based on the limited scope of the work of the criminal justice system, it may be useful to make referrals to the appropriate services and intervention programs. An understanding of the intersections broadens the relationships with legal advocacy programs, domestic violence and sexual assault programs, and criminal justice system programs to better address the safety, justice, and healing needs of survivors of IPSV. Based on an intersectional approach, the work towards creating Community-Coordinated Response (CCR) programs in communities would, by definition, include culturally specific organizations and community leaders who could assist in fully addressing the needs of marginalized families (DePrince et al. 2012).

## Understand the cultural lens

It is important to understand how societal messages about sex and abuse within relationships may resonate within communities of color and other marginalized groups. First and foremost is the idea that rape cannot exist in a marriage or ongoing relationship. This of course then becomes extended to include anyone who has ever had consensual sex. The notions of "wifely duty" and our cultural obsession with coupling further solidify this message.

For individuals who rely on their spirituality for support and affirmation, IPSV is a spiritual violation. Yet many survivors still get the message from their faith community leader that to leave is a sin and that forgiveness should be their goal (see Chapter 14). This disconnect is potentially damaging and can be addressed through the development of relationships between IPSV advocates and spiritual leaders so that survivors can have full access to the strength of spirituality in their healing process. Among a group of black survivors of IPV, researchers found that higher scores on the spirituality scale were correlated with better mental health statuses (Paranjape and Kaslow 2010).

The media often portrays minority women as promiscuous (Carraway 1991; Easteal 1997). Consider the history of sexual abuse endured by slaves at the hands of their slave-owners. Black women were depicted as "Jezebels"—promiscuous and overtly sexual—as a way to justify rape. Consider how this may play into modern-day victimization. One of the many ways that racism and sexism collide is that women of color, under this paradigm, may be perceived as more deserving of rape and in need of being controlled. It is crucial to integrate an understanding of how cultural beliefs may allow for acceptance of violence within intimate relationships and, further, how these beliefs hinder a survivor's access to help and resources.

## Cultural factors that exacerbate intimate partner sexual violence

Culture and background play a role in how survivors experience the impact of violence. While a survivor's culture and social system may offer resources for safety and healing, they can also be the source of messages that can be misused to further isolate a survivor and condone a perpetrator's behavior (Easteal 1996).

Cultural taboos against discussing issues related to sex, sexuality, and sexual abuse are widespread and act as barriers to disclosure across many cultures. It should be remembered though that not every person from a given culture or background adheres to the predominant cultural norms to the same degree. Referring back to the example of Milagros, we can imagine that she was socialized to keep the family together and defer the role of breadwinner and provider to her husband. The degree to which she accepted and lived by this cultural standard probably affected her decision about staying and living with the abuse or leaving and starting a new life. Likewise, the degree to which her immediate support network—her mother, friends, and acquaintances—accepted this standard probably affected her decision as well.

Other culturally based beliefs may also influence a survivor's decision to remain in or leave a relationship with her abusive partner. Studies have shown that women are compelled to stay in relationships to maintain the family unit, protect the children, safeguard their partners from a society that discriminates against them, and to avoid being ostracized from their communities (Lacey 2010; Lipsky et al. 2006; Nash 2005). A study examining the attitudes of Chinese American immigrants' views on domestic violence found that even with the belief that domestic violence is a crime, many felt that it is a family matter that should be kept private (Yick 2000). Due to cultural traditions and beliefs, women may refrain from seeking help and reporting IPSV to the authorities. It is important for practitioners and counselors who provide relief services to victims of IPSV to recognize the barriers that restrict survivors from seeking help.

Another component of this issue is directly related to how comfortable women from marginalized communities feel with sharing personal information with counselors or other service providers who identify with a different racial, religious, or socioeconomic group than their own. Survivors may feel isolated and unsafe about sharing information out of fear of being judged or being treated based on stereotypes. A study found that black women might maintain their relationships with abusive partners to avoid the stigma of being a single mother (Potter 2008). These restrictions are an indirect consequence of historical racism embedded in American society and the persistent negative portrayal of black families. The effects of IPSV are then made worse by added shame, isolation, and difficulties in accessing assistance and seeking help (Easteal 1997). When survivors refrain from seeking help and speaking with members of the community to create a safety plan, you can begin to see how the oppression is compounded by these external factors.

## Implications for domestic violence and sexual assault advocates

Anyone who works with survivors of either domestic or sexual violence should develop a foundational understanding of IPSV and the intersectionality of oppressions and privileges. Cross-training initiatives are a beginning to this process (see Chapter 9), while ongoing approaches that include program design, training, think-tank approaches, and case studies are also essential. Advocates need to understand not only the steps within the system, but at a deeper level the ways that the decisions, options, concerns, and priorities of survivors of IPSV may be impacted by the complexity of the abuse. Therefore, integration of issues of IPSV must be supported and structured into ongoing management structures at every level of organization. Policy groups including coalitions, community task forces, and roundtables are also key to this process. IPSV is not solely a training issue for individual advocates, but an organizational issue, as well as a movement issue. This broad approach is needed in order to ensure that issue development happens at the level of individual advocates, prevention educators, managers, board and advisory groups, and policy makers, and that consideration of cross-cultural factors is always included.

## Service provider skills and tools based on an intersectional approach

In order to understand how best to assist and support a survivor of IPSV, we must look at a wide range of cultural, historical, religious, and sociological factors. Service providers often look for a clear set of guidelines: a set of dos and don'ts. Understand that there is no "one right way" to support survivors of IPSV. Rather, focus on an integrated approach that starts with an awareness of societal factors, informed by an awareness of the role of oppression and privilege in your own life, and an integrated view of a survivor's life and cultural background. Understand the context of the oppression by looking at the cultural taboos and cultural expectations imposed by the survivor's background. Recognizing the effects of culture on behavior can help you understand the context of the abuse for someone whose experience is different from your own. Reflect on your own experience and acknowledge how your own identity can influence your perception of the survivor. When you place yourself within this framework, the survivor's needs and actions become clearer.

Your identity and role as a service provider have direct implications on your relationship with the survivor. Your economic status, gender identity, race, religion, and other factors define your life experience and affect how you understand the influence of sexual orientation, age, ability, and mental health status on survivors' experiences and coping behaviors. Service provision across race and cultures requires each of us to constantly and intentionally be open to learning and to our own transformation as professionals. Milagros' story is one of many that reflect the complexity of needs and issues presented by survivors of IPSV with culturally rich backgrounds. The challenge we all must accept is to embrace that complexity and operate from a perspective that is open to the needs and experiences of each survivor.

# References

Bell, M.E., Perez, S., Goodman, L.A., and Dutton, M.A. (2011) "Battered women's perceptions of civil and criminal court helpfulness: the role of court outcome and process." *Violence Against Women 17*, 1, 71–88.

Bent-Goodley, T.B. (2007) "Health disparities and violence against women: why and how cultural and societal influences matter." *Trauma, Violence, & Abuse 8*, 2, 90–104.

Carastathis, A. (2008) *Intersectionality & Feminism.* Montreal, Canada: Girls Action Foundation's Young Women's Network. Available at www.kickaction.ca/en/node/1499, accessed February 23, 2013.

Carraway, G.C. (1991) "Violence against women of color." *Stanford Law Review 43*, 6, 1301–1309.

Crenshaw, K.W. (1989) "Demarginalizing the Intersection of Race and Sex: A Black Feminist Critique of Antidiscrimination Doctrine, Feminist Theory and Antiracist Politics." In University of Chicago (ed.) *Legal Forum 1989—Feminism in the Law: Theory, Practice and Criticism.* Chicago: University of Chicago.

DePrince, A.P., Belknap, J., Buckingham, S., Labus, J., and Gover, A. (2012) "The impact of community-based outreach on psychological distress and victim safety in women exposed to intimate partner abuse." *Journal of Consulting and Clinical Psychology 80*, 2, 211–221.

Easteal, P. (1996) "Shame and Secrecy and Isolation: The Experience of Sexual Assault." In *Many Voices, Different Stories: Speaking Out About Cultural Diversity and Sexual Assault.* Liverpool: Fairfield Multicultural Family Planning.

Easteal, P. (1997) "Marital rape: conflicting constructions of reality." *3 Women Against Violence: An Australian Feminist Journal,* 23–30.

Kimala, P. (2010) "What is reproductive justice? How women of color activists are redefining the pro-choice paradigm." *Meridians: Feminism, Race, Transnationalism 10,* 2, 42–65.

Lacey, K.K. (2010) "When is it enough for me to leave? Black and Hispanic women's response to violent relationships." *Journal of Family Medicine 25,* 669–677.

Lipsky, S., Caetano, R., Field, C.A., and Larkin, G.L. (2006) "The role of intimate partner violence, race, and ethnicity in help-seeking behaviors." *Ethnicity and Health 11,* 1, 81–100.

Nash, S.T. (2005) "Through black eyes: African American women's construction of their experiences with intimate male partner violence." *Violence Against Women 11,* 11, 1420–1440.

Paranjape, A. and Kaslow, N. (2010) "Family violence exposure and health outcomes among older African American women: do spirituality and social support play protective roles?" *Journal of Women's Health 19,* 10, 1899–1904.

Potter, H. (2008) *Battle Cries: Black Women and Intimate Partner Abuse.* New York: New York University Pres.

Pro-Choice Public Education Project (2004) *She Speaks: African American and Latino Women on Reproductive Health and Rights.* New York: The Pro-Choice Public Education Project. Available at www.protectchoice.org/downloads/She%20Speaks%20Report%20Full.pdf, accessed March 23, 2013.

SisterSong (2013) *Why is Reproductive Justice Important to Women of Color?* Available at www.sistersong.net/index.php?option=com_content&view=article&id=141&Itemid=81, accessed February 10, 2013.

Smith, A. (2005) "Beyond pro-choice versus pro-life: women of color and reproductive justice." *National Women's Studies Association Journal 17,* 1, 119–140.

Sokoloff, N.J. and DuPoint, I. (2005) "Domestic violence at the intersections of race, class, and gender: challenges and contributions to understanding violence against marginalized women in diverse communities." *Violence Against Women 11,* 1, 38–64.

Tjaden, P. and Thoennes, N. (2000) *Full Report of the Prevalence, Incidence, and Consequences of Violence against Women: Findings from the National Violence against Women Survey.* Washington, DC: US Department of Justice.

West, C. (2004) "Black women and intimate partner violence: new directions for research." *Journal of Interpersonal Violence 19,* 12, 1487–1493.

Yick, A. (2000) "Predictors of physical spousal/intimate violence in Chinese American families." *Journal of Family Violence 15,* 3, 249–267.

CHAPTER 20

# Immigrant Women and Intimate Partner Sexual Violence

Bushra Sabri, Veronica Barcelona de Mendoza,
and Jacquelyn C. Campbell

## Prevalence of intimate partner sexual violence among immigrant groups

Although sexual violence (SV) commonly occurs in intimate partner relationships, limited research exists on the cultural context in which violence occurs (Abraham 1998), such as intimate partner relationships in immigrant communities (Allimant and Ostapiej-Piatkowski 2011; Easteal 1996).

According to a 2010 American Community Survey, there were nearly 40 million foreign-born individuals in the US, and women accounted for nearly half of the foreign-born population (Grieco *et al.* 2012). Although intimate partner violence (IPV) or intimate partner sexual violence (IPSV) affects women everywhere, immigrant women are especially vulnerable (Wong *et al.* 2011). Abused immigrant women are often unable to negotiate and engage in safe sex, or to protect themselves from sexual risk from abusive partners, which increases their risk for STD/HIV (Gonzalez-Guarda 2008). Immigrant women with IPSV experiences have been found to be more likely than nonabused women to report multiple sexual health concerns. Raj and colleagues (2005), in their study of 208 South Asian women, discovered abused women were 2.6–3.4 times more likely to report discolored vaginal discharge, burning during urination, and unwanted pregnancy in their current relationships than nonabused women.

Immigrant women may be more vulnerable to IPSV than nonimmigrant women as they maintain traditional patriarchal values from their country of origin. Further, immigrant women are at increased risk for IPSV because of their position of subordination within the family, fear of ostracism by community members if they leave their abuser, religious beliefs, economic dependence, or lack of familiarity with the legal provisions to protect victims of IPSV (Mindlin *et al.*

2010). Immigrant women may not identify an experience of forced sex as rape due to the traditional view of sex as a marital obligation. Women's subordination to men is legitimized by some religious beliefs or texts, and therefore victimization of women by IPV remains hidden or unacknowledged. Women are expected to please their marital partners, which often results in the objectification of women, and normalization of their experiences of IPSV (Abraham 1998, 1999). Among South Asian immigrant groups, sex in marital relationships was found to be considered the masculine right of husbands. Husbands, therefore, were socialized to give little attention to the sexual desire and needs of their wives. They controlled women's choice and access to contraceptives, right to get pregnant, or right to an abortion (Abraham 1999). Such factors underscore the need to better understand the issue of IPSV among immigrant women.

In addition, although IPSV poses a risk to women's safety and health, religious and cultural values related to sex may prevent women from seeking professional help. An unsympathetic response from the community—due to shame, stigma, and traditional religious or cultural values—makes it more difficult for immigrant women to escape their dangerous abusive situations (Weil and Lee 2004; Wong *et al.* 2011), or to address their health concerns related to IPSV.

## Risk factors for intimate partner sexual violence

Understanding the following risk factors can help identify various opportunities for prevention.

### Culture: traditional gender norms and power imbalances in intimate partner relationships

Some research points to the hierarchical and patriarchal nature of families among certain immigrant groups, such as Asian Americans (Nguyen 2005; Runner, Yoshihama, and Novick 2009). Cultural attitudes about men's rights and privileges in intimate partner relationships and women's adherence to such cultural beliefs place them at risk for IPSV (Bhuyan *et al.* 2005; Gage and Hutchinson 2006). Women may suffer punishment, pestering, and fear of increased SV when refusing sex to their partners (Logan, Cole, and Shannon 2007). Among Sri Lankan Tamil Canadian immigrants, refusing husbands' requests for sex was reported as a justifiable reason to discipline a woman (Guruge and Humphreys 2009). Women's endorsement of traditional norms concerning husbands' rights to use violence to discipline their wives has been found to be one of the strongest risk factors for IPSV (Gage and Hutchinson 2006). Latina immigrants report that culturally based gender inequalities, often referred to as *machismo*, result in the man feeling entitled to sex by virtue of being in the relationship, or feeling that he owns the woman, thereby devaluing the woman's value as a person (Gonzalez-Guarda 2007).

Other risk factors include psychological abuse in the form of jealousy and controlling behavior. In a study of Haitian women, Gage and Hutchinson (2006) found a significant positive relationship between husbands' jealousy and controlling behavior and women's exposure to IPSV. Such abusive behavior has a disempowering effect on women's ability to negotiate sex with their husbands (Gage and Hutchinson 2006). IPSV perpetrators have a great desire to exert control over women, and to enhance their own sexual pleasure (Purdie, Abbey, and Jacques-Tiura 2010). They decide where and when to have sex, prohibit birth control, and coerce female sterilization. Some men accuse their wives of sexual inadequacy, especially by making comparisons with American women (Abraham 1998, 1999; Raj and Silverman 2002). Thus, gender inequity in intimate partner relationships is a risk factor for IPSV.

Many immigrant cultures in the US are community-oriented and consider family as a unit of central importance. For instance, in Latino communities, the concept of *marianismo* values women who sacrifice for their families and are submissive (Shetty and Kaguyutan 2002). Immigrant women endure the pain and suffering of abuse, and feel reluctant to disclose for fear of bringing shame and dishonor to the family or fear of breaking up the family (Mindlin *et al.* 2010; Runner *et al.* 2009; Weil and Lee 2004). Additionally, disclosure of IPSV may seem dangerous to women due to the lack of power that they experience within family and societal systems (Singh 2006). Patriarchal social structure and community and family expectations play a major role in silencing women from seeking help for IPSV.

Immigrant women also may have trauma from experiences prior to migration; they may have a history of childhood sexual abuse, or have fled from countries where rape, marginalization, or systematic trauma such as rape and torture were commonplace. Women are at increased risk for abuse from previously nonabusive partners after emigrating from their home countries (Guruge, Khanlou, and Gastaldo 2010).

## Stresses of immigration

In the Western world, immigrants who experience IPSV are representative of the diversity of background and languages of the world. As most immigrants emigrate from their countries because of lack of economic opportunity, political reasons, or more generally in search of a better life, they may be under the false impression that life is easier, jobs are more plentiful, and pay is higher. Many immigrants from Latin America, Asia, and Africa may be unaware of laws that may protect them in their destination country, inasmuch as their abuser may be unfamiliar with the no-tolerance policy to intimate partner violence of most countries to which they have emigrated.

One of the reasons for IPV within immigrant communities is the stress of assimilation and acculturation, and the shift of power in family roles. Immigrants who have lived in the US longer are more economically, psychologically, and socially established, and their adjustment reduces the risk for IPV (Nguyen 2005). Many immigrant women enter the US as dependents. They are dependent upon their husbands for immigration status and visa sponsorships. Limited education, economic dependence on husbands, and lack of social support increase the risk of IPV. "Most women are unaware of the Violence Against Women Act (VAWA) (National Task Force to End Sexual and Domestic Violence Against Women 2013), and survivors of IPV or IPSV with lower acculturation are less likely to access services (Nava 2013). Immigrant women face myriad barriers in seeking help for IPSV, and the near-universal stigma of SV worldwide further complicates this picture.

A characteristic sign of abuse is social isolation, and this is often pronounced in relationships when one or both of the partners are undocumented immigrants. Perpetrators of abuse control behaviors, such as where the woman goes and with whom she interacts. Immigrant women often have limited social networks, and may already feel guilt related to leaving other children and family members in their home country in search of better opportunities. Social isolation may be increased because of the highly individualistic nature of American society, which may be a source of cultural shock for the woman who is used to knowing everyone in her community and having generations of family and friends nearby. This limited social network, made worse by the abuser limiting a woman's social interactions, and a foreign society where the pervasive culture and language are unfamiliar, make for a potentially lethal combination of fear, control, and abuse.

## Obstacles to seeking or receiving help

Cultural barriers such as strictly defined gender roles and religious beliefs about divorce or breaking up families may also prevent women from accessing social and medical services. Latinas often value their children highly, and an abuser may threaten to take away a partner's children or report her to immigration or law enforcement to get her deported, which may be a powerful deterrent to seeking help. West African immigrant women in Australia reported reluctance to seek help for abuse out of fear that their husbands would be deported, leaving them to be the sole caretakers of their children (Ogunsiji et al. 2012). Abused women from Arab cultures may hold to the beliefs that family is first and that divorce is culturally unacceptable (Abu-Ras 2007). Further, Arab immigrant women who report IPV may be at increased risk of abuse from in-laws. Going outside of the family for help often results in a loss of family support, and this may increase women's self-blame and justification of abusive behavior (Abu-Ras 2007).

Level of acculturation is another potential barrier to seeking care. Acculturation encompasses proficiency in the language of the host country, ease with which the woman navigates her community and social systems, and familiarity with local cultural practices and beliefs. Social support networks have been shown to be more limited for immigrant women who experience IPSV, and women may fear further alienation from their communities if they report the abuse (Vives-Cases et al. 2010). As women become more integrated into the culture of the host country, they may find increased support for reporting abuse; however, reluctance to trust outside help may persist (Ogunsiji et al. 2012).

In many countries, the legal immigrant status of the woman influences the support she may receive. For example, in the US, the Violence against Women Reauthorization Act (VAWA) of 2013 makes available legal protections for women who are in abusive relationships, regardless of their immigration status. However, implementation difficulties remain with VAWA. For instance, immigrant women needing help through VAWA (battered spouse) petitions are hampered by barriers such as stringent good moral character requirements and need for documentation to prove that the marriage was entered with good faith. Women who have been divorced also find it difficult to prove that the divorce was connected to the violence or cruelty through the marriage (Benach Ragand LLP 2013).

Length of residency in the host country and level of acculturation are also factors that often influence a woman's decision to seek care. Legal services are often costly and may be complicated by marital status and the burden to prove abuse. In addition, it is not uncommon for immigrants to be paid by their employers in cash, making it difficult for women to set aside money in the home without their partners' knowledge.

Many immigrants face discrimination and racism upon arrival in a new country and experience language barriers and discriminatory social isolation. Since September 11, 2001, anti-Muslim and anti-Arab sentiment has grown in the US and has led to decreased utilization of social services by Arab communities, further isolating women into families and abusive relationships (Padela and Heisler 2010). Recent political and social issues in the US, such as laws passed in Arizona which allow law enforcement to stop anyone who "looks" Latino or undocumented, may have public health consequences, such as fomenting a culture of fear that an abuser may easily use to his advantage (Hardy *et al.* 2012).

IPV may be culturally acceptable in the woman's country of origin and the woman may not know that services such as shelters, counseling, and emergency assistance exist in the host country.

## Issues with health services

Limited or difficult access to health care and social services is an additional barrier for women who experience IPSV. Women may not be independently able or allowed by abusers to access services, or they may be hindered by financial constraints. Once they arrive at health services, the high cost of health care or social services may dissuade women from attending. Insurance status is another potential barrier, as undocumented women have varying levels of coverage and access to health care, depending on the host country's health care infrastructure and laws. Women may not be appropriately screened or treated for SV if payment or reimbursement is a concern for the treating institution.

Once an IPSV survivor has achieved entry into the health care system, her needs may not be met by the staff for a variety of reasons. Women may encounter cultural and linguistic barriers when seeking medical care or help for IPSV. Cultural competence is an ongoing process, and not a discrete achievement that can be completed by health care providers. Providers may use unqualified interpreters, or utilize friends, family members, or even a woman's own children to interpret into her native language. These unethical practices may result in increased abuse risk due to lack of confidentiality in interpretation, inaccuracies in interpretation, and compromised quality of care.

Negative perceptions and mistrust of medical systems and social service providers are additional barriers for women seeking help. Fragmented service delivery may present another barrier for women, as they may not be willing to go to another clinic for care or counseling when services are not co-located, because of mistrust or fear.

Without a strong, trusting relationship between women and health care providers, these important factors may never be known. Shame related to SV must not be overlooked as a powerful barrier to women seeking help.

## Barriers to legal services

Unique barriers exist for immigrant women in accessing legal services as well. Immigrant women with limited financial resources may not have identification from their own countries necessary in order to seek legal help. Many women may have difficulty producing paperwork, paying to hire a lawyer, and obtaining childcare. Language barriers, low literacy, and limited social networks may further complicate this picture.

Immigration law may enable perpetrators of abuse to continue their behavior and exert their power over their spouses, as women must stay in the country in order to obtain residency (Sundari Anitha 2011).

# Recommendations for practitioners

The complexity of IPSV requires a multi-pronged approach, involving traditional and nontraditional community services. Health care, justice/ legal systems, education, and social services (including advocacy programs) should collaborate to increase community awareness of the problem. Recommendations for providers in assisting immigrant victims of IPSV will be presented in the context of primary, secondary, and tertiary prevention, and appropriate interventions proposed for the individual, family, community, and society.

## Primary prevention

Because many women who suffer from IPSV have been previously sexually abused (Basile 2008; Black *et al.* 2011), primary prevention efforts are paramount. Immigrant women who have experienced IPSV report that changing cultural norms, beginning with parenting, is a key way to stop IPV. Women report that they themselves have responsibility for not perpetuating the cultural norm of *machismo* among Latinos (Gonzalez-Guarda 2007).

Parenting education should include risk factors for child sexual abuse and changing cultural norms to value the worth of a female child as much as that of a male. Parents can allow young boys to show emotion, teach them coping mechanisms for anger, and encourage communication rather than physical violence. Promotion of healthy, respectful relationships in families helps to foster healthy intimate relationships among adults (Black *et al.* 2011).

Service agencies should form partnerships with culturally specific organizations in order to ensure that community voices are heard and respected in the prevention process. Agencies that provide resources, counseling, and a sense of community for immigrant women are an important community-based intervention. These agencies can promote acculturation for new arrivals and increase awareness of the host country's laws and expectations regarding IPV and IPSV.

Another important step is to provide universal, comprehensive sex education. Sexuality should be discussed as a normal part of human development and adolescents should learn the characteristics of healthy romantic relationships, including negotiation within a sexual relationship. This should be taught in schools, with encouragement and reinforcement from parents. It is ironic that we are unable as Western societies to have open discussions about sexual abuse and rape, while music, television, and other media routinely display the positive sides of sexual relationships. Cultural norms must change in order to have open, honest discussions and to provide more accurate and complete sex education.

Religion has been found to be a mitigating factor in IPSV. In many communities, an effective intervention for treatment of IPSV is to utilize religious leaders to point out how religions strictly prohibit violence against women, and that it is never justified or acceptable (Abu-Ras 2007). Open, public discussions of physical and sexual violence can help in communities where these behaviors are culturally prevalent (Latta and Goodman 2005). Among Haitian immigrants, these discussions have proven helpful in integrating religious beliefs and talking openly about violence as a way to dispel the shame associated with SV (Latta and Goodman 2005).

## Secondary prevention

Screening and early detection of sexual violence within relationships is the key in secondary prevention of IPSV. Nurses and other health care providers working in women's health, emergency departments, public health, and pediatric settings should first ensure that their agency has a policy regarding universal assessment of women for physical and sexual violence, and then become aware of community resources available for referral. Schools also play an important role in early detection, as social workers and school counselors may be uniquely positioned to identify children who have witnessed violence in their homes, and to screen for child sexual and physical violence. Providers working in mental health and/or with war veterans should also consider IPSV screening due to the relationship between IPSV and posttraumatic stress disorder (Campbell 2002). Assessing for pre-migration trauma or trauma directly related to immigration is also important.

Strengthening health care resources that are vital to screening and assessment for women who experience IPSV is another key intervention. Improving cultural competence is an ongoing task for health care providers and organizations. This process should include continuing education for providers as well as training of staff and nonmedical personnel, and should incorporate members of the target community to build trust between the community and health care providers, as well as ensuring accuracy of the information taught (Latta and Goodman 2005). Hospitals and clinics should utilize trained, professional interpreters who speak key languages which represent the communities served. Policies to support health care providers' use of interpreters and institutional backing for their implementation are crucial to providing high quality care.

## *Tertiary prevention*

Once women have been identified as suffering from IPSV, providers should first offer safety planning and counseling, assisting those who wish to leave their abusers to find shelters.

Professionals working with immigrants are well positioned to influence advocacy and policy development on a larger scale. Additional aid and funding should be dedicated to agencies to ensure the necessary resources to provide universal screening. Professionals should be aware of political discourse and participate to support legislation that protects our vulnerable populations. Service providers' involvement in national organizations that support equal access to health care and education for immigrants and immigrant women is important or further marginalization will occur. Advocacy should include access to family planning and social services, especially emergency shelters and counseling. Service providers must also be aware of culturally and linguistically appropriate advocacy agencies and services in their local community to maximize the probability that referrals will be utilized and well received by women. It is also important to link women with other social and medical services that these agencies provide and that they may not be already receiving.

There is also a need for further research on the relationship between abuse in childhood and adult IPSV to better develop prevention programs. Research on effective interventions to change norms, attitudes, and cultural beliefs related to stalking, IPV, and IPSV is needed as well.

# Conclusion

In conclusion, immigrant women are at increased risk of IPSV and have greater problems accessing help due to lack of social networks, pre-migration trauma, low socioeconomic status, and cultural values that condone violence against women. Solutions to change this cultural phenomenon must be applied at all levels, from the individual and family level to communities and societies, with a focus on primary prevention and improved services for those women and families affected by IPSV.

# References

Abraham, M. (1998) "Speaking the unspeakable: marital violence against South Asian immigrant women in the United States." *Indian Journal of Gender Studies 5*, 2, 215–241.

Abraham, M. (1999) "Sexual abuse in South Asian immigrant marriages." *Violence Against Women 5*, 6, 591–618.

Abu-Ras, W. (2007) "Cultural beliefs and service utilization by battered Arab immigrant women." *Violence Against Women 13*, 1002–1028.

Allimant, A. and Ostapiej-Piatkowski, B. (2011) *Supporting Women from CALD Backgrounds Who Are Victims/Survivors of Sexual Violence: Challenges and Opportunities for Practitioners.* Melbourne: Australian Institute of Family Studies. Available at www.aifs.gov.au/acssa/pubs/wrap/wrap9/index.html, accessed December 7, 2012.

Basile, K.C. (2008) "Histories of violent victimization among women who reported unwanted sex in marriages and intimate relationships: findings from a qualitative study." *Violence Against Women 14*, 1, 29–52.

Benach Ragland LLP (2013) *Congress Re-authorizes VAWA but Falls Short on Immigration Provisions.* Washington, DC: Benach Ragland LLP. Available at http:// liftedlamp.com/2013/03/06/congress-reauthorizes-vawa-but-falls-short-on-immigration-provisions/, accessed August 19, 2013.

Bhuyan, R., Mell, M., Senturia, K., Sullivan, M. *et al.* (2005) "Women must endure according to their karma: Cambodian immigrant women talk about domestic violence." *Journal of Interpersonal Violence 20*, 8, 902–921.

Black, M.C., Basile, K.C., Breiding, M.J., Smith, S.G. *et al.* (2011) *The National Intimate Partner and Sexual Violence Survey: 2010 Summary Report.* Atlanta, GA: National Center for Injury Prevention and Control; Centers for Disease Control and Prevention. Available at www.cdc.gov/ViolencePrevention/pdf/NISVS_Report2010-a.pdf, accessed December 1, 2012.

Campbell, J.C. (2002) "Health consequences of intimate partner violence." *The Lancet 359*, 1331–1336.

Easteal, P. (1996) "Double jeopardy: violence against immigrant women in the home." *Family Matters 45*, 26–30.

Gage, A.J. and Hutchinson, P.L. (2006) "Power, control, and intimate partner sexual violence in Haiti." *Journal of Sexual Behavior 35*, 1, 11–24.

Gonzalez-Guarda, R.M. (2007) "Addressing intimate partner violence among Hispanic women: The importance of incorporating qualitative research methods." *Hispanic Health Care International 5*, 1, 1–2.

Gonzalez-Guarda, R. (2008) "HIV risks, substance abuse, and intimate partner violence among Hispanic women and their intimate partners." *Journal of the Association of Nurses in AIDS Care 19*, 4, 252–266.

Grieco, E.M., Acosta, Y.D., de la Cruz, G.P., Gambino, C. *et al.* (2012) *The Foreign Born Population in the United States: 2010.* American Community Survey Reports. Available at www.census.gov/prod/2012pubs/acs-19.pdf, accessed December 5, 2012.

Guruge, S., and Humphreys, J. (2009) "Barriers affecting access to and use of formal social supports among abused immigrant women." *Canadian Journal of Nursing Research 41*, 3, 64–84.

Guruge, S., Khanlou, N., and Gastaldo, D. (2010) "Intimate male partner violence in the migration process: intersections of gender, race and class." *Journal of Advanced Nursing 66*, 1, 103–113.

Hardy, L.J., Getrich, C.M., Quezada, J.C., Guay, A. *et al.* (2012) "Call for further research on the impact of state-level immigration policies on public health." *American Journal of Public Health 102*, 7, 1250–1253.

Latta, R.E. and Goodman, L.A. (2005) "Considering the interplay of cultural context and service provision in intimate partner violence: the case of Haitian immigrant women." *Violence Against Women 11*, 1441–1464.

Logan, T.K., Cole, J., and Shannon, L. (2007) "A mixed-methods examination of sexual coercion and degradation among women in violent relationships who do and do not report forced sex." *Violence and Victims 22*, 1, 71–94.

Mindlin, J., Orloff, L.E., Pochiraju, S., Baran, A. *et al.* (2010) *Dynamics of Sexual Assault and the Implications for Immigrant Women.* New York: Legal Momentum. Available at http://iwp.legalmomentum.org/cultural-competency/dynamics-of-violence-against-immigrant-women/1%20Dynamics.pdf, accessed December 9, 2012.

National Task Force to End Sexual and Domestic Violence Against Women (2013) *VAWA Fact Sheets.* Available at http://4vawa.org/the-facts-about-vawa, accessed May 28, 2012.

National Task Force to End Sexual and Domestic Violence Against Women (2012) *VAWA Endangers Immigrant Victims.* Available at http://4vawa.org/pages/hr-4970-endangers-immigrant-victims, accessed May 23, 2012.

Nguyen, T.D. (2005) "Overview: Asian American Communities and Domestic Violence." In T.D. Nguyen (ed.) *Domestic Violence in Asian American Communities: A Cultural Overview.* Lanham, MD: Lexington Books.

Ogunsiji, O., Wilkes, L., Jackson, D., and Peters, K. (2012) "Suffering and smiling: West African immigrant women's experience of intimate partner violence." *Journal of Clinical Nursing 21*, 11–12, 1659–1665.

Padela, A.L. and Heisler, M. (2010) "The association of perceived abuse and discrimination after September 11, 2001, with psychological distress, level of happiness, and health status among Arab Americans." *American Journal of Public Health 100*, 2, 284–291.

Purdie, M.P., Abbey, A., and Jacques-Tiura, A.J. (2010). "Perpetrators of intimate partner sexual violence: are there unique characteristics associated with making partners have sex without a condom?" *Violence Against Women 16*, 10, 1086–1097.

Raj, A. and Silverman, J. (2002) "Violence against immigrant women: The roles of culture, context, and legal immigrant status on intimate partner violence." *Violence Against Women 8*, 3, 367-398.

Raj, A., Liu, R., McCleary-Sills, J., and Silverman, J.G. (2005) "South Asian victims of intimate partner violence more likely than non-victims to report sexual health concerns." *Journal of Immigrant Health 7*, 2, 85-91.

Runner, M., Yoshihama, M., and Novick, S. (2009) *Intimate Partner Violence in Immigrant and Refugee Communities: Challenges, Promising Practice and Recommendations.* Available at www.futureswithoutviolence.org/userfiles/file/ImmigrantWomen/IPV_Report_March_2009.pdf, accessed November 28, 2012.

Shetty, S. and Kaguyutan, J. (2002) *Immigrant Victims of Domestic Violence: Cultural Challenges and Available Legal Protections.* National Resource Center on Domestic Violence. Available at www.vawnet.org/applied-research-papers/print-document.php?doc_id=384, accessed December 18, 2012.

Singh, A.A. (2006) "Resilience strategies of South Asian women who have survived child sexual abuse." *Counseling and Psychological Services Dissertations,* Paper 4. Available at http://digitalarchive.gsu.edu/cps_diss/4, accessed December 17, 2012.

Sundari Anitha, S. (2011) "Legislating gender inequalities: the nature and patterns of domestic violence experienced by South Asian women with insecure immigration status in the United Kingdom." *Violence Against Women 17,* 10, 1260–1285.

Vives-Cases, C., Gil-Gonzalez, D., Ruiz-Perez, I., Escriba-Aguir, V. *et al.* (2010) "Identifying sociodemographic differences in intimate partner violence among immigrant and native women in Spain: a cross-sectional study." *Preventive Medicine 51,* 85–87.

Weil, J.M. and Lee, H.H. (2004) "Cultural considerations in understanding family violence among Asian American Pacific Islander families." *Journal of Community Health Nursing 21,* 217–227.

Wong, F.Y., DiGangi, J., Young, D., Huang, Z.J. *et al.* (2011) "Intimate partner violence, depression, and alcohol use among a sample of foreign-born Southeast Asian women in an urban setting in the United States." *Journal of Interpersonal Violence 26,* 2, 211–229.

CHAPTER 21

# Sexual Assault in Intimate Same-sex Relationships

Janice Ristock

*I am still healing or coming to terms with the sexual abuse, the sexual assault. It affected me so significantly. The main thing is that I feel marked by it. I feel somehow that this incident specifically marks me as being different from other people and somehow different from other lesbians... I have really internalized the idea that it was somehow because I was a lesbian that this happened.* (Samantha)

## The silence of sexual abuse in same-sex relationships

The opening quotation is from a woman whom I interviewed as part of a larger research project that examined lesbian women's experiences of domestic violence in same-sex intimate relationships (Ristock 2002). The 102 women that I interviewed reported a range of abuse including emotional, verbal, financial, physical, and sexual. Most experienced a combination of emotional, verbal, and physical abuse. For those who experienced sexual abuse in their relationships, it was apparent that when one is already viewed negatively by a homophobic dominant culture, being humiliated or sexually violated by a partner can have a tremendous negative impact on one's sexual identity, leaving one feeling "marked" by the sexual assault and internalizing the belief that it happened because you were a lesbian.

While many advances have been made over the last 30 years in terms of human rights and social gains for lesbian, gay, bisexual, and transgender (LGBT) people, homophobia, transphobia, and heterosexism still exist and create contexts where people are stigmatized and marginalized. This can make it difficult for people to talk about abuse or sexual violence in their relationships or seek any kind of support services because they fear they will encounter negative reactions or experience discrimination.

Further, many people in same-sex relationships may not identify their relationship as abusive because they associate the experience of abuse and the related terms with heterosexuals (Hester and Donovan 2009; Ristock 2005). This may in fact be more pronounced for women talking about sexual assault and coercion in their lesbian relationships (Girshick 2002; Wang 2011). Accordingly, women—often and understandably—had great difficulty talking about this in their interviews with me. They often expressed shame that another woman could have abused them in this manner. Some felt that the term "sexual assault" did not apply to their experiences even though their partner had sexually violated them, because they associated that language with the behavior of male perpetrators (Ristock 2002). For example, this quotation is from a woman who described how her partner would come home and wake her up to assault her:

> She'd come home, wake me up, and say "I want to do this or that" and it's like "No," you know. And she used to give me bruises all over my arms when she'd come on the waterbed and hold my arms down...and stuff like that.
>
> [Would she be forcing you to have sex?]
>
> Yeah, now there's something new, I hadn't really seen that. (Wanda)

What is revealing is that Wanda had not considered this to be an experience of forced sex until asked the question directly as part of the interview. However, if I had asked her if she had ever been sexually assaulted in that relationship, she would have likely said no.

## The nature of the sexual violence

Sexual violence reported by women in my sample included: forced sex or rape (where women described being sexually violated and forced against their will), sexual coercion (which involved engaging in sex as a result of pressure), and emotional sexual abuse (which included having certain body parts demeaned, being sexually rejected, and/or having partners who were verbally sexually controlling in nonconsensual ways). In my study, 20 of the 102 women spoke of a rape or sexual assault occurring within their relationships. This was most often a one-time occurrence. Nineteen women reported sexual coercion and 32 women talked about experiencing emotional sexual abuse. The sexual abuse described in these women's stories was rarely simple. (See Ristock 2002, pp.51–55, for more detailed information.)

For example, here is how one woman described how she began to feel emotionally and sexually violated:

> *When we were really intimate and we felt a lot for each other, that is when she felt she was losing control or whatever…she had this compulsive or obsessive behavior where she would scratch herself [her vagina] and she'd scratch and scratch like to the point she'd bleed and I would take her hands and say, "Stop it, you're going to bleed" and she'd pull away and go, "No, no, I have to do it" and she'd push me away. We had just been intimate and I'm feeling totally rejected and vulnerable. I didn't know what was going on. Then she'd say, "Give me a hug, a cuddle" and I would be like, "Two seconds ago you pushed me away, this is really hard for me to understand." And then she would swear at me and say, "Well, what was this to you? Just some kind of fuck?"… It made being intimate very difficult. That was the start of the breakdown because I couldn't feel intimate with her without feeling violated. (Anita)*

Anita described feeling rejected and humiliated while at the same time acknowledging the internalized homophobia that may have fueled her partner's behavior.

Further, a few women spoke of experiencing confusing sexually coercive behaviors that occurred in the context of consensual sadomasochistic (s/m) relationships. While clearly not all s/m relationships are abusive, I interviewed seven women who identified as engaging in s/m sex within their relationship with another woman, and of those, three women felt the abusive dynamics included crossing the line from consensual s/m into nonconsensual acts. They were confused by the dynamics because in these three cases their partners were introducing them to s/m and they had no context within which to assess their own desires and limits, and the actions of their partners. This is evident in the following example:

> B: *And during sex she was pushing some of my boundaries. Initially it was just kind of like getting me to try things, sort of light things, light s/m things, and it was all stuff that I was okay with. But then she started saying things like, "Oh, I think you can take it harder. I think you can take more." That kind of thing, and I was thinking, "No, I don't think so" even that was too much. And you know she just started doing it anyway.*

> Interviewer: *It didn't matter what you said?*

> B: *Yeah, and then you know in certain situations you can't exactly do anything about it… It was something that was really, like, very new to me… It was frightening, and I think that was the hardest thing afterwards to work through on my own because, I mean, it is so easy to get hang-ups about sex*

*anyway... That kind of put me back at a place I was never even at before, you know?* (Bonita)

These three women, in addition to feeling shame and experiencing an impact on their sexuality, blamed themselves for getting into an s/m relationship and felt they would be judged negatively if they told anyone about what had happened.

From these examples, we see the differing forms of sexual violence that women have encountered in their intimate relationships with other women and we see the common feelings of shame and the negative impact on their lesbian sexual identity (see Ristock 2002, pp.54–55).

In a more recent research project, Diane Hiebert-Murphy, Doug Brownridge, and I interviewed women about their perceptions of what put them at risk for violence. Of the ten in-depth qualitative interviews that we conducted with women in same-sex relationships, six women reported sexual violence. Those who reported sexual abuse most often did not wish to go into any detail about the nature of the assault, reminding us again of the pronounced underlying shame that surrounds these experiences. For example, the interviewer would ask: "Did she force you into any unwanted sexual activities by threatening you, holding you down, or hurting you in some way?" Examples of the brevity of the responses in those six interviews are as follows:

Interview #01: *Everything was very sexually orientated with her, so yeah she'd pinch me and stuff.*

Interview #02: *Yes.*

Interview #03: *Yes.*

Interview #04: *One time, yes.*

Interview #05: *Yes, she did sexually assault me.*

Interview #06: *Yeah, on many occasions.*

While it was still difficult, women would elaborate far more when speaking about the other forms of violence that they experienced in their relationship (Hiebert-Murphy, Ristock, and Brownridge 2011). Given the difficulties that women face in talking about this form of violence, I remain mindful of the lack of knowledge we have of the motivations, forms, and impact of sexual violence in same-sex intimate relationships.

## The varied experiences of sexual violence within intimate lesbian, gay, bisexual, and transgender relationships

In addition to my own research, several other important studies have been undertaken that are useful to review. One of the first studies to specifically address woman-to-woman sexual assault was conducted by Lori Girshick (2002). She interviewed 70 lesbian and bisexual women about their experiences and found that her respondents were confronted with homophobia and discrimination, had difficulty pressing charges because of the language of rape laws that assumed male perpetrators, and suffered emotionally (including depression, posttraumatic stress disorder, and suicidality) from the negative impact of their assaults.

More recently Emily Rothman, Deinera Exner, and Allyson Baughman (2011) conducted a review of 75 studies (published between 1989 and 2009) that examine the prevalence of sexual assault victimization among gay or bisexual men and lesbian or bisexual women in the US. They found that the reported prevalence of lifetime sexual assault ranged from 12 percent to 54 percent for gay and bisexual men and from 16 percent to 85 percent for lesbian and bisexual women. They suggest that gay, lesbian, and bisexual people may in fact be at greater risk for sexual violence victimization compared to their heterosexual counterparts when considering the combined prevalence estimates for child sexual assault, adult sexual assault, intimate partner sexual assault, and hate-crime-related sexual assault. They also note that it is difficult to know what the reported rates of intimate partner sexual assault actually reflect, since many studies do not identify whether the assault being reported occurred in a same-sex or opposite-sex relationship. Further, they suggest that there may be underreporting of sexual assault within same-sex relationships due to the fear of reporting this form of abuse and the fact that the unwanted sexual contact may not be perceived or reported as coercive.

Rebecca Stotzer's (2009) review of violence against transgender people in the US indicates that they experience a high frequency of sexual assault and rape that often starts at a young age. Her review shows the largest percentage of perpetrators is comprised of people who are known to the victims, including family members, intimate partners, and dates. What stands out is that transgender people often experience a lifetime of violence at home, at work, and in the public sphere.

Other large comparative survey studies are important to consider. A report based on the US National Violence Against Women Survey (Tjaden and Thoennes 2000) compared intimate partner victimization rates between same-sex and opposite-sex couples. The researchers conducted a telephone survey with a nationally representative sample of 8000 women and 8000 men about their experiences as victims of various forms of violence including intimate partner violence. They found that women living with female partners experience less intimate partner violence than women living with male partners. Nearly 25 percent of surveyed women said they were raped and/or physically assaulted by their male partner. Slightly more than 11 percent of the women who lived with a woman reported being raped, physically assaulted, and/or stalked by their female intimate partner. On the other hand, men living with male intimate partners reported more violence than men who lived with female intimate partners. Approximately 15 percent of the men who have lived with a male intimate partner reported being raped, physically assaulted, and/or stalked by a male partner, while 7.7 percent of men who lived with women reported such violence by their female partner. These findings are very interesting and suggest certain gendered patterns in terms of what men and women experience. They also point to some differences in the experiences of the types and forms of violence within heterosexual, gay, and lesbian relationships.

Most recently the National Intimate Partner and Sexual Violence (NISVS) study was released and again confirms many of the findings of the aforementioned National Violence Against Women Survey (Tjaden and Thoennes 2000). NISVS results are based on interviews with 16,507 adults (9086 women and 7421 men). According to Walters, Chen, and Breiding (2013), the NISVS found that bisexual women had the highest lifetime prevalence rates for rape and sexual violence when compared to both heterosexual women and lesbians. They also found that lesbian women and gay men reported levels of intimate partner violence and sexual violence equal to or higher than the heterosexual respondents in their sample. What is also interesting is the data that shows the sexual violence experienced by lesbians, gay men, bisexual men and women, and heterosexual women was mainly by male perpetrators.

Another more recent study that compares domestic violence experiences was conducted in the UK. Here, researchers Marianne Hester and Catherine Donovan (2009) designed a survey that was distributed in LGBT communities. It included items that could then be compared to the data collected in the British Crime Survey on heterosexual domestic violence. Hester and Donovan received 800 responses to their community survey and reported on the similarities and differences of experiences. Overall, those 20–25 years of age are more likely to report having experiences of domestic abuse. They also found that many respondents reported experiencing abuse after separating or ending the relationship. This was similar to the experiences reported by heterosexual women (see Chapter 5). In terms of differences, in same-sex relationships the respondents in their survey reported more emotional and sexual abuse than physical abuse in comparison to those reporting heterosexual domestic violence. The researchers also found that gay and bisexual men were more likely to report being forced into sexual activity, being hurt during sex, and being threatened with sexual assault when compared to lesbians and bisexual women. Thus, we again see that we cannot simply describe the experiences of LGBT people as if they are a homogeneous group.

More recently, a few research studies have been conducted that also show the need to consider the particular and specific contexts that surround LGBT people's experiences of sexual assault in intimate relationships. This research reveals the ways that violence is reinforced in a larger context of social structures that create inequalities, disadvantages, and vulnerabilities to violence. For example, Yu-Wei Wang (2011) offers a case study of woman-to-woman sexual violence in a rural community. The case study demonstrates how the context of this sexual assault occurring in an isolated rural community, within a conservative, fundamentalist culture, and a small, insular gay, lesbian, and bisexual community, intersects with personal and relational factors affecting a sexual assault survivor's recovery process.

José Toro-Alfonso and Sheilla Rodríguez-Madera (2004) examined the experiences of Puerto Rican gay men with sexual coercion in the context of the HIV epidemic. They surveyed 302 Puerto Rican gay males (half of whom report having a steady partner) and found that 48 percent reported experiences of emotional violence in their relationships, 26 percent reported physical violence, and 27 percent reported sexual violence. They found a positive correlation between three variables: being anally penetrated without a condom, the need to please the partner, and being HIV positive. They conclude that the manner in which violence is constructed and perceived by men may be related to their vulnerability to sexual coercion and possibly HIV infection.

What emerges from this review is the fact that we cannot treat all cases of sexual violence in LGBT intimate relationships as equivalent and interchangeable. Differing social contexts, social positionings, and geographic locations affect the motivations for sexual violence, the experiences of sexual violence, and the responses to it.

Finally, when considering the research on sexual violence in LGBT relationships, it is also important to recognize the larger context of violence and oppression that affects LGBT people's lives. The practice of so-called "corrective rape" as a means of "curing" LGBT individuals of their nonheteronormative, nonconforming sexual orientation and/or gender identity is a very blatant example of the need to consider the impact of the larger context of oppression and violence facing LGBT people. Most often we hear about the practice of "corrective rape" occurring in South Africa where lesbians, in particular, are targeted by men who violently sexually assault them. In South Africa, gay marriage is legal and the rights of gays and lesbians are part of the constitution, yet it appears that being a lesbian is an intolerable and punishable threat to masculinity and male dominance in spite of legal advances that suggest societal acceptance (Price 2011). It is also important to recognize that these same hate crimes happen in other nations—by family members and by strangers. For example, the Hollywood film *Boys Don't Cry* depicted the real case of Brandon Teena who was raped and murdered for being transgender. Thus, any understanding of sexual assault/violence within LGBT relationships must also consider the ways in which interlocking systems of power and privilege work to sustain, support, and give meaning to violence. Some LGBT people may feel relatively safer in a sexually abusive intimate relationship than in other areas of their lives.

## The need for better responses to sexual assault in same-sex relationships

We know that people in same-sex relationships remain more likely to turn to friends or to counselors for therapy rather than call the police, use the criminal justice system, access health care services, or turn to anti-violence services. There are also very few places that gay and bisexual men or female-to-male transgender people can specifically turn to as victims of violence. These experiences also depend on where the person lives—it is more difficult to access or find services in rural locations and there are generally more options in large urban centers with visible LGBT communities. Further, these experiences can be confounded by discrimination based on race and class, making it more difficult for LGBT people of color and poor people to get support services (Duke and Davidson 2009; Durish 2011; Renzetti 1992; Ristock 2003; Turell and Herrmann 2008).

My discussions with service providers (Ristock 2001, 2002) reveal that some of the barriers that LGBT people experience when accessing services are the result of funding structures and prescribed service mandates. For example, in Canada the battered women's shelter movement addresses domestic violence, while the anti-rape movement focuses on sexual assault. The result of this siloed approach is that sexual assault gets constructed as something separate and outside of violence in relationships. These institutional practices serve to further marginalize LGBT people. They leave LGBT people who have been victimized by violence in a quandary as to how to best define their experience. Was it sexual assault? Was it partner assault? What if it was both? Where do you go for help?

In order to achieve more nuanced understandings of sexual violence in same-sex relationships, we need to practice what I have called an "ethics of response" (Ristock 2002). An ethics of response involves taking a self-reflexive stance when thinking about intimate partner sexual violence so that you imagine working from a place of multiplicity that considers the particular people involved, the varied social and discursive spaces in which violence occurs, and the need for diverse responses. This ethical stance works against the tendencies in social services, in laws and policies, and in individual practices of homogenizing, normalizing, and thereby creating exclusionary effects when responding to LGBT people who have experienced sexual assault.

Specifically for addressing sexual assault in LGBT relationships, I have found it helpful to remember the following:

- Listen to LGBT people's differing experiences of sexual assault in intimate relationships and think about the social contexts in which they occur.

- Think through multiple frameworks (gender, intersectional, critical race, etc.) in order to hear differing stories and to keep this work rooted in larger anti-oppression and social justice efforts.

- Remember that sexual assault and violence in same-sex relationships are political issues that can be used against LGBT people to support homophobic and transphobic views.

- Resist the tendency to create universalizing (one size fits all) approaches that assume and enforce sameness.

- Imagine new responses that do not force diversely situated people into limited and/or binary forms of heterosexist and gender identities.

Finally, we need to position ourselves as allies who are committed to working to end all forms of systemic, symbolic, and individual violence if we are to truly support sexual assault survivors and disrupt cultures of oppression and hate.

*Author's note: This research was supported by a grant from the Lesbian Health Fund of the Gay and Lesbian Medical Association and from the Social Sciences and Humanities Research Council of Canada. A portion of this chapter is based on: Janice L. Ristock (2002)* No More Secrets: Violence in Lesbian Relationships. *New York: Routledge, pp.51–55. All interviewees' names are pseudonyms.*

# References

Duke, A. and Davidson, M. (2009) "Same sex intimate partner violence: lesbian, gay and bisexual affirmative outreach and advocacy." *Journal of Aggression, Maltreatment and Trauma 18*, 795–816.

Durish, P. (2011) "Documenting the Same Sex Abuse Project, Toronto, Canada." In J. Ristock (ed.) *Intimate Partner Violence in LGBTQ Lives*. New York: Routledge.

Girshick, L. (2002) *Woman-to-Woman Sexual Violence: Does She Call It Rape?* Boston: Northeastern University Press.

Hester, M. and Donovan, C. (2009) "Researching domestic violence in same sex relationships—a feminist epistemological approach to survey development." *Lesbian Studies 13*, 161–173.

Hiebert-Murphy, D., Ristock, J., and Brownridge, D. (2011) "The Meaning of 'Risk' for Intimate Partner Violence Among Women in Same-Sex Relationships." In J. Ristock (ed.) *Intimate Partner Violence in LGBTQ Lives*. New York: Routledge.

Price, P. (2011) *Corrective Rape: A Growing Trend in South Africa*. Available at www.digitaljournal.com/article/313566, accessed July 25, 2012.

Renzetti, C. (1992) *Violent Betrayal: Partner Abuse in Lesbian Relationships.* Thousand Oaks, CA: Sage Publications.

Ristock, J. (2001) "Decentering heterosexuality: feminist counselors respond to abuse in lesbian relationships." *Women and Therapy 23,* 3, 59–72.

Ristock, J. (2002) *No More Secrets: Violence in Lesbian Relationships.* New York: Routledge.

Ristock, J. (2003) "Exploring dynamics of abusive lesbian relationships: preliminary analysis of a multi-site, qualitative study." *American Journal of Community Psychology 31,* 3, 329–341.

Ristock, J. (2005) "Relationship violence in lesbian/gay/bisexual/transgender/queer [LGBTQ] communities: moving beyond a gender-based framework." *Violence Against Women Online Resources.* Available at www.mincava.umn.edu/documents/ lgbtqviolence/lgbtqviolence.html, accessed December 7, 2012.

Rothman, E., Exner, D., and Baughman, A. (2011) "The prevalence of sexual assault against people who identify as gay, lesbian, or bisexual in the United States: a systematic review." *Trauma, Violence, & Abuse 12,* 2, 55–66.

Stotzer, R. (2009) "Violence against transgender people: a review of United States data." *Aggression and Violent Behavior 14,* 170–179.

Tjaden, P. and Thoennes, N. (2000) *Full Report of the Prevalence, Incidence, and Consequences of Violence Against Women: Findings from the National Violence Against Women Survey.* Washington, DC: US Department of Justice.

Toro-Alfonso, J. and Rodríguez-Madera, S. (2004) "Sexual coercion in a sample of Puerto-Rican gay men." *Journal of Gay and Lesbian Social Services 17,* 1, 47–58.

Turell, S. and Herrmann, M. (2008) "'Family' support for family violence: exploring community support systems for lesbian and bisexual women who have experienced abuse." *Journal of Lesbian Studies 12,* 2–3, 211–224.

Walters, C., Chen, J., and Breiding, M.J. (2013) *The National Intimate Partner and Sexual Violence Survey (NISVS): 2010 Findings on Victimization by Sexual Orientation.* Atlanta, GA: National Center for Injury Prevention and Control, Centers for Disease Control and Prevention.

Wang, Y. (2011) "Voices from the margin: a case study of a rural lesbian's experience with woman-to-woman sexual violence." *Journal of Lesbian Studies 15,* 2, 166–175.

CHAPTER 22

# Issues Faced by Intimate Partner Sexual Violence Survivors in Rural Areas

Debra Parkinson and Claire Zara

## Introduction

The rural landscape is changing under the weight of relentless economic and climatic assault (Mission Australia 2006). Although rural communities differ (Hogg and Carrington 2003; Neame and Heenan 2004) depending on population, location, wealth, values, and traditions, the exodus of young people to cities emphasizes a long-standing rural/urban divide (Australian Bureau of Statistics 2013). The social conservatism associated with rurality (Neame and Heenan 2004) sharpens as populations whittle down to the stoic and the loyal. Services diminish, from hospitals to schools to banking (Lewis 2003; Mission Australia 2006). Public transport has rarely been viable for country people, relying as they must on private vehicles and the vicissitudes of petrol pricing to overcome distance and isolation (Alston *et al.* 2006; Slama 2004).

Regular documentation of inferior health and welfare services in rural Australia depicts a correlation between extent of rurality and quality of health care (Alston *et al.* 2006). As distance from cities increases, health outcomes diminish (Australian Institute of Health and Welfare 2008). Specialist services are few and fragmented despite the greater prevalence of violence and drug and alcohol use, and high rates of depression, anxiety, trauma, and suicide (Alston *et al.* 2006; Department of the Attorney General 2009). Yet the current political discourse centers on an individual—and even biomedical—focus, ignoring the reality of rural social experience and the determining impact of the socio-political environment on people (Alston *et al.* 2006).

The theory of intersectionality (Crenshaw 1991; see also Chapter 19) describes the complex relationship of the factors that shape women's experience, including ethnicity, migration status, class, location, age, sexuality, and motherhood. The social determinants of health theory explain further that life chances predominantly rely on early access to health services, housing, education, and money (Marmot and Wilkinson 2006). The personal is indeed political, as women's experiences result from this complex mix much more than their personal qualities or decisions. Being rural and being female are potent determinants of women's life course, particularly in rural areas characterized by masculine hegemony (Alston *et al.* 2006; Hogg and Carrington 2003).

The default position is that men inherit farms, and their work as farmers is reified (Barclay, Foskey, and Reeve 2007), while women's contribution both on the farm and outside to augment family income is disregarded—perhaps to avoid bringing notice to a failure (in patriarchal terms) of men to provide. Women are helpmates, often without decision-making power in families and farms (Australian Government 2011; Barclay *et al.* 2007). This conceptualization sometimes extends to their role within the intimate partner relationship.

> *Living in the country, there's still a whole belief system in the marital ownership of women... it's a really silent belief system... Men are not in there fighting for us. They are quite happy to hold the power.* (Health professional #1)

The impact of intimate partner sexual violence (IPSV) is deeply felt by women in cities and in rural and remote areas alike (Neame and Heenan 2004). Across all locations, women will be helped or hindered by the quality of the response from professionals. The nub for rural women is isolation, denial of wrongdoing, and a prevailing conservative environment (Boyd 2008; Parkinson 2008).

Current partners were responsible for 45 percent of rapes reported to a UK survey, and the prevalence of partner rape in the US and Australia is around one in ten women (Finkelhor and Yllo 1985; Myhill and Allen 2002; National Council to Reduce Violence against Women and their Children 2009). The known barriers to women reporting (Australian Law Reform Commission 2010; Department of the Attorney General 2009; Lievore 2003) are even more formidable for rural women—therein implying a higher hidden rate in rural areas (Lewis 2003). It is clear that reported domestic violence rates rise commensurate with increasing rurality (Victoria Police 2011). Yet, service-use data for both sexual assault and domestic violence do not reflect the reality of rural violence for two key reasons: (1) because specialist sexual assault and domestic violence services either do not exist or are inaccessible, and (2) because there are formidable barriers to rural women reporting, including conformity to rural ideologies and surveillance of women (Lewis 2003).

## Our research

The quotations from survivors and professionals in this chapter are derived from our research described in Chapter 11, unless otherwise stated.

### Nature of rural violence

While lack of effective service response to rural violence reflects funding levels and is indicative of broader rural disadvantage (Australian Institute of Health and Welfare 2008), community culture can excuse violence (Inter-Agency Standing Committee 2005; National Council to Reduce Violence against Women and their Children 2009; Taylor and Mouzos 2006). Although rural areas are not homogeneous, common threads are conservatism and patriarchy, where men are seen to head households and farms and to support dependent women (Barclay et al. 2007). Further, rural constructions of masculinity have been linked to gendered violence (Hogg and Carrington 2003).

> We don't have zero tolerance here... We have 100 percent tolerance of violence. (Health professional #12)

Sexist peer norms and cultures have been identified as contributing to sexual violence, with the male bonding and aggression associated with sport enhancing risk (Dyson et al. 2007). In rural areas, social activities often revolve around sport and football in particular—its competitive nature leading to "intense local bonds" (Tonts 2005, p.147). Tonts (2005) noted that "sport is a binding thread in rural areas, contributing to local identity, sense of community and a spirit of egalitarianism" (p.137). However, its influence is not always positive, as women are mostly relegated to low-status, servile tasks—cooking and cleaning—and then unwelcome at training sessions and "booze ups" (p.147). While a strong drinking culture is characteristic of many rural areas, it is most apparent after sport, with research noting "a culture of excessive and unsafe drinking" associated with country sporting clubs—the smaller the population, the higher the consumption (Drug Info Clearinghouse 2008, p.5).

Sport, drinking, and sex are indeed the preferred mix for a Saturday night in many rural communities. Football violence feeds into domestic violence for men shaped by a particular masculine construct (Braaf and Gilbert 2007). The culture of heavy drinking after sport may lead to demands for sex that some men see as their right.

> *If there's football on, they find that their partner can be more violent towards them. It's that whole drinking culture, they go out with the football, they come back, they're pissed and want to have sex. So I think this whole elevation of the football culture is really closely linked to, "It's OK to be violent."* (Health professional #12)

James, Seddon, and Brown (2002) described violent men's inability to view their violence from the victim's perspective. They described men choosing behaviors that fit the dominant and competitive masculine culture they grew up in (James *et al.* 2002). Echoing this, none of the women in our research believed their partner would recognize his actions as rape, or even wrong—an unsupportable belief in the light of vicious and criminal attacks resulting in deep physical and emotional injury.

Hogg and Carrington (2003) note violence in the white rural family is hidden, the culture profoundly masculinist, and ownership of guns high, underpinning intimidation.

> *Recently, a woman on a farm...actually said to me that if she's found dead not to let people pass it off without investigation. And she's told her family the same thing. Again, I've tried to encourage this woman to consider leaving and she said that she would be petrified to leave him, that he would kill her—that he would find her and he would kill her. And this is a woman who already had a sutured face and major injuries on the farm. She feels she can't be protected, and this is a very, very capable woman. The police have known, a local friendly policeman has been and seen the injuries, but nothing's happened.* (Health professional #8)

## Community attitudes

Public opinion lags behind legislative reforms—snared in outdated notions of private terrain, and sustained by an apparent absence of legal consequences (Daly 2011).

*There's a strong Protestant ethic that the male is the be-all-god and the woman knows her place...those nineteenth-century thought processes where the male is dominant and the female is submissive. We see it a lot in the farming community. The women see it as normal because they've been conditioned to see it that way.* (Health professional #3)

This sense of entitlement seems to pervade some men's thinking and is nurtured by our society's complicity with a man's rights as husband and head of the house. This is more extreme in rural areas where traditional roles remain the norm in many families.

*I think it's the culture, the patriarchal "women have their place, which is to meet the sexual needs of men and raise the children and clean the house." Women are very, very silenced here.* (Health professional #9)

Many cling to the notion that men have a right to control women. Too many with this opinion are in positions of power.

*[The priest] actually told me that my responsibility as a wife was to do whatever my husband told me to do, and so that put me in a worse place than I was before because...my husband told me all the time that it was my fault anyway. So that just reaffirmed the fact.* (Louise)

Rural women rely on their community. Friends, family, and neighbors are all part of the web that compensates for limited professional services. Transport and childcare options are few, and opportunities are limited (Australian Institute of Health and Welfare 2008; Hogg and Carrington 2003). Ironically, this dependence on community and deep sense of belonging can also be the factor that keeps women trapped in violent relationships (Hogg and Carrington 2003).

The women in our research suffered rape that was clearly criminal. They were unlawfully detained, they feared for their lives, and they had grievous physical injury. Even in these circumstances, justice was not served. For Aboriginal and Torres Strait Islander women, too, the justice system does not live up to its name (Atkinson 2002). Since colonization, they have been deprived of their cultural identity through the dispossession of land, child removal policies, loss of right to Aboriginal lore, and economic exclusion. The result is inherited grief, entrenched poverty, redundant male roles, alcohol and drug abuse, and breakdown of family kinship systems (Victorian Law Reform Commission 2006). This reality forms the backdrop for violence in intimate relationships. Greater visibility sits alongside extensive underreporting, reflecting mistrust of a white justice system

(Hogg and Carrington 2003), exacerbated by ethnocentric attitudes and the tragedy of Aboriginal deaths in custody (Hogg and Carrington 2003; Victorian Law Reform Commission 2006). For some of the issues faced by Native American women in the United States, please see Chapter 19 in this work.

> *I do a lot of work in the Koori community and it's not just confidentiality, but if a woman was to make a complaint and that man was to end up in jail then she would feel a heap of a lot of guilt and she would have a lot of blame put on her if he was to self-harm in jail. She would shame the community.* (Health professional #8)

Clearly, loyalty to the community is an imperative for all rural women.

## *Entrapment and surveillance*

Where "everyone knows everyone," there is greater opportunity for surveillance and control (Parkinson, Burns, and Zara 2004). The "goldfish bowl" (Slama 2004), together with financial insecurity, present fundamental impediments to escaping partner rape. Migrant and refugee women with insecure residency status are at increased risk through fear of deportation and limited access to services (Allimant and Ostapiej-Piatkowski 2011; see also Chapter 20). The universally high emotional and practical costs associated with the task of leaving, for example, are exacerbated, as rural women must move some distance away to another town to avoid the perpetrator and community gossip (Neame and Heenan 2004). Everything must change. Survivors moving within urban and suburban areas may benefit from more anonymity and continuity in services and relationships (Neame and Heenan 2004).

The economics of farming can mean that family assets are tied up in property and linked to (usually male) inheritance—effectively limiting cash flow (Hogg and Carrington 2003). A woman may be part of a wealthy farming family but totally dependent on the funds meted out for household expenses. She may hold no bank accounts in her own name, and several members of the family might have an economic interest in the farm. Her decision-making capacity may be negligible. Other control mechanisms identified by Alston *et al.* (2006) alarmingly include forced imprisonment on the farm, and denial of access to transport and significant friends and family. Mileage may be checked and movements monitored. Community members may unwittingly collude by casually passing on information. Help-seeking may be aborted as professionals may be friends or acquaintances of the abuser (Neame and Heenan 2004).

> *Where do you go? Your family doctor, especially if the man you're married to is well known, could be [his] best mate. You've got no-one.* (Amanda)

Even at a professional level, where confidentiality is required in doctor/patient communication or lawyer/client dealings, this was not assured for two of the women in our research. One commented:

> *Going to GPs [general practitioners] was not an option because I knew my story would go with me. When I did go to a lawyer, there was not an option to go to another if I didn't like him, because of conflict of interest... There were always obstacles. I've tried to consider that a lot of people don't know. But all the lawyers know. This stuff about confidentiality—information does get shared around.* (Victoria)

The fear of not being believed, indeed being ostracized by the very community that a rural woman relies on, is often enough to keep her passive and silent. Fear of the "whole bloody town knowing" (SOCAU officer) is both a real deterrent and a genuine likelihood.

Understandably, rural women are particularly reluctant to disclose rape and seek a medical or legal response, fearing reprisal from others in the community who may side with the abusive partner (Easteal and McOrmond-Plummer 2006; Lewis 2003).

> *I only know three or four police and they are the ones...we are affiliated with, and they say, "He's the leader of this great organization, he wouldn't do that."* (Sandie)

> *If the husband is the only GP in town, for his wife to say, "He raped me," she's going to be ostracized, because they see him as an outstanding member of community.* (Uniformed officer)

In our study, this professional silencing could condemn women to a life of abuse and, sometimes, to a label of mental instability which "proves" the man's innocence. The stoicism and self-reliance valued by rural communities had the effect of magnifying harsh judgment of women who spoke of violence against them. Private torment became public condemnation, as such women were seen as undermining the idyllic rural lifestyle, and even as "deviant" (Cowan 2008; Neame and Heenan 2004). A health professional from the city reported:

> *You'll sit and listen to the psychiatric workers say, "She's making it up," or "She's imagining it," or "She's psychotic," or "She deludes," "Look at the way*

*she acts"... It's the culture amongst the churches, in the education system, in medicine, in psychiatry.* (Health professional #9)

Four women in our study who reported rape by their partner to police stated they were no better off for having done so. Five women reported physical abuse to police and purposely did not mention the rapes. Another ten women said they would not report it to police, some quoting treatment received by women in high-profile cases (e.g. the Geoff Clark trial in 2006–2007). Police themselves spoke of the burden of proof preventing partner rape cases getting to court and achieving conviction, well documented in the literature (Daly 2011; Lievore 2003).

# Conclusion

Societal complicity in partner rape traverses both urban and rural experiences, and the scarce recognition of damage by sexually violent men is evident in the negligible legal consequences for this criminal behavior. For any woman suffering partner rape in rural areas, her ability to speak of the violence against her and the willingness of others to support her will be compromised by both the practicalities of rurality and by the strength of her community's values. As diverse as rural communities are, stronger patriarchy and traditional constructs of masculinity are common threads. Aspects of rural living that may be idyllic, such as social cohesion and closer ties, can offer positive experience or they can deny autonomy and options. Although women's experience is mediated by other factors related to their privilege and social standing, there is no getting around the profound challenges presented by distance, isolation, limited opportunities, and lack of anonymity.

## Changing the status quo

Change is possible despite the seemingly entrenched conservative nature of rural life. There are clear strategies for beginning this cultural shift. First steps will be to raise awareness in the community about violence against women. Next is to challenge men's privilege and restate the criminality of IPSV. In tandem with this social marketing is addressing the structural nature of discrimination against women. The most obvious undertaking is to recognize rural women's limited access to higher education and training and offer financial support with fees, childcare, transport, technology, and books. Strategies to begin to achieve these higher-level objectives include the following:

- Educate health professionals (including police, physicians, and allied health practitioners) about partner rape through training and encourage them to use the "Four Steps" (see Chapter 11).

- Adapt the Four-Step Postcard to include local, statewide, or national referral details and distribute through service networks as well as in public locations such as libraries and community centers.

- Create culture change in rural areas by engaging men in activities that explicitly state violence against women will not be tolerated, such as "White Ribbon Day," and recruiting "No to Violence" ambassadors. Target sporting clubs, service organizations, emergency management groups, and churches.

- Deliver community education and school-based education on women's sexual and reproductive rights, and respectful relationships.

- Address the growing use of technologies which portray unrealistic and misogynistic messages about sex and consent; for example, online pornography and the use of sexting.

- Address violence against women at its root cause—the inequality between women and men, in particular women's lesser access to money and resources. In practical terms, increase women's understanding about their financial position and entitlements. Provide information seminars on farm income and entitlements, superannuation, and farm succession and inheritance.

The question is who will undertake this work. Culture change can begin with anyone. As Margaret Mead famously said, "Never doubt that a small group of committed people can change the world. Indeed, it is the only thing that ever has."

## References

Allimant, A. and Ostapiej-Piatkowski, B. (2011) *Supporting Women from CALD Backgrounds who are Victim/Survivors of Sexual Violence: Challenges and Opportunities for Practitioners*. ACSSA Wrap No. 9. Melbourne: Australian Institute of Family Studies.

Alston, M., Allan, J., Dietsch, E., Wilkinson, J. *et al.* (2006) "Brutal neglect: Australian rural women's access to health services." *Rural Remote Health 6*, 1. Available at www. rrh.org.au/publishedarticles/article_print_475.pdf, accessed July 16, 2012.

Atkinson, J. (2002) "Voices in the wilderness—restoring justice to traumatised people." *UNSW Law Journal 25*, 233–241.

Australian Bureau of Statistics (2013) Regional *Population Growth, Australia,* 2011–12. Available at http://www.abs.gov.au/ausstats/abs@.nsf/Products/3218.0 ~2011-12~Main+Features~Main+Features?OpenDocument#PARALINK0, accessed August 11, 2013.

Australian Government (2011) *Women's Budget Statement 2011–2012.* Available at www.resources.fahcsia.gov.au/budget/2011-12/Womens_Budget_2011.pdf, accessed July 15, 2012.

Australian Institute of Health and Welfare (2008) *Rural, Regional and Remote Health: Indicators of Health Status and Determinants of Health.* Rural Health Series No. 9. Cat. No. PHE 97. Canberra: Australian Institute of Health and Welfare.

Australian Law Reform Commission (2010) "Family violence—a national legal response." *Australian Law Reform Commission Report 114.* Sydney: Australian Law Reform Commission.

Barclay, E., Foskey, R., and Reeve, I. (2007) *Farm Succession and Inheritance. Comparing Australian and International Trends.* Report to the Rural Industries Research and Development Corporation, Institute for Rural Futures, University of New England, Armidale. Available at www.rirdc.gov.au/fullreports/hcc.html, accessed July 16, 2012.

Boyd, C. (2008) "Research review: where is care in the country?" *ACSSA Aware 16.* Melbourne: Australian Centre for the Study of Sexual Assault. Available at www. aifs.gov.au/acssa/pubs/newsletter/n16.html#where, accessed July 16, 2012.

Braaf, R. and Gilbert, R. (2007) *Domestic Violence Incident Peaks: Seasonal Factors, Calendar Events and Sporting Matches.* Stakeholder Paper 2. Sydney: Australian Domestic and Family Violence Clearinghouse.

Cowan, S. (2008) *Expose the Hidden—Rape is Rape.* Wangaratta, Victoria: Women's Health Goulburn North East.

Crenshaw, K.W. (1991) "Mapping the margins: intersectionality, identity politics, and violence against women of color." *Stanford Law Review 43*, 6, 1241–1299.

Daly, K. (2011) "Conventional and innovative justice responses to sexual violence." *ACSSA Issues No. 12.* Melbourne: Australian Centre for the Study of Sexual Assault.

Department of the Attorney General (2009) *Family and Domestic Violence—Equality Before the Law: Benchbook.* Perth: Department of the Attorney General.

Drug Info Clearinghouse (2008) *Prevention of Harm from Alcohol Consumption in Rural and Remote Communities.* Available at www.druginfo.adf.org.au/attachments/346_PRQ04Feb08_final.pdf, accessed July 15, 2012.

Dyson, S., Flood, M., Mitchell, A., and Fox, C. (2007) "AFL Respectful Behaviours in Sport: Building Cultures of Respect and Non-violence—A Review of Literature." In Australian Football League, VicHealth, and the Australian Research Centre, *Sex, Health and Society.* Melbourne: La Trobe University.

Easteal, P. and McOrmond-Plummer, L. (2006) *Real Rape, Real Pain: Help for Women Sexually Assaulted by Male Partners.* Melbourne: Hybrid Publishers.

Finkelhor, D. and Yllo, K. (1985) *License to Rape: Sexual Abuse of Wives*. New York: The Free Press.

Hogg, R. and Carrington, K. (2003) "Violence, spatiality and other rurals." *Australian & New Zealand Journal of Criminology 36*, 3, 293–319. doi:10.1375/acri.36.3.293

Inter-Agency Standing Committee (2005) *Guidelines for Gender-based Violence Interventions in Humanitarian Settings Focusing on Prevention of and Response to Sexual Violence in Emergencies*. Geneva: Inter-Agency Standing Committee. Available at www.humanitarianinfo.org/iasc/downloadDoc.aspx?docID=4402, accessed July 16, 2012.

James, K., Seddon, B., and Brown, J. (2002) *Using It or Losing It: Men's Constructions of their Violence towards Female Partners*. Research Paper 1. Sydney: University of New South Wales, Australian Domestic and Family Violence Clearinghouse.

Lewis, S. (2003) *Sexual Assault in Rural Communities*. VAWnet, National Sexual Violence Resource Center. Available at www.ncdsv.org/images/VAWnet_SAinRuralCommunities_9-2003.pdf, accessed July 16, 2012.

Lievore, D. (2003) *Non-Reporting and Hidden Recording of Sexual Assault: An International Literature Review*. Canberra: Australian Institute of Criminology.

Marmot, M. and Wilkinson, R.G. (eds.) (2006) *Social Determinants of Health*, Second Edition. New York: Oxford University Press.

Mission Australia (2006) *Rural and Regional Australia: Change, Challenge and Capacity*. Sydney: Mission Australia.

Myhill, A. and Allen, J. (2002) *Rape and Sexual Assault of Women: Findings from the British Crime Survey*. London: Home Office. Available at www.aphroditewounded.org/Myhill and Allen.pdf, accessed July 4, 2013.

National Council to Reduce Violence against Women and their Children (2009) *Time for Action: The National Council's Plan for Australia to Reduce Violence against Women and their Children, 2009–2021*. Canberra: ACT Commonwealth of Australia.

Neame, A. and Heenan, M. (2004) "Responding to sexual assault in rural communities." *ACSSA Briefing 3*, 1–23.

Parkinson, D. (2008) *Raped by a Partner: A Research Report*. Wangaratta, Victoria: Women's Health Goulburn North East.

Parkinson, D., Burns, K., and Zara, C. (2004) *A Powerful Journey: Women Reflect on What Helped Them Leave*. Wangaratta, Victoria: Women's Health Goulburn North East.

Slama, K. (2004) "Rural culture is a diversity issue." *Minnesota Psychologist*, January, 9–13.

Taylor, N. and Mouzos, M. (2006) *Community Attitudes to Violence Against Women Survey 2006: A Full Technical Report*. Canberra: Australian Institute of Criminology.

Tonts, M. (2005) "Competitive sport and social capital in rural Australia." *Journal of Rural Studies 21*, 137–145.

Victoria Police (2011) Family incident reports. Data extracted from LEAP on July 18, 2011. Melbourne.

Victorian Law Reform Commission (2006) *Review of Family Violence Laws Report*. Melbourne: Victorian Law Reform Commission.

CHAPTER 23

# Addressing Intimate Partner Sexual Violence in Teen Relationships

Jennifer Y. Levy-Peck

## Defining teen intimate partner sexual violence

Sexual violence in teen relationships is often discussed as an aspect of "teen dating violence," a term so popular it now has its own awareness month—February—in the United States. However, "dating violence" is not the most accurate description of the problem. Teen relationships are so varied that the traditional notion of dating does not reflect the current reality. In addition, the term "violence" tends to evoke images of physical abuse. The sexual violence that teens experience varies from harassment to rape, and teens often do not recognize or label what has happened to them as a violation. The term "adolescent relationship abuse" more accurately reflects the range of coercion and assault that occurs in teen (and even pre-teen) relationships (California Adolescent Health Collaborative 2011).

Intimate partner sexual violence (IPSV) takes many forms in teen relationships. It may consist of sexually derogatory verbal abuse, pressure to have sex for fear of disappointing or angering a partner, threats (implicit or explicit), or attempted or completed rape. It can include deceiving a teen into thinking a romantic relationship exists, only to force her into sex trafficking; threatening to "out" a gay or bisexual teen in order to force a sexual act; or sabotaging a partner's contraception to gain control.

As with adults, sexual violence perpetrated by a partner may or may not be accompanied by physical violence. There are a variety of strategies whereby an offender can control or coerce a victim, including deception, social pressure, intimidation, and preying on an individual's sexual naiveté. Teens are exceptionally vulnerable to these pressures because of their natural desire to fit in with their peers and the fact that they are still learning about the realities of life, sex, and relationships.

## Prevalence of teen intimate partner sexual violence

Teen IPSV is a hidden and under-researched issue for a number of reasons. Because it is difficult to define in a way that is both understandable to teens and standardized in research studies, the literature shows widely varying statistics regarding the prevalence of partner sexual assault or coercion. The National Intimate Partner and Sexual Violence Survey (Black *et al.* 2011) states that more than half (51.1%) of women who experienced rape in their lifetime and 75 percent of women who experienced lifetime sexual coercion were assaulted by current or former intimate partners. In this survey, 42 percent of female victims experienced their first rape before the age of 18, and 75 percent of the victims were first raped before age 25.

Harner (2003), having conducted an extensive literature review, concludes that, excluding sexual abuse by a parent or caregiver, "most sexual victimization experienced by young women is perpetrated by dating partners or acquaintances and may occur in the context of other dating violence, including physical and emotional abuse" (p.2). Silverman *et al.* (2001) surveyed high school students and found that one in five female students reported experiencing physical and/or sexual violence by a dating partner. Since some older teens are in college, it is noteworthy that the percentage of college women who are victims of attempted or completed rape "might climb to between one-fifth and one-quarter" (Fisher, Cullen, and Turner 2000, p.10). Clearly, teen girls are at risk for IPSV.

While this chapter focuses on teen girls in heterosexual relationships, LGBTQI (lesbian, gay, bisexual, transgender, queer/ questioning, and intersex) youth are also victimized by dating partners (Winters 2009). Boys in heterosexual relationships may be pressured or coerced into sexual activity as well (Harner 2003). Programs and professionals that address teen IPSV should use inclusive language, be aware of the additional barriers that LGBTQI and male survivors may face in getting help, and partner with community agencies to facilitate understanding and outreach.

## Context of teen intimate partner sexual violence

To a certain extent, teens live in their own subculture, which is highly influenced by the commercialization of sex. It is critical to understand the connection of teen IPSV to the cultural norms and messages to which adolescents are exposed. According to a study by the Kaiser Family Foundation (Kunkel *et al.* 2005), 70 percent of the television shows most watched by teens contain sexual content, and nearly half contain sexual behavior. Teens watch actors and singers who behave and dress in a sexually suggestive manner. Girls' magazines are filled with advice about being attractive to boys. And yet, teen girls are also expected to be the sexual "gatekeepers," restricting sexual activity, while boys are surrounded by cultural messages that equate masculinity with sexual prowess (Friedman and Valenti 2008).

Hird and Jackson (2001) conducted extensive group discussions with adolescents in England and New Zealand and stated:

> On the one hand, girls are barraged through popular media with the idea that they ought to be having sexual intercourse in order to establish their status as adults, but risk being labeled "slut" if they do become actively sexual. (p.33)

The young men in this study believed that males have a strong biological imperative to be sexually forceful, even in the face of resistance by a girl.

> Male sexual need is understood to be so strong as to override what a girlfriend wants and leads to an interpretation of her protests as an impediment to be overcome. Such a construction of male sexuality excuses rape, attributing responsibility to biology rather than any "conscious" decision. (p.36)

The girls in this study were not immune to this point of view, thereby often rationalizing and minimizing their partners' sexual violence.

Brady and Halpern-Felsher (2008) found that both sexually experienced and inexperienced youth felt there were negative consequences of refraining from sexual activity, including: "partner became angry, had a bad reputation, felt regret, felt left out, felt like you let your partner down" (p.164). Consistent with the mixed messages girls receive from society, they were more likely than boys to report higher rates of both negative and positive consequences of refraining from sexual activity. Sexually experienced girls reported higher rates of negative consequences from refraining than those who were inexperienced, suggesting that, once teens become sexually active, it is harder for them to draw back from sexual activity. The responses regarding partners becoming angry or disappointed as a consequence of sexual refusal take on a more ominous feeling in physically or emotionally abusive relationships, and reveal the types of sexual pressure that teens may feel.

IPSV among teens may be concealed from parents and other adults. Teens often use technology, such as cell phones and online messaging, to communicate with their partners. Parents are often unaware of these communications (Liz Claiborne, Inc./Teen Research Unlimited 2008). In addition, teens at risk for IPSV may be involved in activities that they do not wish to reveal to adults, such as drinking or dating older partners. In combination with the isolating tactics common to abusers, these factors may allow abuse to persist undetected.

## Teen relationships

Despite the modern phenomena of online relationships, "hooking up," and other nontraditional arrangements, teens still identify themselves as being involved in romantic relationships. The Add Health study asked adolescents about involvement in romantic relationships in the previous 18 months. Approximately 25 percent of 12-year-olds, 50 percent of 15-year-olds, and 70 percent of 18-year-olds answered affirmatively (Carver, Joyner, and Udry 2003). Ryan, Manlove, and Franzetta (2003) found that 85 percent of teens stated their first sexual relationship was with a romantic partner; however, approximately one quarter of these teens reported verbal and/or physical violence during their first sexual relationship.

Any approach to teen IPSV must take into account the variety of possible relationships in which it may occur. Manning, Giordano, and Longmore (2006), in reviewing a large-scale study of adolescents, observed that "more than three fifths of sexually active adolescents eventually have sexual encounters outside of a traditional dating context with partners ranging from strangers to friends to former boyfriends or girlfriends" (Liace, Nunez, and Luckner 2011, paragraph 3). Manning and colleagues (2006) noted that 61 percent of sexually active teens had sex outside of a dating relationship. The potential for sexual victimization exists in these encounters as well as in ongoing relationships.

Adolescent relationships are influenced by developmental factors as well. Teens' brains are still forming, affecting the capacity for good judgment and the ability to consider long-term consequences. The story of Romeo and Juliet attests to the intensity of young love and its imperviousness to the opinions of adults. At the same time, teens are highly sensitive to peers' perceptions, which may include acceptance of behaviors and values that contribute to IPSV, such as male entitlement to unlimited sexual access with a partner or a certain level of physical violence in a relationship (Hyman, Lucibello, and Meyer 2010).

## Age and vulnerability

Because power and control issues are central to abusive relationships, it is important to note that 20 percent of teen girls have a partner who is four or more years older, and 50 percent of girls who become sexually active at age 14 or earlier have a partner who is at least two years older (Ryan *et al.* 2003). While a mature 19-year-old with a 23-year-old boyfriend may have a reasonably egalitarian relationship, a 13-year-old who is dating an 18-year-old is at risk of being dominated and controlled.

A study of youth ages 11 to 14 found that one out of three who had sex by age 14 reported physical abuse by a partner, 36 percent said they were pressured into having oral sex when they did not want to, and 34 percent said they were pressured into unwanted intercourse (Liz Claiborne, Inc./Teen Research Unlimited 2008). Younger adolescents may have a harder time identifying coercive behaviors because they have less experience with relationships. They may also be more vulnerable because they wish to conceal their sexual activity, knowing that parents will disapprove. Abusers may target young teens because of their increased vulnerability.

## Reproductive coercion

Even in nonabusive relationships, adolescents may struggle to negotiate birth control use with their partners. To discuss contraception effectively, an individual must have sufficient knowledge, adequate communication skills, and the ability to assert himself or herself in a safe environment. Teens in abusive relationships may be pressured or forced to become pregnant, to continue or terminate a pregnancy, or to engage in risky sexual practices such as sex without condoms

(Miller *et al.* 2010). The result may be an unintended pregnancy or a sexually transmitted infection, both of which can have a major impact on a young person's life.

## Teen pregnancy and parenting

In general, teens have more options than older women for leaving an abusive partner, because they are less likely to be married or to have children in common. Teens who are pregnant or have children are a notable exception. Teen mothers are more likely than other teens to be abused (Buell 2002), and young women in abusive relationships are more likely to have another pregnancy within months of giving birth (Jacoby *et al.* 1999; Raneri and Wiemann 2007). They may be emotionally or financially dependent on their abusers, and may wish to maintain a relationship between the child and his or her father. When an abuser is the father of the survivor's child, he may insist on contact with his former partner and have more leverage for coercion.

## Prevention with teens and their parents

Many sexual violence prevention programs for adolescents fail to focus appropriately on sexual assault and coercion within intimate relationships. In addition, the approach is often focused on avoiding victimization, rather than preventing perpetration and changing the societal underpinnings of sexual violence. This reinforces the message that somehow the responsibility for reducing sexual assault belongs to girls.

Effective prevention programs should be evidence-based, address issues such as gender stereotypes that lay the foundation for sexual violence, and emphasize healthy relationships and the need to obtain clear consent for any sexual interaction (Berkowitz 2001). Prevention programming should take into account the context of sexual violence, including media messages and online interaction, and include bystander intervention strategies, since peers are often the first to know about teen victimization (Tabachnick 2009).

In addition to learning the elements of healthy and safe relationships, teens need a strong foundation of basic sexual knowledge and an understanding of all the nuances of giving and receiving consent. They need to know their legal rights and responsibilities (such as "age of consent" laws) and be able to identify danger signals and grooming behavior.

Parents need to learn skills for discussing healthy sexuality and relationships with their children, starting early in life. A positive parent–child relationship is a protective factor, and open communication makes it more likely that teens will disclose relationship concerns before problems escalate to abuse. The Washington Coalition of Sexual Assault Programs (2010) has developed a series of resources on *Parenting to Keep Teens Safer from Sexual Violence in Relationships* to address this need.

## Barriers to intervention

Ashley and Foshee (2005) studied the help-seeking behaviors of 225 victims and 140 perpetrators of "dating violence" and found that the majority (60% of victims and 79% of perpetrators) sought no help whatsoever. However, those who did seek help turned to friends and family members first and foremost. While this study included only adolescents in rural North Carolina, and thus may have limited generalizability, education about partner violence is important in reaching both victims and perpetrators. If teens and parents can identify various forms of abuse and respond appropriately to disclosures, and if they are aware of resources, the information is more likely to reach those who need it.

The effects of trauma on teens' behavior may create additional barriers to seeking help. As the Adverse Childhood Experiences Study (Centers for Disease Control 2012) demonstrates, young people may have experienced multiple forms of trauma. In this large-scale survey, 41 percent of women reported two or more adverse experiences in childhood, including various forms of abuse, neglect, or household dysfunction. Nearly 23 percent of college rape victims were raped more than once (Fisher *et al.* 2000). Additional victimization experiences may leave IPSV survivors with cumulative effects of trauma. Teens may respond to the trauma of IPSV, in combination with any past stressors, by abusing drugs or alcohol, self-injuring, developing mental health symptoms, or becoming withdrawn or angry (Silverman *et al.* 2001). Because the essence of IPSV is betrayal by the very person the survivor believed to be most trustworthy, trusting others (including well-intentioned service providers) may be very difficult. Teens are also vulnerable to accepting the verbal abuse that usually accompanies IPSV, leading to impaired self-concept and difficulty believing effective action is possible.

One factor that undermines response to teen IPSV is the belief of some authorities that it is simply the result of miscommunication—the boy or man did not understand the girl was not willing. While miscommunication may occur, it is often rooted in attitudes of male entitlement and disregard for obtaining clear consent. Abusers who commit acts of sexual violence against intimate partners may engage in "grooming" behaviors, lulling the victim into thinking she is a valued partner. In a study of male college students, Lisak and Miller (2002) found that among a subgroup of men whose self-reported behaviors met the legal definition of rape or attempted rape but who had never been charged, the majority had committed multiple acts of sexual violence, averaging 5.8 rapes each. This certainly calls into question the common perception that "acquaintance rape" is a simple misunderstanding between two young people.

## Reaching the perpetrator

Therefore, effective intervention for teen IPSV should focus not only on providing support and services to survivors, but also on creating accountability and effective change for perpetrators. Sadly, there is little movement toward this goal. Very few of these cases enter the criminal justice system, because they are complex, difficult to prosecute, and often re-traumatize survivors. Teen survivors may avoid making police reports or pursuing criminal options for many of the same reasons cited by adult survivors (embarrassment, fear of retaliation, or an expectation they will not be believed). In addition, teens may not wish to reveal their circumstances to their parents or may be actively discouraged from legal action by parents or peers. One remedy is effective advocacy addressing these individual concerns as well as the larger issue of creating integrated, survivor-friendly responses from various service systems.

Even when cases go to court, there are few programs specifically for young abusers and victims. Buel (2002) recounts some new efforts to intervene with "juvenile batterers," teens who are violent to parents or intimate partners. Hyman *et al.* (2010) describe two promising programs in California and New York. The common factors are:

- strong professional collaborations
- "significant and specific" victim services targeted to the needs of teens
- batterer intervention programs specific to adolescents
- "reasonably fast" dispositions of cases.

## Services for survivors

Sexual assault and domestic violence advocacy programs have the potential to offer effective support to teen IPSV survivors, whether or not they are involved in the legal process. Teens may not utilize advocacy services for a number of reasons: (1) they don't identify what is happening to them as abuse; (2) the term "domestic violence" doesn't seem to apply to them; (3) they may have access concerns because of transportation problems or the wish to maintain secrecy from their parents; (4) discussing sexual activity with an adult may be daunting; and (5) the programs' messaging and appearance may appeal to adults rather than teens. Advocacy programs can benefit from working with existing teen advisory groups (such as those run by Planned Parenthood) or establishing their own advisory group to obtain input on creating appropriate outreach messages and a welcoming, teen-friendly environment and approach. Partnerships with educators and with other professionals who work with adolescents may increase the number of teens who seek advocacy services.

Health care professionals and mental health clinicians (as well as advocates) will be able to provide more effective interventions by educating themselves on teen sexual coercion and specifically on IPSV. In order to create a trusting relationship between the teen and the provider, it is crucial that all youth-serving professionals learn about mandatory abuse reporting requirements and communicate this information to teens in a straightforward manner before providing services. Service providers can offer *all* teen clients useful, effective information about IPSV identification and resources. This can help teens who are not yet ready to disclose abuse, as well as those who have friends in abusive relationships.

# Specific recommendations for various disciplines
## Health care providers

- See adolescent patients alone, without accompanying parents or partners, for at least a portion of each visit. This offers the opportunity for the patient to discuss sensitive concerns safely.

- Consider using the "Hanging Out or Hooking Up" cards developed by Futures Without Violence (2010) and recommended in a document co-sponsored by the American College of Obstetricians and Gynecologists (Futures Without Violence 2012) to provide information to young patients and to prompt discussion of relationship issues.

- Incorporate information about sexual coercion into any visit concerning contraception, sexually transmitted infection prevention, pregnancy concerns, or postpartum issues.

- Develop relationships with community-based advocacy programs and learn about their services for teens so that you can make informed referrals.

## Mental health clinicians

- Consider the possibility of IPSV as an underlying factor in depression, anxiety, posttraumatic stress disorder, eating disorders, and substance abuse (Silverman et al. 2001).

- Educate teen clients and their parents about IPSV.

- Include IPSV topics in presentations to professionals or community members.

- Consider cross-training opportunities with local advocacy programs to share information and develop a comfortable relationship, making the referral process easier.

## Sexual assault and domestic violence advocates

- Learn as much as possible about teen IPSV.

- Use teen "consultants" to ensure your program's messages, facilities, and services are teen-friendly.

- Be clear about limits of confidentiality and mandated reporting requirements, and communicate this information prior to providing services.

- Include information about IPSV in outreach and prevention programming.

- Work with high schools and colleges to develop sexual assault policies and services.

- Consider offering a support group for teen IPSV survivors.

## *Criminal justice professionals*

These recommendations were summarized from Hyman *et al.* 2010.

- Consider the need for specialized services for adolescent victims and perpetrators.

- Focus on accountability and effective intervention for young perpetrators.

- Engage the community.

## Conclusion

Adolescents are vulnerable to IPSV. Because they are in a period of change and growth, it is especially vital that their relationships remain safe and healthy. Professionals who work with teens can create a collaborative community environment to help teens receive consistent messages about relationship abuse and to direct survivors to appropriate resources. While these efforts represent a substantial investment of time and energy, they offer teens positive options for safety and wellbeing.

## References

Ashley, O.S. and Foshee, V.A. (2005) "Adolescent help-seeking for dating violence: prevalence, sociodemographic correlates, and sources of help." *Journal of Adolescent Health 36*, 25–31.

Berkowitz, A. (2001) "Critical Elements of Sexual Assault Prevention and Risk-Reduction Programs for Men and Women." In C. Kilmartin (ed.) *Sexual Assault in Context.* Holmes Beach, FL: Learning Publications, Inc.

Black, M.C., Basile, K.C., Breiding, M.J., Smith, S.G. et al. (2011) *The National Intimate Partner and Sexual Violence Survey (NISVS): 2010 Summary Report.* Atlanta, GA: National Center for Injury Prevention and Control, Centers for Disease Control and Prevention. Available at www.cdc.gov/violenceprevention/pdf/nisvs_executive_summary-a.pdf, accessed June 2, 2013.

Brady, S.S. and Halpern-Felsher, B.L. (2008) "Social and emotional consequences of refraining from sexual activity among sexually experienced and inexperienced youths in California." *American Journal of Public Health 98*, 1, 162–168. doi: 10.2105/AJPH.2006.097923

Buel, S.M. (2002) "Why juvenile courts should address family violence: Promising practices to improve intervention outcomes." *Juvenile and Family Court Journal, 53*, 2, 1-16.

California Adolescent Health Collaborative (2011) *Adolescent Relationship Abuse.* Oakland, CA: California Adolescent Health Collaborative. Available at www.californiateenhealth.org/health-topics/adolescent-relationship-abuse, accessed June 20, 2012.

Carver, K., Joyner, K., and Udry, R.J. (2003) "National Estimates of Adolescent Romantic Relationships." In P. Florsheim (ed.) *Adolescent Romantic Relationships and Sexual Behavior: Theory, Research, and Practical Implications.* Mahwah, NJ: LEA.

Centers for Disease Control (2012) *Adverse Childhood Experiences Study.* Available at www.cdc.gov/ace/index.htm, accessed June 5, 2012.

Fisher, B.S., Cullen, F.T., and Turner, M.G. (2000) *The Sexual Victimization of College Women.* Washington, DC: National Institute of Justice.

Friedman, J. and Valenti, J. (2008) *Yes Means Yes: Visions of Female Sexual Power & a World without Rape.* Berkeley, CA: Seal Press.

Futures Without Violence (2010) *Hanging Out or Hooking Up: Teen Safety Cards.* Available at http://www.futureswithoutviolence.org/content/features/detail/1653, accessed August 11, 2013.

Futures Without Violence (2012) *Hanging out or hooking up: Clinical guidelines on responding to adolescent relationship abuse.* San Francisco: Futures Without Violence. Available at http://www.futureswithoutviolence.org/userfiles/file/HealthCare/Adolescent%20Health%20Guide.pdf, accessed on 2 February 2012.

Harner, H. (2003) *Sexual Violence and Adolescents.* VAWnet: The National Online Resource Center on Violence Against Women. Available at http://new.vawnet.org/Assoc_Files_VAWnet/AR_Adolescent.pdf, accessed June 4, 2012.

Hird, M. and Jackson, S. (2001) "Where 'angels' and 'wusses' fear to tread: Sexual coercion in adolescent dating relationships." *Journal of Sociology 37*, 27-43.

Hyman, E.W., Lucibello, W., and Meyer, E. (2010) "In love or in trouble: examining ways court professionals can better respond to victims of adolescent partner violence." *Juvenile and Family Court Journal 61*, 40, 17–37.

Jacoby, M., Gorenflo, D., Black, E., Wunderlich, C. and Eyler, A.E. (1999) "Rapid repeat pregnancy and experiences of interpersonal violence among low-income adolescents." *American Journal of Preventive Medicine, 16*, 4, 318-321.

Kunkel, D., Eyal, K., Finnerty, K., Biely, E. *et al.* (2005) *Sex on TV 4: A Kaiser Family Foundation Report.* Available at www.kff.org/other/sex-on-tv-4-report, accessed June 1, 2012.

Liace, L.K., Nunez, J.B., and Luckner, A.E. (2011) "Casual sex in adolescence: outcomes and implications for practice." *Communiqué Online 39*, 6. Available at www.nasponline.org/publications/cq/39/6/casual-sex-in-adolescence.aspx, accessed June 8, 2012.

Lisak, D. and Miller, D.M. (2002) "Repeat rape and multiple offending among undetected rapists." *Violence and Victims 17*, 1, 73–84.

Liz Claiborne, Inc./Teen Research Unlimited (2008) *Teen/Tween Dating Relationships Survey*. Available at www.loveisnotabuse.com/web/guest/search/-/journal_content/56/10123/83545, accessed May 2, 2012.

Manning, W.D., Giordano, P.C., and Longmore, M.A. (2006) "Hooking up: the relationship contexts of 'nonrelationship' sex." *Journal of Adolescent Research, 21*, 459–483.

Miller, E., Decker, M.R., McCauley, H.L., Tancredi, D.J. *et al.* (2010) "Pregnancy coercion, intimate partner violence, and unintended pregnancy." *Contraception 81*, 4, 316–322.

Raneri, L. G. and Wiemann, C. M. (2007) "Social ecological predictors of repeat adolescent pregnancy." *Perspectives on Sexual and Reproductive Health, 39*, 1, 39-47.

Ryan, S., Manlove, J., and Franzetta, K. (2003) *The First Time: Characteristics of Teens' First Sexual Relationships*. Washington, DC: ChildTrends. Available at http://www.childtrends.org/wp-content/uploads/2003/08/First-Time.pdf, accessed August 11, 2013.

Silverman, J.G., Raj, A., Mucci, L.A., and Hathaway, J.E. (2001) "Dating violence against adolescent girls and associated substance use, unhealthy weight control, sexual risk behavior, pregnancy, and suicidality." *JAMA 286*, 5, 572–579.

Tabachnick, J. (2009) *Engaging Bystanders in Sexual Violence Prevention*. Enola, PA: National Sexual Violence Resource Center.

Washington Coalition of Sexual Assault Programs (2010) *Parenting to Keep Teens Safer from Sexual Violence in Relationships*. Available at www.wcsap.org/ipsv-resources-publications, accessed May 4, 2012.

Winters, M. (2009) "Making the Connections: Advocating for Survivors of Intimate Partner Sexual Violence." In Washington Coalition of Sexual Assault Programs (ed.) *Intimate Partner Sexual Violence: Sexual Assault in the Context of Domestic Violence*. Olympia, WA: Washington Coalition of Sexual Assault Programs.

# CHAPTER 24

# Effective Approaches to Helping Intimate Partner Sexual Violence Survivors in Prison

Debbie Kilroy

## The complex experiences of women in prison

Women in prison are not a homogeneous group, yet despite this, many of them share a history which includes being a victim of violence and sexual abuse. While this experience has undoubtedly affected their entrance into the criminal justice system as well as their response to service provision, it must be noted at the outset that it is not the experience of violence and sexual abuse alone which shapes a woman's needs; it is also her unique personal resources, values, and motivations. Effective service provision will always begin with supporting women to identify their *own* needs and goals.

Notwithstanding the potentially low reporting rate of intimate partner sexual violence (IPSV), the prevalence of a history of domestic violence and sexual assault is high within the community, and even more so with incarcerated women. For incarcerated women, the prevalence is dramatically high, with 60 percent experiencing some form of child abuse and 80 percent being the victim of violent abuse as an adult (Johnson 2004). The high prevalence of abuse is particularly salient for Aboriginal and Torres Strait Islander women in prison in Australia, where 75 percent have experienced childhood sexual abuse, 50 percent have experienced sexual abuse as an adult, and 80 percent have experienced family violence (Taylor and Putt 2007).

Violent physical and sexual abuse of women can set victims on a path which leads to their own criminalization. While victimization can mark the beginning of a pathway into criminalization, the effects of victimization can also negatively impact a woman's ability to cope with the stress and strain of life in prison. Furthermore it can increase the risk that women will reoffend when released, particularly if they are not well supported to avoid situations where they may be revictimized.

Many of the pathways into criminalization described above relate to the pragmatic response of many women to victimization; however, there are a range of emotional and cognitive impacts on women who experience IPSV which also shape their behavior and capacity to make choices.

## Complicating factors

In addition to violent antecedents, many women prisoners have additional factors which may further impact their experiences and response to service provision. Some of these factors include the following:

- As many as 85 percent of the women in prison are mothers of dependent or young children and were their sole caregivers prior to being incarcerated (Anti-Discrimination Commission Queensland 2006).

- Around half of all women prisoners are dependent on illicit drugs (Johnson 2004).

- Many of the women in prison come from economically and socially disadvantaged backgrounds with high rates of unemployment and low rates of education and training (Kilroy 2004).

- Up to 85 percent of women in prisons have a diagnosable mental illness (Tye 2002, as cited in Cerveri et al. 2005).

- Up to half of the women in prison have some form of learning disability or cognitive impairment (Anti-Discrimination Commission Queensland 2006).

- Thirty-five percent of female inmates in an Australian study reported at least one head injury with a loss of consciousness (Rushworth 2011).

Women with pre-existing strong mental health who do not abuse alcohol or drugs may be more resilient to both victimization and criminalization. However, women who lack economic resources and are predisposed to mental health issues or substance abuse, and/ or have cognitive difficulties, may be more vulnerable to repeated victimization as well as the short- and long-term negative effects of being victimized. Similarly they may be more negatively affected by the experience of criminalization, and their risk of reoffending may be higher. Also, recognition of the impact of additional considerations for Indigenous women (and American Indian, Native Alaskan, and Canadian First Nations women) is integral to effective service delivery to this special population. Therefore, it is important that service provision is flexible and provides a holistic response to the many complex issues these women have experienced.

## Intimate partner sexual violence— coping and consequences

There are a range of consequences and responses for women who have experienced IPSV. While there is often a misconception in the community that women who are in abusive relationships are passive, this may be a gross misrepresentation of reality. "Women living with and leaving violent men say that they want the violence to stop and are often actively engaged in trying to protect themselves and their children" (Norman and Barron 2011, p.13). These women are often proactively trying to deal with their situation with the resources they have available to them. However, these resources may be even more limited for women who have had adverse contact with the criminal justice system, as there is evidence that they may be less likely to seek help from mainstream community services for fear of police and child protection involvement (Rumgay 2004). Therefore, these women may find it even harder to escape the abuse. While this section outlines some of the potential symptoms of victimization, it is important to recognize that these women are also survivors.

### *Consequences of trauma and posttraumatic stress disorder*

It is important to understand the different responses to IPSV which women in prison may demonstrate. Often, the level of symptoms experienced is not based on the severity of the trauma, but on the individual response of each woman and the level of support or intervention received after the trauma. Women should be supported based on the type and severity of symptoms they experience, rather than the type of trauma they experience. Therefore, understanding the different potential symptoms is important.

There are a range of physical and psychological symptoms associated with trauma. Some of these combine to form the basis of a clinical diagnosis of a mental illness; however, some women experience symptoms of trauma yet do not meet the clinical threshold for a mental health disorder. Additionally, not all symptoms may cause women personal distress, and therefore they may either not acknowledge the symptom or not desire any "treatment" of the symptom. Substance abuse is a good example of this. Therefore, it is not only important to recognize that each woman will have a unique set of symptoms from her trauma, but women will also have differing perspectives on their needs in relation to addressing these "symptoms."

While low self-esteem and blaming themselves for the abuse is common among female victims of IPSV, these effects can become even more serious when they are paired with or part of a broader mental health disorder such as depression, anxiety, or posttraumatic stress disorder (PTSD). Research demonstrates that exposure to high levels of ongoing stress has a negative physiological impact on both the body and the brain and can lead to greater rates of neurologically based depression (Higgins and George 2007). Therefore, women who live in abusive relationships have a higher risk of developing depression, which can include symptoms such as diminished motivation, increased agitation, and feelings of worthlessness or excessive guilt (American Psychiatric Association 2000). These thoughts and feelings can impact abuse survivors' risk of offending, their ability to cope within a prison environment, and if untreated their ability to successfully return to the community.

Similarly, constant exposure to stress can increase the risk of developing an anxiety disorder which can be characterized by irritability, difficulty concentrating, and feeling constantly "keyed up" (American Psychiatric Association 2000). As with depression, living within a prison environment may exacerbate these symptoms or even be sufficient to cause them. Furthermore, it can be difficult to identify what is a "normal" response to the prison environment; for example, decreased motivation due to the lack of available and relevant goal-directed activities, or feeling constantly "keyed up" due to constant monitoring and the inherent threats of prison life. Additionally, women with anxiety may feel that their symptoms serve a functional purpose which supports their survival in the prison environment, and therefore may not be interested in receiving services aimed at reducing their symptoms while they are still incarcerated.

PTSD shares some symptoms with depression and anxiety; however, there are three unique components to this disorder.

First, women with PTSD *re-experience their trauma*, either through flashbacks, recurring intrusive thoughts, nightmares, or intense psychological and physiological reactions to stimuli which remind them of the trauma. Second, women with PTSD *avoid remembering* the event, either consciously or unconsciously, and this may be observed as memory loss, feelings of detachment, dissociation (disconnection), or even substance use. Finally, women with PTSD may also experience a constant state of *alertness and arousal*, which can result in sleep disturbances, agitation, outbursts, or an exaggerated startle response (National Institute of Mental Health 2013). As with symptoms of anxiety, these final symptoms may be part of an expected response to very real stressors in the prison environment.

Given that an essential feature of PTSD is the avoidance of remembering the trauma and the re-experiencing of the trauma when memories are triggered, it is important that service delivery is extremely sensitive to the possibility of activating trauma memories to avoid revictimization. Any psychotherapy (such as exposure therapy) aimed at reducing PTSD symptoms must be undertaken with care so as not to unduly exacerbate the individual's distress while she is also coping with the difficult and possibly even dangerous environment in prison.

## *Exacerbating symptoms with strip searching*

While women in prison have disproportionately experienced physical and sexual abuse within domestic and family relationships, they continue to experience institutional victimization with frequent routine strip searching. Strip searching is often mandatory before and after any visit with family or even legal counsel. In one extreme example, women in a unit in the Townsville Women's Correctional Centre were required to strip six times per day (Anti-Discrimination Commission Queensland 2006).

Strip searching may create a serious detrimental effect on the health, well-being, and choices of all women in prison, with minimal justification for its contribution to identifying contraband items (Kilroy 2004). However, for the many women in prison who have been sexually abused, strip searching revictimizes them and risks severely exacerbating their symptoms of trauma. They may subsequently avoid situations, such as family visits, whereby they will be required to be strip searched. This not only doubly punishes the women involved, but also punishes their family—which often includes children.

# Service delivery

## Identifying needs and goals for service delivery

The starting point for any effective service delivery is to ensure that the goals of the recipient and provider are aligned. Being able to identify and set their own goals is an empowering process for women in prison and may be one of the few aspects of their life over which they have any choice. Therefore, it is important that the agendas of the prison authority, the funding providers, and the prison counselors or therapists are put aside and a woman is allowed to explore the range of options available to her. An effective way to facilitate this process early in a counseling relationship is through motivational interviewing, a counseling approach largely developed by Miller and Rollnick (2012). This practice adopts the perspective that a woman will only make changes in areas of her life where she is motivated. The motivation may come from fear of the consequences of not changing, or from a desire for the benefits of change. While training in motivational interviewing is recommended, the basic principles and their application to eliciting goals for service provision to incarcerated women who have experienced IPSV are outlined below:

1. *Qualities of the worker.* To facilitate a motivational interview it is important that the worker is nonjudgmental, supportive, and nonconfrontational (Miller and Rollnick 2012). Being nonjudgmental applies equally to the woman's past and current behavior, as well as her choices for herself in the future. For example, if a woman desires to return to an abusive relationship upon release, it is important that she feels comfortable enough to express this and not feel she will be disappointing or angering her worker. In the event that she does not feel comfortable expressing it, then it is likely she will return to the situation anyway and may even cease contact with the worker after her release. However, if she is able to honestly communicate her desire to her worker without judgment, then the worker can assist her to think through both the consequences and benefits of returning, and assist her in safety planning ahead of her release.

2. *Empathy:* While very few counselors will ever understand the experience of being victimized, criminalized, and incarcerated, a genuine effort to understand the perspective of women in

prison is crucial. It is important during a motivational interview that the worker expresses empathy for the experiences and challenges that women in prison have experienced and continue to experience (Miller and Rollnick 2012). For example, even where workers believe that there may be a way out of the abuse and offending cycle, they also need to empathize with the feeling that there is no way out.

3. *Explore discrepancy*: The key to motivational interviewing is supporting women to gently explore discrepancies among their values, thoughts, and behavior. However, this should not be done in a confrontational or challenging way. A good starting point is to realize that we all have discrepancies in our values, thoughts, and behaviors; however, these discrepancies may be more salient for women in prison who have experienced IPSV. For example, they may have competing values relating to the welfare of their children and their personal safety in an abusive relationship. Similarly, they may have different thoughts on what is necessary for survival in prison versus what is necessary for survival in the community. Effective exploration of these discrepancies will assist a woman to identify what values, thoughts, and behaviors will inform her short-term goals while she is incarcerated and what values, thoughts, and behaviors will inform her long-term goals when she has returned to the community. This may be a long and overwhelming process, and it may be helpful to concentrate on one small area at a time, beginning with emotionally safer areas such as employment and training, and then move to more challenging areas such as family and relationships.

4. *Avoid arguing*: While this applies to all good counseling, it is particularly important within the context of motivational interviewing (Miller and Rollnick 2012). As soon as a woman feels that you may be arguing with her perspective, she may adopt a polarized perspective or refuse to engage further. Arguing with her perspective may not always be as obvious as saying "You are wrong because…" Often it will emerge in more subtle ways such as statements like "Yes, but…" In these instances the intention of the worker is not important. Rather the emphasis should be on how a woman perceives the

situation and whether she feels that she is being coerced or convinced into seeing a certain perspective.

5. *Roll with resistance:* Resistance is a very powerful therapeutic tool and is very helpful in motivational interviewing if it is used effectively. Where a woman is resistant to the idea of a particular concept, it is quite useful to explore this resistance and identify what is maintaining the value, thought, or behavior (Moyers and Rollnick 2002). With the example of a woman who wishes to return to an abusive relationship, she may be resistant to leaving for many reasons, such as cultural values against divorce, financial dependence on the abuser, guilt about leaving, and often the potential impact on her children. In this instance she may believe that the benefits of leaving, such as the abuse ceasing, may not outweigh the consequences of leaving, such as losing contact with children or being ostracized from the community. Without exploring and understanding these issues from the perspective of the woman, a worker cannot begin to support her to problem-solve. Therefore it is important that workers identify resistance and endeavor to understand and appreciate where the resistance is coming from.

6. *Support self-efficacy:* The most important aspect of motivational interviewing to elicit goals is to recognize that women in prison who have experienced IPSV are survivors. Therefore it is important to ensure that they realize their own strengths that have allowed them to survive and utilize these to build the life that they choose for themselves. Allowing a woman to make her own choices about goals for service delivery is a good starting point for supporting self-efficacy and communicates to the woman that the worker believes the woman is best placed to make decisions about her life. This is particularly important for women who have experienced IPSV, whereby an integral element of abuse is the power and control of the abuser.

7. *Potential goals of service delivery:* The impact and consequences of IPSV may contribute to a woman's initial offense, level of coping within prison, and risk of reoffending. However, effective service delivery may not necessarily focus on the experience of IPSV; rather, it will deliver services which meet the individual goals of each woman, with sensitivity to their

experiences of IPSV. There is a range of goals which may be explored, and the most effective counseling will support women to pursue one or many of these goals within a time frame which suits the women receiving the service, irrespective of the constraints of funding or judicial orders.

Some of the possible goals are outlined below:

1. *Pragmatic goals*: Women may be primarily interested in pursuing pragmatic goals to minimize the risk of revictimization, minimize the risk of becoming reinvolved with offending cycles, or simply to enhance their life and sense of well-being. These goals are a good starting point to build relationships and trust between a worker and a woman, and may include things such as:

   • enrolling in training or education while incarcerated

   • identifying and accessing post-release housing options

   • identifying and accessing post-release income support

   • accessing legal support in regard to personal legal issues or child protection matters.

2. *Personal values*: As the relationship between a worker and a woman develops, the woman may be interested in exploring some goals related to personal values, such as being a good mother or being financially independent. Some of these goals may be able to be acted upon while the woman remains incarcerated, and some may be goals for the future. It is important that women are not only empowered to consider these goals for themselves, but also encouraged to change goals or add new ones over time. These goals may be more challenging to discuss and achieve than the pragmatic goals; however, they are a good framework for developing a woman's sense of self-efficacy and assisting her to feel more positive about the future.

3. *Therapeutic goals*: As described, women who have experienced IPSV may have a range of emotional and psychological consequences to work through. Depression and anxiety can be successfully treated with medication, and psychotherapy is often an effective adjunct or alternative treatment. Women will have differing opinions on the use of both medication

and psychotherapy, and the most effective treatment will always be the one that a woman is most likely to commit to and comply with. Therefore, support and referrals should be based not only on women's symptoms, but should also include consideration of their personal values and beliefs about mental health treatment. Furthermore, medication alone is not an effective treatment for the recovery of PTSD, particularly where there is no co-morbidity with depression (Oltmans and Emery 2004). Therefore, one of the most effective evidence-based treatments continues to be exposure therapy (American Psychological Association 2003), but this may, as we have seen, be inappropriate in the prison context. Women in prison who suffer PTSD as a consequence of IPSV may be better supported through psychoeducation and referral to therapy post-release, or through therapy that is designed with sensitivity to their need to cope in the prison environment. In addition to this, it is important that advocacy around issues such as strip searching is maintained to limit the damaging impact of the prison environment on these women.

## *The role of advocacy*

The final point to highlight reinforces the importance of advocacy within any service delivery framework. This includes both individual advocacy and systemic advocacy.

### Individual advocacy

This form of advocacy centers on supporting women to have their existing rights met. First, it involves informing women of their rights and the process by which they can enforce their rights, such as the right to seek Victims' Compensation. Second, it involves designing advocacy services to meet the expressed needs and concerns of the individual woman, and being sure to ask what the woman would like to work on with the advocate. While some women may have their rights breached, there may be personal or strategic reasons for avoiding the reinstatement of their rights. Personal advocacy should always be based on the desires articulated by the woman herself rather than the worker's desires for the woman.

## Systemic advocacy

This form of advocacy centers on expanding the existing recognized rights of women. While international conventions may recognize human rights, these are not always recognized within governmental institutions, and systemic advocacy may draw attention to this in an attempt to rectify it. An example of such advocacy is Sisters Inside's campaign against the routine strip searching of women. Sisters Inside is an organization that provides woman-directed individual and system advocacy. It is hoped that the final outcome of such advocacy results in the reduction of the revictimization of women in prison through strip searching. However, equally important is the message behind such advocacy, which highlights to all women in prison that no form of violence or sexual abuse against women is acceptable even when sanctioned by the state. This is an important message for women who have experienced IPSV at the hands of more powerful and controlling abusers, and challenges any notions that they may have in regards to the abuse being deserved, justified, or in any way acceptable. Therefore, it is important that effective service delivery goes beyond meeting the needs and goals of women in prison and attempts to address the systemic forces which continue to victimize them.

# References

American Psychiatric Association (2000) *Diagnostic and Statistical Manual of Mental Disorders, Fourth Edition, Text Revision (DSM-IV-TR)*. Arlington, VA: American Psychiatric Association.

American Psychological Association (2003) *Exposure Therapy Helps PTSD Victims Overcome Trauma's Debilitating Effects*. Washington, DC: American Psychological Association. Available at www.apa.org/research/action/exposure.aspx, accessed March 16, 2013.

Anti-Discrimination Commission Queensland (2006) *Women in Prison: A Report by the Anti-Discrimination Commission Queensland*. Brisbane: Anti-Discrimination Commission Queensland. Available at www.adcq.qld.gov.au/human-rights/women-in-prison-report, accessed August 11, 2013.

Cerveri, P., Colvin, K., Dias, M., George, A. *et al.* (2005) *Request for a Systematic Review of Discrimination Against Women in Victorian Prisons*. Victoria: The Federation of Community Legal Centres and the Victorian Council of Social Service.

Higgins, E.S. and George, M.S. (2007) *The Neuroscience of Clinical Psychiatry: The Pathophysiology of Behavior and Mental Illness*. Philadelphia, PA: Lippincott Williams & Wilkins.

Johnson, H. (2004) *Drugs and Crime: A Study of Incarcerated Female Offenders*. Canberra: Australian Institute of Criminology.

Kilroy, D. (2004) *Submission of Sisters Inside to the Anti-Discrimination Commissioner for the Inquiry into the Discrimination on the Basis of Sex, Race and Disability Experienced by Women Prisoners in Queensland.* Brisbane: Sisters Inside.

Lynch, M., Buckman, J., and Krenske, L. (2003) *Youth Justice: Criminal Trajectories.* Canberra: Australian Institute of Criminology. Available at http://www.aic.gov.au/documents/6/3/2/%7B6327DF90-1459-4D7E-9A8B-F69D7662AA6F%7Dtandi265.pdf, accessed February 28, 2013.

Miller, W. and Rollnick, S. (2012) *Motivational Interviewing: Preparing People for Change,* Third Edition. New York: Guilford Press.

Moyers, T. and Rollnick, S. (2002) "A motivational interviewing perspective on resistance in psychotherapy." *Journal of Clinical Psychology 58,* 185–193.

National Institute of Mental Health (2013) *Post-Traumatic Stress Disorder.* Bethesda, MD: National Institute of Mental Health. Available at www.nimh.nih.gov/health/publications/post-traumatic-stress-disorder-ptsd/what-are-the-symptoms-of-ptsd.shtml, accessed March 16, 2013.

Norman, N. and Barron, J. (2011) *Supporting Women Offenders who have Experienced Domestic and Sexual Violence.* Bristol: Women's Aid Federation of England. Available at www.womensaid.org.uk/domestic_violence_topic.asp?section= 0001000100220048&sectionTitle=Women+in+prison, accessed February 28, 2013.

Oltmans, T. and Emery, R. (2004) *Abnormal Psychology,* Fourth Edition. Saddle River, NJ: Pearson Prentice Hall.

Rumgay, J. (2004) *When Victims Become Offenders: In Search of Coherence in Policy and Practice.* London: Fawcett Society.

Rushworth, N. (2011) *Out of Sight, Out of Mind: People with an Acquired Brain Injury and the Criminal Justice System.* Sydney: Brain Injury Australia. Available at www.bia.net.au/docs/CJSpolicypaperFINAL.pdf, accessed March 16, 2013.

Taylor, N. and Putt, J. (2007) *Adult Sexual Violence in Indigenous and Culturally and Linguistically Diverse Communities in Australia.* Canberra: Australian Institute of Criminology. Available at www.aic.gov.au/publications/current%20series/tandi/341-360/tandi345.html, accessed February 28, 2013.

# PART 5

# Conclusion

CHAPTER 25

# Conclusion

## BRINGING IT ALL TOGETHER

Jennifer Y. Levy-Peck, Patricia Easteal AM,
and Louise McOrmond-Plummer

Intimate partner sexual violence (IPSV) is a manifestation of abuse of power at the personal level. It is shrouded in secrecy and maintained by shame and societal stigma. It is an ugly subject—just hearing about it may cause vicarious traumatization in helping professionals, and living with it has damaged the lives of many individuals, primarily women. Why, then, do we need to dwell on this unpleasant topic? Why are we asking every service provider who may come in contact with the recently victimized or longer-term survivors of IPSV to pay attention, to learn, and to respond differently?

It is because, as Louise McOrmond-Plummer says in Chapter 3, there is "a hole in the knowledge." Over the past few decades, the community at large and service providers in particular have become aware of the widespread and devastating nature of domestic and sexual violence. Yet at the intersection of these very personal forms of abuse there is still a secret: women and teens (and some men) are being coerced into distasteful sexual acts by the very partners who are supposed to love and protect them. We can't turn away from this ugliness because it is part of the lived experience of so many people. We have learned, in the case of domestic violence and sexual assault, that we must name and recognize abusive behavior in order to address it. IPSV is no different.

We need to "dwell on this unpleasant topic" for another reason. There are still so many entrenched community and practitioner beliefs that contribute to a lack of understanding about coercion and negation of consent within intimate relationships. Such "fictions" create a myriad of visible and invisible hurdles for the victims of partner rape in accessing assistance. Our contributors illustrate this potential problematic labyrinth and the potential for secondary wounding as well. They do far more than that, though, and provide a means of translating the "fictions" into victim-based reality documentary and models of best practice.

Accordingly, in Part 2 of this book, we ask the question, "How serious is IPSV?" Jocelyn C. Anderson, Jessica E. Draughon, and Jacquelyn C. Campbell answer that question by describing the medical and emotional havoc IPSV can wreak in survivors' lives, and by pointing out that IPSV can be a marker for fatality risk. Emma Williamson helps us understand how so many women feel they must acquiesce to sexual coercion to maintain their physical safety, and how abusive partners wrest away control of one of the most profound choices a woman has: whether or not to have a child. Walter S. DeKeseredy offers a clear response to the question that some service providers are still asking: "Why doesn't she just leave?" She doesn't leave because her abuser makes it clear to her that she will suffer unimaginable horrors if she does. She doesn't leave because IPSV is a fundamental attack on her sense of self and her sense of effectiveness. She doesn't leave because she has been socialized with the common fictions and has difficulty in naming the crime. She doesn't leave because she feels ashamed and responsible for the rape. She doesn't leave because she doesn't know that there are services that can help her. She doesn't leave because she fears for her children's safety and well-being. She doesn't leave because she has justifiable fears about housing, finances, or immigration status; she doesn't leave because she is likely to be raped or perhaps even killed if she does. How serious is IPSV? Deadly serious.

What is it, then, that professionals must do differently to meet the needs of IPSV survivors? First, they must consider IPSV in the context of the social-ecological model of violence prevention (Centers for Disease Control and Prevention 2009). This model locates violence within four levels: individual, relationship, community, and societal. All four levels must be addressed in order to understand the nature of violence. Isabelle Kerr knows that for counselors and advocates to help survivors, they have to see the big picture. Debra Parkinson and Susie Reid demonstrate the value of looking at all levels to prevent IPSV. Gender-based violence is a global phenomenon, and sexual terror is used as a method of power and control worldwide. While service providers need and want to help individual survivors, they must understand that the causes and solutions for IPSV must take place at the societal, community, and relationship (with the focus on the abuser) levels. Gender role perception, legislation, community attitudes and support systems, provider response, and barriers to service access must change before IPSV can diminish. As we help individual survivors, we must ensure that they understand IPSV is not "their" problem. Although they live with the consequences, they do not cause their own victimization. This may seem obvious, but the voices of survivors throughout this book demonstrate that women are still being blamed for being victims and continue to feel the shame of self-blaming.

With the overarching understanding of the societal and community factors that create the climate for sexual assault within relationships, each profession has its own opportunity to offer enlightened and innovative responses to IPSV. Too often, interventions for those affected by IPSV have been inadequate because of our fragmented service system. Di Macleod's approach to cross-training for domestic violence and sexual assault workers emphasizes the integrated, multidisciplinary approach that is essential to meeting survivors' needs. Jennifer Y. Levy-Peck describes the challenges and opportunities for IPSV advocacy, and points out the value of IPSV-specific support groups as a mechanism for helping survivors overcome the harm of having been violated by a partner, while at the same time raising community awareness of the issue.

Medical and mental health responses to IPSV need to be nuanced and effective. Charlotte Palmer and Vanita Parekh explain that even forensic medical response to IPSV must be deeply rooted in an understanding of the dynamics of partner sexual abuse, the numerous and varied effects it may have on a survivor's health and well-being, and the risk for further violence. These themes are carried further by Elizabeth Layton, who requires the same depth of understanding for professionals who counsel women who have suffered IPSV. She emphasizes the overall context of IPSV as a necessary backdrop to interventions with individual survivors.

An understanding of the denial and stigma surrounding IPSV and the shortcomings of the criminal justice system in responding to this crime inform Mike Davis' recommendations on effective response by law enforcement as well as Lynn Hecht Schafran's guidance for the courts on handling IPSV cases. Effective prosecution of these cases may rely on accurate forensic medical assessment, as addressed by Vanita Parekh and Angela Williams. Patricia Easteal AM brings the desire for fair treatment of victims by the criminal justice system into the practical realm with her specific advice for criminal justice staff and advocates. Barbara Roberts illuminates the way in which clergy and pastoral counselors may be affected by the same societal distortions as the general public, and how their leadership can transform community response to IPSV survivors. For every category of service provider mentioned in this book, the compassionate support of those victimized by IPSV must be coupled with a broader view of this form of injustice.

Viewing IPSV as a form of oppression leads us to examine the particular concerns and barriers faced by certain survivors. Recognizing the cultural context of IPSV, as depicted by Marianne Winters and Isabel Morgan, allows service providers to offer culturally sensitive interventions and thereby to reduce barriers to service access. This theme is explored further in Bushra Sabri, Veronica Barcelona de Mendoza, and Jacquelyn C. Campbell's discussion of how factors associated with immigration can make it more likely that individuals will be sexually victimized by their partners and less likely that they will be able to find appropriate services. Janice Ristock's description of sexual assault in same-sex relationships is also firmly rooted in her analysis of the everyday oppression faced by lesbian, gay, bisexual, and transgender (LGBT) individuals and how their victimization experiences are shaped by the communities and societies in which they live.

Context matters in understanding IPSV. Adolescents who experience sexual coercion or assault by a partner are affected not only by developmental issues, Jennifer Y. Levy-Peck points out, but also by the many societal influences on teens and the specific subculture in which they live. Women who live in rural areas are affected by geographic isolation, economic stressors, community norms, and practical access barriers, according to Debra Parkinson and Claire Zara. Finally, as Debbie Kilroy discusses in Chapter 24, incarcerated women are a group with an extremely high likelihood of past victimization, including by IPSV.

Thus, each of the authors in this book offers a clear view of IPSV as a manifestation of societal gender inequality, damaging community attitudes, and distorted relationship values, resulting in severe harm to victims. Story after story tells of survivors being misunderstood, blamed, treated poorly by those to whom they turned for help, and having to live with the consequences not only of the abuse itself but also of inadequate responses to the search for help.

And help is necessary. Sexual assault by a partner results in long-term trauma and physical harm. Children of women who are sexually abused by partners are also affected, starting with the possibility that the child may have been conceived in rape or as a result of reproductive coercion, and continuing with the effects of living in a family whose dynamics are warped by abuse and fear. Women who have children in common with their abusers have special challenges in achieving safety and autonomy. Teens, with their intense emotions and limited experience, are vulnerable to entrapment by abusive partners, and the consequences may resonate throughout their lives.

As disturbing as these facts and patterns are, there is hope in the pages of this book. IPSV no longer needs to be an unrecognized, unaddressed problem. Around the world, researchers and service providers are identifying this troubling issue, studying its nature, crafting more effective responses, and sharing their knowledge with survivors and with other professionals. Increasingly, abusers are no longer getting a free pass to disregard the choices of their partners with regard to sexual activity. Resources such as this book are being developed to increase accountability, to support survivors, and to educate community members and service professionals. Education (information) is a requisite key to effecting any real change. This is evidenced, for example, in the law, where we see that law reform intended to remove a partner's license to rape is limited by the gatekeepers' interpretation and implementation.

Understanding the many levels of causation and perpetuation of IPSV can lead us to despair, feeling overwhelmed by the magnitude of the problem. We do need to work on the underlying causes of exploitation of women as they relate to sexual violence within relationships. We do need a global perspective, strong public policy, and changes in institutions such as the courts. Yet, at the same time, we need to respond to what is happening in our communities and among individuals and families. A resonant theme from the authors of this book is that our understanding of the root causes of IPSV is a necessary component of our response to this issue at crime scenes, in courtrooms, in advocacy programs, in medical and therapeutic settings, and in our houses of worship.

Our vision for this book was to assemble strong voices from different countries and different disciplines in order to move the field forward. There is still work to be done. We need a more detailed and comprehensive view of abusers themselves, and how to hold them accountable and offer pathways to change. We need to expand our understanding of IPSV survivors throughout the lifespan, with strategies for assisting older individuals who are vulnerable to victimization.

As they are often the first port of call, health practitioners working in general practice, reproductive care, and/or in emergency rooms need to understand IPSV so that they can better identify those at risk. Clergy of all denominations need direction in supporting survivors and speaking out against abuse. Police and prosecutors too must be taught to identify and better assist survivors. And of course the findings of researchers need to be translated into specific service strategies by sexual assault workers, domestic violence workers, and the other potential practitioner helpers, as this book has begun to do.

Survivors deserve safety for themselves and their children, economic justice, autonomy in their decisions, and respect from their communities. The work has begun; we have much more work to do.

# Reference

Centers for Disease Control and Prevention (2009) *The Social-Econological Model: A Framework for Prevention.* Atlanta, GA: Centers for Disease Control and Prevention. Available at www.cdc.gov/violenceprevention.overview/social-econologicalmodel.html, accessed March 12, 2013.

# Resources

## Web resources

*Aphrodite Wounded*: A website for IPSV survivor support and IPSV education for students, professionals, and others. Contains an extensive list of resources and references for professionals. www.aphroditewounded.org

*Assisting Older Victims of Intimate Partner Sexual Violence*: A forum containing very important information about a neglected survivor group. http://ovc.ncjrs.gov/ovcproviderforum/asp/sub.asp?Topic_ID=167

*End Violence Against Women International*: The mission of End Violence Against Women (EVAW) International is to "inspire and educate those who respond to gender-based violence." Their website includes an Online Training Institute, free webinars, and other resources that support the work of law enforcement and other professionals in holding offenders accountable while providing effective and sensitive victim response. Their materials debunk the myth that most sexual assault is stranger assault and emphasize the need for a multidisciplinary approach. www.evawintl.org

*Intimate Partner Sexual Abuse: Adjudicating This Hidden Dimension of Domestic Violence*: A comprehensive and *free* online course offered by the National Judicial Education Program of Legal Momentum. www.njep-ipsacourse.org.

*Marital Rape*: A free online course by Raquel Bergen. Developed for VAWnet; 30 minutes' duration. www.vawnet.org/elearning/MaritalRape/player.html

*Private Nightmares, Public Secrets: Sexual Assault by Intimate Partners*: The 40-page manual is a guide for developing presentations for groups on the topic of sexual assault by intimate partners. It includes handouts, notes for trainers, and overhead materials. Can be purchased from Jane Doe Inc. www.janedoe.org/learn_more/publications

*Stalking Resource Center:* The National Center for Victims of Crime Offers information for professionals and for victims, online courses, awareness materials, publications, and videos. www.victimsofcrime. org/our-programs/stalking-resource-center

*Technology Safety:* An extensive array of web-based technology safety resources from the National Network to End Domestic Violence's (NNEDV) Safety Net: National Safe and Strategic Technology Project. www.nnedv.org/resources/safetynetdocs.html

*Real not Rare—a cross-sectoral training program to recognize and respond to intimate partner sexual violence:* Two-day program available from Gold Coast Centre Against Sexual Violence Inc. www.stopsexualviolence. com

*Washington Coalition of Sexual Assault Programs (WCSAP)* is at the forefront of several excellent IPSV initiatives. They are as follows:

- *Intimate Partner Sexual Violence: Sexual Assault in the Context of Domestic Violence*—publication available for download at www. wcsap.org/sexual-assault-context-domestic-violence. Features several interesting articles for professionals, including:
  - *Making the Connections: Advocating for Survivors of Intimate Partner Sexual Violence* by Marianne Winters.
  - *Making Marital Rape a Crime: A Long Road Traveled, a Long Way to Go* by Lynn Hecht Schafran, Stefanie Lopez-Boy, and Mary Rothwell Davis.
  - *Prosecuting Intimate Partner Sexual Assault* by Jennifer Gentile Long.
  - *Successfully Investigating IPSV: Considerations for Law Enforcement* by the National Center for Women and Policing.
- *WCSAP Training Tools:*
  - *Building an Effective Parent Education Program to Prevent Intimate Partner Sexual Violence in Teen Relationships.* www. wcsap.org/building-effective-parent-education-program-prevent-intimate-partner-sexual-violence-teen
  - *IPSV Train the Trainer kit*—IPSV training workshop. www. wcsap.org/ipsv-train-trainer-kit

- *Leadership for a Successful IPSV Support Group.* www.wcsap. org/leadership-successful-ipsv-support-group
  - *Screening Questions: A Guide for Developing Tools to Assess for Sexual Assault within the Context of Domestic Violence.* www. wcsap.org/screening-questions
  - *Sexual Assault and Coercion in Teen Relationships (2011)—* Webinar. www.wcsap.org/sexual-assault-and-coercion-teen-relationships
  - *WCSAP Online Courses (free) at http://learn.wcsap.org:*
    - *Intimate Partner Sexual Violence* (a component of the Advocate Core online class).
    - *IPSV Advocacy Strategies* (under Ongoing Advocacy Training).

*When the Rapist is Her Partner* – An Australian full-day IPSV training workshop for professionals, presented by Louise McOrmond-Plummer and Helen Newman. For further information, see www. aphroditewounded.org/workshops.html.


# DVDs

*Partner Rape: Know About It, Respond Effectively, Prevent It.* This is a free resource, presenting a multidisciplinary approach to IPSV. Testimonies from survivors; appearances by police, medical and counseling professionals, and other experts. Although it is Australian, the perspectives offered will be applicable anywhere. Can be viewed chapter-by-chapter online at www.whealth.com.au/work_partner_rape.html. Copies may also be requested.

*Project Plan to Empowerment.* Available for purchase at www.rickyhunter. org/eworks.html. Three-hour workshop put together by survivor Ricky Hunter about domestic violence and featuring Louise McOrmond-Plummer discussing topics about IPSV for professionals such as:

- the challenges that survivors face when help-seeking
- helpful and unhelpful responses
- the differences between IPSV and other domestic/sexual violence
- common effects of IPSV for professionals to be aware of

- why women experiencing IPSV stay
- support needs of women who stay
- support needs for women who leave
- why peer support for survivors may be important.

# Contributors

## Jocelyn C. Anderson

Jocelyn C. Anderson, M.S.N., R.N., has been involved in forensic nursing since 2008 when she began working toward completing her master's degree in nursing with a clinical nurse specialist and forensic nursing concentration. She is currently enrolled in the Ph.D. program at Johns Hopkins University School of Nursing and is working with faculty mentors Jacquelyn C. Campbell, Nancy Glass, and Daniel Sheridan on a number of projects aimed at improving the health care outcomes of women who have experienced domestic violence and sexual assault.

## Veronica Barcelona de Mendoza

Veronica Barcelona de Mendoza has worked in several different capacities with underserved populations, with a primary focus on maternal-child health issues in Latina/Hispanic women. She is bilingual in English and Spanish and has done pregnancy and family planning education and clinical service delivery in maternal-child health in community-based health centers and health departments. Ms. Barcelona de Mendoza worked internationally on a maternal mortality reduction initiative in Latin America for the Pan American Health Organization, in La Paz, Bolivia, for the State Department, and in the National Health Service hospital system in the UK. She earned master's degrees in community health nursing and public health from Johns Hopkins University, and is ANCC certified as an advanced public health nurse. She is now a full-time doctoral student in reproductive epidemiology at Tulane University School of Public Health and Tropical Medicine.

## Jacquelyn C. Campbell

Jacquelyn C. Campbell, Ph.D., R.N., is the Anna D. Wolf Chair and a Professor in the Johns Hopkins University School of Nursing with a joint appointment in the Bloomberg School of Public Health, as well as being the National Program Director of the Robert Wood Johnson Foundation Nurse Faculty Scholars program. Since 1980, Dr. Campbell has been conducting advocacy policy work and research in the area of violence against women and women's health, publishing more than 220 articles and seven books.

# Mike Davis

Mike Davis is a police sergeant for the Vancouver, Washington Police Department, where he helped establish the City of Vancouver's first Domestic Violence Unit and served as the first Domestic Violence Sergeant. In 2004, he was named Outstanding Law Enforcement Officer by the Clark County Prosecuting Attorney's Office for service to victims of domestic violence. From 2006 to 2012, he coordinated the city's response to domestic violence crimes. Sergeant Davis has presented at the regional and national level on domestic violence and intimate partner sexual violence.

# Walter S. DeKeseredy

Walter S. DeKeseredy is Anna Deane Carlson Endowed Chair of Social Sciences, Department of Sociology and Anthropology, West Virginia University. He has published 18 books and more than 140 journal articles and book chapters on violence against women and other social problems. In 2008, the Institute on Violence, Abuse and Trauma gave him the Linda Saltzman Memorial Intimate Partner Violence Researcher Award. He also jointly received the 2004 Distinguished Scholar Award from the American Society of Criminology's (ASC) Division on Women and Crime and the 2007 inaugural UOIT Research Excellence Award. In 1995, he received the Critical Criminologist of the Year Award from the ASC's Division on Critical Criminology (DCC), and in 2008 the DCC gave him the Lifetime Achievement Award.

# Jessica E. Draughon

Jessica E. Draughon, Ph.D., M.S.N., R.N., is a Postdoctoral Fellow at the University of California San Francisco. Her area of research is the intersection between HIV and gender-based violence. She has presented at national and international conferences and is a member of the Sigma Theta Tau International Honor Society for Nursing.

# Patricia Easteal AM

Patricia Easteal AM, Ph.D., is a legal academic, author, and advocate, who was named the Australian Capital Territory Australian of the Year in 2010 and was made a member of the Order of Australia the same year. In 2012, she was a finalist for the Australian Human Rights Community Award (Individual). She has published 14 books and well over 130 academic journal articles with a primary focus on access to justice for women. She is currently completing a book with a colleague in the UK looking at violence against women, society, and the law.

## Isabelle Kerr

Isabelle Kerr has been working in the field of violence against women since becoming a volunteer with Glasgow Rape Crisis Centre in 1981. She was a founder member of the Aberdeen Rape Crisis Centre and worked directly with survivors for more than ten years. In 2006, Isabelle became Centre Manager of the Rape Crisis Centre in Glasgow. In 2009, Isabelle set up DF Consultancy and Training, working with NHS Scotland on patient screening for domestic abuse and childhood sexual abuse. The consultancy has delivered gender-based violence training to a range of other services and produced training materials for both practitioners and managers.

## Debbie Kilroy

Debbie Kilroy, O.A.M., L.L.B., B.Soc.Wk., G.Dip. For.M.H.—a psychotherapist and Australian Human Rights Medal Winner in 2004— is a former prisoner. As the Director of Sisters Inside, she has successfully built it into a thriving community-based organization which advocates and provides services to criminalized young people, and women in and from prison, throughout Australia. Its management is comprised of women who are still currently imprisoned, augmented by a select few former politicians, lawyers, academics, and other professionals. Debbie also works as a criminal defense lawyer in Queensland. She is the first person with serious criminal convictions admitted to practice law in Australia.

## Elizabeth Layton

Elizabeth Layton is a mental health professional working as a counselor from her home practice. She earned a diploma in counseling from the Institute of Natural Healing, Somerset, UK. She is a survivor of marital rape and domestic violence and has for the last six years been a passionate advocate of raising awareness about the issue of intimate partner sexual violence. Her counseling practice has always been specifically geared towards women who have experienced sexual violence within partnerships and who may also be experiencing domestic violence. Elizabeth continues to be committed to social justice and to helping support survivors of IPSV through her counseling and research.

# Jennifer Y. Levy-Peck

Jennifer Y. Levy-Peck is a clinical psychologist working for the Washington Coalition of Sexual Assault Programs, a statewide nonprofit organization in the US. She provides training and develops resources on a number of topics related to sexual victimization, including intimate partner sexual violence. Dr. Levy-Peck has worked with trauma survivors and in program development for the past 30 years, including co-founding a domestic violence program. She is the author of an IPSV support group manual and a book, *Healing the Harm Done: A Parent's Guide to Helping Your Child Overcome the Effects of Sexual Abuse*. She provides training for national audiences on IPSV and related topics.

# Di Macleod

Di Macleod has worked in the area of violence prevention and intervention for 33 years. She has a social science degree and is completing a master of management (community management). Di previously worked in a women's refuge and is currently Director of the Gold Coast Centre Against Sexual Violence Inc., which she founded in 1990. In 2000, Di developed a cross-training program on intimate partner sexual violence which addresses the need for education and collaboration between domestic violence workers, sexual assault workers, and women's refuges to better respond to this issue.

# Louise McOrmond-Plummer

Louise McOrmond-Plummer survived domestic violence which included repeated rape and threats to her life by a partner who later murdered somebody else. After gaining her freedom, she studied for an associate diploma in welfare studies (La Trobe University, Victoria) and has devoted 20 years to the study of intimate partner sexual violence, supporting survivors and making resources available for both survivors and professionals. She is co-author with Patricia Easteal AM of the book *Real Rape, Real Pain: Help for Women Sexually Assaulted by Male Partners*, and runs the intimate partner sexual violence support and educational website Aphrodite Wounded (www.aphroditewounded.org). Her expertise with respect to IPSV is internationally recognized. Ms. McOrmond-Plummer currently presents a day-long professional training workshop, When the Rapist is her Partner. She is also a director of Pandora's Project (www.pandys.org), a well-known and celebrated online peer-support resource for survivors of rape and sexual assault.

# Isabel Morgan

Isabel Morgan is currently a junior at Mount Holyoke College studying anthropology and preparing for careers in public health and medicine. She has experience as the communications assistant at Safe Passage, a nonprofit domestic violence organization in western Massachusetts. She has served in a leadership role on campus, where she is currently a senior community advisor, working to build community within the residence halls. Isabel also works in the anthropology and sociology department at Mount Holyoke College. Isabel has received several honors and awards to recognize both her academic and nonacademic achievements, most notably as a Caribbean American Medical and Scientific Association Scholar in 2012. Isabel plans to graduate in December 2013 and begin a degree program in public health the following spring.

# Charlotte Palmer

Charlotte Palmer's academic qualifications include the following degrees: B.Med.Sci. (psychological medicine); M.B.B.S.; Grad. Dip. Forensic Medicine; D.R.A.C.O.G.; and F.R.A.C.G.P. She has been in clinical medical practice for 40 years, the majority of that time in the Australian Capital Territory, and has worked in both a therapeutic and forensic capacity with women who have experienced interpersonal violence. Currently in general practice, she is all too aware of the exigencies and possibilities of that discipline.

# Vanita Parekh

Vanita Parekh is a senior staff specialist medical practitioner in sexual health and forensic medicine based at the Canberra Hospital. She is Director of the Clinical Forensic Medical Services. She has a number of research interests within the areas of sexual assault and clinical forensic medicine. She holds a senior lecturer position at the Australian National University, an honorary senior lecturer position at Monash University, and is an adjunct associate professor at the University of Canberra. Her qualifications include Fellowship of the Australasian Chapter of Sexual Health Medicine, a masters in forensic medicine, graduate certificate in higher education, and diplomas in family planning and venereology.

# Debra Parkinson

Debra Parkinson is a social researcher who is committed to feminism and social justice. Her research focus with Women's Health Goulburn North East (WHGNE) has been women leaving violent relationships and partner rape.

Debra has an M.A., B.Litt., and B.A., and is currently a Ph.D. candidate at Monash University, researching post-disaster violence against women.

## Susie Reid

Susie Reid has worked in education, marketing and promotions, health promotion, and disability. She has been involved in work to prevent violence against women since the early 1990s. Her first foray into the field was with the award-winning *Let's Lift the Lid: Anti-Violence Project*. As Executive Officer of Women's Health Goulburn North East, Susie played a key role in the structure of the integrated family violence service system, and has a continuing role in the Alliance and as auspice of the Family Violence Leadership Position. She has overseen and co-launched the research report *Raped by a Partner*, and she features with other experts in the accompanying DVD.

## Janice Ristock

Janice Ristock, Ph.D., is Vice-Provost (Academic Affairs) and Professor of Women's and Gender Studies at the University of Manitoba. Her research is in three intersecting areas: gender and sexuality, interpersonal violence, and HIV/AIDS and stigma. She has gained international recognition for her research on violence in same-sex relationships and community-based research methodologies. She has authored, co-authored, or co-edited numerous books, chapters, journal articles, and government reports. She serves on several editorial boards and peer reviews for journals and funding agencies both nationally and internationally. She has been active in the feminist, gay, and lesbian anti-violence movement for over 25 years.

## Barbara Roberts

Barbara is a survivor of domestic abuse and author of *Not Under Bondage: Biblical Divorce for Abuse, Adultery and Desertion* (2008). She has personal and peer knowledge of how Christian victims have been helped, or hurt, by church responses to intimate partner abuse, including sexual abuse. She co-administers the blog *A Cry For Justice* with Pastor Jeff Crippen, where they seek to awaken the conservative evangelical church to domestic violence and abuse (http://cryingoutforjustice.wordpress.com). She educates and supports Christian victim-survivors by addressing scriptural misunderstandings that block them from empowered self-agency, and she shares her knowledge of secular resources that will help Christian survivors without running contrary to their faith. She is based in Australia but interacts with survivors all round the world.

# Bushra Sabri

Bushra Sabri, Ph.D., L.M.S.W., A.C.S.W., is a social worker by training, and is a postdoctoral fellow at Johns Hopkins University, Baltimore, Maryland. She has extensive cross-cultural and cross-national experiences in research, health care, and social service settings. She has published numerous papers and presented at various conferences. Her research focuses on interpersonal violence and related lethal and non-lethal effects among at-risk populations, including immigrants and minorities; development of culturally competent risk assessments and interventions; and racial/ethnic and gender disparities in health.

# Lynn Hecht Schafran

Lynn Hecht Schafran is an attorney and Director since 1981 of the National Judicial Education Program (NJEP), a project of Legal Momentum in cooperation with the National Association of Women Judges. Among the judicial education curricula she has published is an extensive web course titled *Intimate Partner Sexual Abuse: Adjudicating This Hidden Dimension of Domestic Violence Cases*. It is available free at www.njep-ipsacourse.org. NJEP's other resources on adult victim sexual assault—publications, DVDs, and online curricula—may be accessed at www.legalmomentum.org/our-work/vaw/njep.html.

# Angela Williams

Angela Williams is a forensic physician with the Victorian Institute of Forensic Medicine and an adjunct senior lecturer in the Department of Forensic Medicine at Monash University in Australia. She has also worked as a certified consultant to the Victorian Forensic Paediatric Medical Service. Dr. Williams has coordinated both medical and nursing postgraduate studies in sexual assault with Monash University, is a fellow of the Faculty of Forensic and Legal Medicine UK, and is a member of the Australasian Association of Forensic Physicians. Her professional interests cover the full span of clinical forensic medicine, but current activities are centered on sexual assault, injury interpretation, child abuse, and forensic medical education. Her qualifications include a masters in forensic medicine and a graduate diploma in law. She oversees the medical sexual assault service for Victoria and educates on this subject matter to doctors, police, lawyers, public groups, and students.

# Emma Williamson

Emma Williamson, Ph.D., P.G.Dip., B.A. (Hons.), is a senior research fellow in gender-based violence at the University of Bristol in the School for Policy Studies. Emma has many years of research experience in the area of gender-based violence, including health, law, social policy, and service interventions. Emma previously worked as the Domestic Violence Information and Membership Manager for Women's Aid, the national domestic violence charity in the UK. Emma's recent projects include: a Home Office project exploring the service and support needs of male, lesbian, gay, bisexual, transgendered, black, and other minority ethnic victims of domestic and sexual violence; a longitudinal study of the needs of homeless women; domestic abuse in military families; and the health needs of male patients who are victims and/or perpetrators of potentially abusive behaviors.

# Marianne Winters

Marianne Winters, M.S., has been an advocate and activist in movements to end violence against women for 25 years. She established consultation practice Praxis for Change after many years as an advocate, counselor, and leader in local, statewide, and national organizations. She also serves as Project Diva for Graphix for Change, a website and design firm that helps social change organizations accomplish their goals using Web 2.0 technologies. She is the Executive Director of Safe Passage in Northampton, Massachusetts.

# Claire Zara

Claire Zara holds a B.A. in media studies and literature (Swinburne University), a Grad. Dip. in literature (Deakin University), and a Grad. Dip. in education (Monash University). Claire's experience in health promotion and violence prevention with Women's Health Goulburn North East includes research, training, and film production. She was co-researcher for *The Way He Tells It: Relationships after Black Saturday*, which revealed the increase of family violence after the 2009 Victoria bushfires. Claire is a Ph.D. student with Monash Injury Research Institute.

# Subject Index

# Author Index